December 2001.

Changing interp

Also in this series:

Education, Adjustment and Reconstruction: Options for Change
Education Reform in the South in the 1990s

Changing international aid to education

Global patterns and national contexts

Edited by Kenneth King and Lene Buchert

Education on the Move
UNESCO PUBLISHING/NORRAG

The authors are responsible for the choice and presentation of the facts contained in this book and for the opinions expressed therein, which are not necessary those of UNESCO and do not commit the Organization.

The designations employed and the presentation of material throughout this publication do not imply the expression of any opinion whatsoever on the part of UNESCO concerning the legal status of any country, territory, city or area or of its authorities, or concerning the delimitation of its frontiers or boundaries.

Published in co-operation with the
Northern Policy Research Review and
Advisory Network on Education and Training

Published in 1999 by the United Nations Educational,
Scientific and Cultural Organization,
7, place de Fontenoy,
75352 Paris 07 SP (France)
Composed and printed by Imprimerie des Presses Universitaires de France,
41100 Vendôme

ISBN 92-3-103514-2

© UNESCO 1999

Preface

Current trends in international development co-operation suggest that there should be a rethinking of relationships between the North and the South before the new millennium. Many international agencies, including UNESCO, have emphasized the primary responsibility of Southern countries for their own development, while both the North and the South recognize the need for a genuine partnership in tackling issues of poverty alleviation, sustainable development and debt relief. Equity and especially gender equity are now a priority in the concrete programmes and policies of UNESCO and other international funding and technical assistance agencies. The same has been true for some years of emphasis upon the protection of the environment, human rights and multi-party politics. Several bilateral and multilateral bodies (including the Swedish International Development Co-operation Agency (Sida), the European Union and UNESCO) have also been stressing the need for a new code of conduct for international agencies in their development co-operation with governments in the South – to be expressed in clear contractual standards and principles of ethics among equal partners. Within the specific field of education and training, there have been parallels to these general trends. It is particularly with the translation of new aid policies into national education and training policies that this book is concerned.

The opportunity for UNESCO to work with the Northern Policy Research Review and Advisory Network on Education and Training (NORRAG) in the production of this book was therefore very appropriate. NORRAG has for the last decade been concerned with the analysis of policies and practices of international funding and technical assistance agencies. Through its newsletter, workshops and monographs, it has sought to disseminate to governments, agencies and the academic community in both the North and the South critical commentary on many of the new trends in international development co-operation. This book is no exception. It is topical, it reflects the thinking of individuals in multilateral and bilateral agencies, as well as in national governments and in academia, and it also points to some of the difficulties in implementing new policies that many governments and agencies in both the North and the South find appealing. The local context and specific conditions in the individual countries in the South are obviously critical factors which will determine many of the outcomes of global aid efforts, however ideal they may initially seem.

The book will hopefully become an important illustration, for the education sector, of the new directions in international development co-operation. It expresses many of the concerns, ideas and ideals of UNESCO, but the views presented in the individual contributions are those of the authors and do not necessarily bear the endorsement of this organization.

Colin N. Power
Assistant Director-General for Education, UNESCO

Contents

11   List of abbreviations
13   Introduction: new challenges to international development co-operation in education, *Kenneth King*

Part One.
Development co-operation
in the context of globalization

31   The new boundaries of international development co-operation, *Jacques Forster*
46   The future of international aid to education: a personal reflection, *Aklilu Habte*
60   Aid, international co-operation and globalization: trends in the field of education, *Michel Carton*
68   Education, development and assistance: the challenge of the new millennium, *Simon McGrath*

Part Two.
New approaches to development co-operation among international funding and technical-assistance agencies

- 93 Educational multilateralism at a crossroads, *Karen Mundy*
- 119 Education and development co-operation: a UNESCO perspective, *Wyn Courtney*
- 132 Development aid in education: a personal view, *Stephen P. Heyneman*
- 147 The Europeanization of aid, *Wolfgang Gmelin*
- 153 Education and geopolitical change in Africa: a case for partnership, *Lennart Wohlgemuth*
- 166 Changing frameworks and practices: the new Department for International Development of the United Kingdom, *Myra Harrison*
- 173 Redefining strategies of assistance: recent trends in Japanese assistance to education in Africa, *Yumiko Yokozeki and Nobuhide Sawamura*
- 182 Non-governmental organizations as partners in Africa: a cultural analysis of North–South relations, *Juliet Elu and Kingsley Banya*

Part Three.
New directions for aid practice: constraints and opportunities

- 209 Aid co-ordination through the other end of the telescope, *Henry Kaluba and Peter Williams*
- 222 Co-ordination of aid to education at the country level: some experiences and lessons from the United Republic of Tanzania in the 1990s, *Lene Buchert*
- 239 Aid co-ordination in theory and practice: a case study of Botswana and Namibia, *Ulla Kann*

Part Four.
**National responses to changes
in international development co-operation**

257 Aid to South African education: a case of the reluctant recipient?
     Kenneth King
280 Educational policies, change programmes and international
     co-operation: the case of Chile, *Cristián Cox and Beatrice Avalos*
298 Issues amidst assistance: foreign aid to education in China,
     Kai-ming Cheng
307 Development assistance to primary education in India:
     transformation of enthusiastic donors and reluctant recipients,
     Jandhyala B. G. Tilak

319 Contributors

List of abbreviations

ACLE	Actividades Curriculares de Libre Elección
ACP	African, Caribbean, Pacific Group
ADB	Asian Development Bank
ADB	African Development Bank
ADEA	Association for the Development of Education in Africa
AIDS	Acquired Immune Deficiency Syndrome
CESO	Centre for the Study of Education in Developing Countries
CICE	Centre for the Study of International Co-operation in Education
CSFP	Commonwealth Scholarship and Fellowship Plan
DAC	Development Assistance Committee
DAE	Donors to African Education
Danida	Danish International Development Assistance
DFID	Department for International Development
DGIS	General Directorate for International Co-operation of the Netherlands
DPEP	District Primary Education Programme
EBRD	European Bank for Reconstruction and Development
ECOSOC	Economic and Social Council of the United Nations
EDF	European Development Fund
EIADP	Eastern Area Integrated Agricultural Development Project
EPUs	Educational Policy Units
FAO	Food and Agriculture Organization of the United Nations
FAVDO	Forum of African Voluntary Development Organizations
GATT	General Agreement on Tariffs and Trade
GDP	Gross Domestic Product
GEF	Global Environment Facility
GNP	Gross National Product
GTZ	German Organization for Technical Co-operation
HDI	Human Development Index
IBRD	International Bank for Reconstruction and Development
IDA	International Development Association
IDCC	International Development Co-operation Committee
IDRC	International Development Research Centre, Canada
IIEP	International Institute for Educational Planning

ILO	International Labour Organization
IMF	International Monetary Fund
IWGE	International Working Group on Education
JICA	Japan International Co-operation Agency
JKUAT	Jomo Kenyatta University of Agriculture and Technology
MEC	Ministry of Education and Culture
MOEC	Ministry of Education and Culture
NAFTA	North Atlantic Free Trade Agreement
NCP	National Planning Commission
NEPRU	Namibia Economic Policy Research Unit
NGLS	Non-governmental Liaison Service
NGO	Non-governmental organization
NORAD	Norwegian Agency for Development Co-operation
ODA	Official Development Assistance
OECD	Organisation for Economic Co-operation and Development
OPEC	Oil Producing Export Countries
PEC	Project Executive Committee
PEI	President's Educational Initiative
PEP	Primary Education Programme
RDP	Reconstruction and Development Programme
SADC	Southern African Development Community
SAREC	Swedish Agency for Research Co-operation
Sida	Swedish International Development Co-operation Agency
SIMCE	Sistema de Medición de la Calidad de la Educación
SIP	Sector Investment Programmes
SWAPO	South-West Africa People's Organization
TICAD	Tokyo International Conference on African Development
UNCTAD	United Nations Conference on Trade and Development
UNDP	United Nations Development Programme
UNEP	United Nations Environment Programme
UNFPA	United Nations Population Fund
UNHCR	United Nations High Commissioner for Refugees
UNICEF	United Nations Children's Fund
UNIN	United Nations Institute for Namibia
USAID	United States Agency for International Development
USSR	Union of Soviet Socialist Republics
WGESA	Working Group on Education Sector Analysis
WGTP	Working Group on the Teaching Profession
WFP	World Food Programme
WTO	World Trade Organization

Introduction: new challenges to international development co-operation in education
Kenneth King

An analysis of changes in international development co-operation in education is inseparable from the more general changes in development assistance that have become evident in the mid to late 1990s. The purpose of this first chapter is to underline how significant some of these tendencies may potentially be and how they have the possibility to alter out of recognition the shape of the aided educational universe as it is currently known. On the other hand, it seems entirely possible that these new trends may remain more at the level of rhetoric than implementation, with the result that the older patterns of relationship between aid provider and recipient will continue.

In this chapter, some of the main elements of potential change in international co-operation are set out, looking first at these in the North and then at their implications for the South. The sources of these changes are not to be found in a single text on co-operation or in the proposals of a single agency. Rather, this new thinking about North–South relations can be identified in non-governmental organizations, in multilateral agencies such as the World Bank and, especially, in several bilateral agencies. In this new phase of development co-operation, trends are not coming simply from the North and being imposed on the South: the role of the South in the identification of the new thinking is also critical.

Development co-operation and change in the North

One of the more far-reaching changes is the recognition that development co-operation is not just about new actions in the South and by the South: it is also about change in the North. This is important to stress because it is tempting to conclude that any new aid paradigm has principally to do with the better co-ordination of international funding and technical-assistance agencies in the countries in the South, with new modalities of delivering co-operation in the South, or with renewed commitment and conditions among the aid recipients.

Decline in proportion of official development assistance

By contrast, it is worth recognizing that there are several apparently almost contradictory trends becoming visible in the North. The first of these is not strictly speaking a change, but is important since it sets the background against which to measure the feasibility of some of the other changes. It is the fact that, for countries that are members of the Organisation for Economic Co-operation and Development (OECD), official development assistance (ODA) fell from a high of 0.61 per cent of gross national product (GNP) in 1961 to a low of 0.27 in 1995. This proportion of ODA is still falling on average, despite the handful of relatively small countries that have for several years far exceeded the United Nations target of 0.7 per cent set as long ago as 1970 and the fact that, as outlined by Forster in this book, the number of potential recipients of development assistance has greatly increased in Eastern Europe and the former Soviet Union. Thus, Germany contributed no less than 0.13 per cent of its GNP for the benefit of Eastern European countries in 1993, and as much as 5 per cent of Germany's GNP (around DM 150 billion) has been transferred annually to its own developing eastern sector since unification. This figure, covering some 15 million people in Germany, is 40 per cent higher than the entire development aid effort of all international funding and technical assistance agencies for all recipients worldwide (3 billion people). It raises a timely question whether aid efforts can, on their present basis, be concerned with transformation or only with reaching some minimalist poverty alleviation goals (Theil, 1996; King, 1996). Habte analyses with some concern the disturbing gap between the North and the South, and between the aspirations of global conferences such as the World Conference on Education for All held in Jomtien, Thailand, in 1990, on the one hand, and the reality of what seems to be a Northern weariness with aid and an inward-looking tendency, on the other.

Introduction: new challenges
to international development co-operation in education
Kenneth King

The emergence of the partnership discourse

Despite the evidence of continuing aid reduction from the North, a second trend which has become evident in the North in recent years is an expressed desire to develop more symmetrical interrelations or partnerships between the North and the South. The thinking about these new partnerships takes different forms in different OECD countries and has perhaps gone furthest in the Nordic countries, and especially in Sweden, with the work it has generated, collaboratively with Africa, in the report *Partnership with Africa* (Sweden. Ministry for Foreign Affairs, 1997a; see Wohlgemuth in this book). There is a parallel discussion about new relationships evident in the British White Paper *Eliminating World Poverty* (United Kingdom. DFID, 1997; see Harrison in this book), as well as in *Japan's Official Development Assistance Summary* (Japan. Ministry of Foreign Affairs, 1997; see Yokozeki and Sawamura in this book). Multilateral agencies and organizations, such as the World Bank and the Development Assistance Committee (DAC) of OECD, have also adopted the discourse about partnership, most notably in World Bank President Wolfensohn's *New Directions and New Partnerships* (1995) and in DAC's *Development Partnerships in the New Global Context* (OECD, 1996). The thrust of these initiatives is to imply that beyond the older world of agency conditionalities and forced structural adjustment policies, there is a brave new situation where 'genuine' partnerships (United Kingdom. DFID, 1997) and 'a more equal and respectful relationship' (Sweden. Ministry for Foreign Affairs, 1997a, p. 22) between North and South can be anticipated. This new language of symmetry suggests that the aid relationship is going to change. For example, Sweden has proposed that there be a new code of conduct for itself as aid provider (Sweden. Ministry for Foreign Affairs, 1997a, p. 21) and even the World Bank, in Wolfensohn's own words, has accepted the idea of listening to recipients in what sounds like a new moral economy: 'To be a good partner, we must be ready to listen to criticism and respond to constructive comment. There is no place for arrogance in the development business' (1995, p. 20).

One cannot be dogmatic about the source and rationale of this new language of partnership. It may, in part, reflect a continuing tendency in the bilateral and multilateral agencies to take over the aspirational language of non-governmental organizations whose discourse for years has described the South as partners rather than recipients or counterparts. In part, it may also be a recognition that too many development co-operation initiatives have in the past been accepted under financial pressure and have not been locally or nationally owned in the South. In this sense the term partnership is an essential corollary and complement to ownership. Ownership has become a standard item in agency language. On its own, it may not always signify any change in the aid relationship except at the rhetorical level, but in the new partnership discourse, recognition of national ownership of projects and programmes by the South is an important counterbalance to the admitted financial dominance of the North.

A third source of the partnership discourse is the South itself. There has in the late 1990s been much discussion about the emergence of a 'New Africa' with a new generation of leaders and policy-makers determined to engage with the world on equal terms (Olukoshi, 1997). This Southern dimension of the partnership discourse has been an evident element in the Swedish exploration of new policies towards Africa. It could be argued that this Southern insistence on a new relationship with the North must itself be a crucial ingredient of any meaningful concept of a development partnership. It is much too early to know how the kinds of aspiration to achieve what Wohlgemuth (1998, p. 42) calls 'a real negotiation where both parties give and take and where no one dictates the conditions for the other' transfer into the reality of day-to-day discussion in recipient countries. But it is sobering to compare the ideal of 'new co-operation relations' and 'genuine partnership' laid out generally for the United Republic of Tanzania in 1996 in its joint co-operation with Finland, Norway, Sweden and Denmark (Sweden. Ministry for Foreign Affairs, 1997*b*) with the particularity of agency co-ordination and the challenge to local ownership so evident in the detailed (and often frustrating) education sector negotiations in the United Republic of Tanzania described by Buchert (in this book), or in the non-governmental organization partnership sphere (see Elu and Banya in this book).

It has been suggested (Dower, 1998) that the new partnership paradigm may not remove selectivity or indirect conditionality. It could merely shift the conditionality from the macro-economic terms associated with the structural adjustment era to a situation where the North chooses partners according to whether they fulfil certain other essential criteria. In what may be termed the 'development texts' in which the new approaches are embodied, it is already evident that there has emerged a set of preconditions for partnership. These include at minimum: pro-poor economic growth strategies in the South; pro-democracy and pro-human rights policies; pro-gender and pro-equity policies; and a pro-environmental sustainability commitment. The emphasis on these partnership criteria differs somewhat from agency to agency. Thus Japan would certainly underline the crucial requirement of local self-help within any such list of priorities:

In particular, the idea that serious self-help efforts by developing countries are the most important element in development's success is based on Japan's own post-war experience and on the experience of the Asian countries that primarily Japan has supported in these development efforts (Japan. Ministry of Foreign Affairs, 1997, p. 17).

None of this enumeration of criteria is meant to suggest that these elements are not important to populations in the South itself. They very clearly are, and civil society in many developing countries has been marked by an increasing intolerance of corruption and autocratic rule, and an insistence on access to basic human freedoms.

Partnership and selectivity. Even if these criteria are powerfully shared by the South, there is a danger that it is the North that is seen to be doing the choosing. Graphically illustrated in President Clinton's choice of six African countries to visit in 1998, this tendency could result in a new set of divisions among developing countries and their relationships to the North. Already there is some evidence that the new approaches may lead to the North having these 'genuine partnerships' with a smaller number of countries.

Expanded version of bilateralism. The proof of the pudding may well be whether countries such as the United Kingdom or Sweden can indeed implement what may be called a new bilateralism, based on agreed criteria and shared values, and end up choosing very different countries from those with which they have traditionally and historically been partners. If part of the partnership conditions must be to have in place the kind of rich, historical legacy of connections between two countries that is laid out in *Partnership with Africa*, then it may well prove difficult to take on quite new bilateral partners even if they do meet the new pro-poor and other pro-democracy criteria.

But the partnership discussion is not solely about this version of bilateralism closely linked to the policies of a Northern and a Southern government. There is another, expanded, version of bilateralism emerging that points not only to the rich historical legacy of connections between two countries, but also to the possibility of multiple connections at many different levels of two societies, not just central government to central government.

There is thus a tension at the heart of the rediscovery of partnership, at least in bilateral relations. In the old (Cold War) version of bilateral relations, it was possible to argue that a long-standing aid relationship (e.g. between Sweden and Ethiopia, between Belgium and the Democratic Republic of the Congo or between the United Kingdom and Malawi) should in some way be maintained despite the changes of government towards more or less democracy. In the new criteria-based version of bilateralism, the shared values that are the explicit bedrock of the partnership include such issues as human and gender rights, freedom of expression and political pluralism, accountability, uncorrupt government and the rule of law. The absence of these, and of other concerns such as pro-poor and pro-equity development strategies, may now appear to put at risk the whole basis of the bilateral relationship. On the other hand, the new expanded version of bilateralism insists that the new partnership should not be entirely a matter of state-to-state relations, but be about strengthening all manner of civil society linkages between two countries. This latter vision of bilateralism encompasses North–South contacts between churches, popular movements, cultural and educational exchanges, environmental co-operation, trade, industry and tourism, and lastly, but very importantly, co-operation between those from the particular Southern country domiciled in the North and their homeland.

This extended vision of bilateralism may also cover local authority linkages with the developing countries, as well as North–South school and town twinning. It may well be that this broader, more multifaceted partnership will eventually come into conflict with the narrower criteria-based state-to-state version.

Coherence and consistency in partnership

The tension between the broader and narrower connections between Northern and Southern countries underlines a third dimension of development co-operation that is beginning to have an impact on the North, namely the discovery of coherence. This concept suggests that the multiplicity of connections with a particular Southern country should be complementary and consistent across the different ministries of a Northern country rather than being at variance. In other words, a partnership relationship mediated by the development co-operation ministry, such as the United Kingdom's Department for International Development (DFID), should ideally not be undermined by the trade policy of a trade and industry ministry, for instance. And as a corollary, the severing of partnership on account of human rights and other criteria should not be paralleled by a continuation of the transfer of weapons or other military expenditures (see Forster in this book). On the other hand, it can be anticipated that an important issue will be which should be the lead agency or ministry on matters of coherence. The choice of the Ministry of Development Co-operation could present problems for the Ministry of Foreign Affairs or of Trade and Industry. And similarly the other way round. This may pose particular problems for a country such as Japan where the aid budget is owned by no fewer than nineteen separate ministries. The question of choice of lead ministry or agency for partnership coherence is also inseparable from a series of changes in Northern ministries concerned with aid, trade, development and foreign affairs (Carton, 1998).

Global sustainability and development targets for both North and South

A last change beginning to have an impact on the North concerns whether international development targets, pro-poor growth and sustainable livelihoods are primarily relevant only for the South or whether they must be globally meaningful. This has implications for the focus of development education and development studies as well. The recognition that development is not exclusively about the South and that poverty is not a condition over which the South has a monopoly suggests that the kind of development education encouraged in schools in OECD member states should not only be about commitment to and awareness of the South, but equally about global responsibility for both North and South (Dower, 1998). In the case of development studies, they have begun to shift from a preoccupation with the South to a concern about common development problems in the North and South (see Forster in this book).

The impact of thinking about sustainable livelihoods has similarly had significant implications for the North. There has been a tendency in the North to project on the South the importance of convergence in respect of human rights and governance issues, but to be much less clear about the South's natural aspirations for Western-style patterns of consumption. In the post-Cold War world, there has, of course, been strong encouragement by Northern agencies and from the World Bank and the International Monetary Fund (IMF) for the South to pursue free market growth and trade liberalization. In general, however, it has not been the development co-operation ministry that has spelled out the implications for the North of what may be called pro-sustainability economic growth. In fact, it is worth noting that the new development texts do discuss the importance of stable and vigorous economic growth for the developing world, but they tend to steer clear of the question of whether Southern growth should aspire to Western standards of living (United Kingdom. DFID, 1997, p. 15). It can be argued, however, that equitable distribution on a global scale has much more radical consequences than rich countries (or their development ministries) are prepared to admit.

This thinking suggests new preconditions (or 'conditionalities') for change in the North if there is to be global sustainability or meaningful partnership. The powerful metaphor in *Caring for the Future* (Independent Commission on Population and Quality of Life, 1996) of the 'carrying capacity of the earth' is certainly not anticipating that equity and sustainability will arrive without a fundamental rethinking of Northern consumption and expenditure patterns. Thus, the burden of responsibility in development education and development awareness (which several European Union member states are concerned about) is not so much related to reigniting the 'caring capacity' of the Northern public for the South. It is more a call for what might be termed 'ecodevelopment education' with direct implications for sustainable lifestyles in both North and South. This could mean that the very valuable mechanism of international development targets (derived from global conventions and synthesized by DAC) should become less a set of minimum standards for economic and social well-being in the South and more explicitly also a set of targets that change the assumptions about the continuity of non-sustainable growth in the North (OECD, 1996).

Introduction: new challenges
to international development co-operation in education
Kenneth King

Rethinking the delivery and co-ordination of development assistance

From donor projects to sector development

Even though the partnership paradigm has some of the above flaws and contradictions, it is already beginning to have some impact on aid delivery in the South. Once an agreement had been reached on the kinds of criteria that lie behind the new partnership thinking, it followed logically that instead of there being a whole series of easily recognizable projects funded by international funding and technical assistance agencies, there is instead a process of agencies buying into a number of nationally owned sector development programmes. This late 1990s agency preference to work with countries that have developed their own policies rather than continue with project enclaves sounds very progressive. No more British, World Bank or Danish flags flying over their own well-known projects. Or, in the words of a 1996 Danish source:

This means in principle that in the future there will not be a 'Danida Sector Programme', but instead Danida will support a national sector framework and specific elements of this framework. Danida will consequently not perform its 'own' projects or programmes in developing countries but support national activities (Madsen, 1996, p. 37).

The recent British White Paper takes a similar line, in emphasizing the role of sector programmes rather than British projects:

Where we have confidence in the policies and budgetary allocation process and in the capacity for effective implementation of the partner government, we will consider moving away from supporting specific projects to providing resources more strategically in support of sector-wide programmes or the economy as a whole (United Kingdom. DFID, 1997, p. 38).

Following this same thinking, it can be anticipated, particularly within the European Union, that there could be an extension of some degree of common policy approach across what are currently highly differentiated traditions of development co-operation within the European Union. Over time, the development of a European Union framework for co-operation may reduce the variety of Northern offers of aid (see Gmelin in this book). This will not be rapid – at least not in harmonizing the distinctions between

European Union member states that can scarcely be said to have an aid programme and those that have had one for decades. The first major attempt at a policy paper, *Resolution on Education and Training in Developing Countries*, only took place in 1994 (*NORRAG News*, 1995). But what is already clear is that, since these guidelines were adopted, there has been, paradoxically, a reduction in the scope for Southern countries to put forward their own aid preferences in discussions with the European Union:

Guidelines were provided for policy and co-ordination of European support to TVET (technical and vocational education and training). This meant that European Community aid to education and training should no longer be determined solely by the priorities of the recipient countries. Instead, the guidelines in the Council Resolution form a basis for dialogue (Working Group for International Co-operation in Vocational and Technical Skills Development, 1997, p. 8).

In other words, it could be argued that in the European Union, and to some extent in the Danish and British examples above, the very process that the North carefully prepares its preconditions for partnership reduces the degrees of freedom for Southern partners. Thus, by 1996, the desire for coherence and co-ordination of European Union aid, including in the education and training sector, had moved a stage further to what the Commission is terming Sectoral Development Programmes. The expected results at the country level are coherent strategic plans which, it can be seen from the following comment, also reflect external priorities:

Tanzania was selected for education. Simultaneously, the Horizon 2000 Education Experts agreed that the European Union should be moving towards co-ordinated sectoral approaches to aid. This has led to assistance to the Tanzanian Government in planning a Sectoral Development Programme. This will include a basic education masterplan, a secondary education masterplan, institutional improvements including the rationalisation of tertiary education, and improved education of disadvantaged groups (Working Group for International Co-operation in Vocational and Technical Skills Development, 1997, p. 8).

In this book, there is the opportunity to tease out further the consequences at the country level of this move towards mechanisms that are meant to give the recipient country greater ownership. The chapter on the United

Republic of Tanzania is a valuable commentary on partnership ideals; equally, it throws light on the processes that were involved in the earlier phases of the development of the basic education masterplan (see Buchert in this book). Similarly, South Africa would appear to have been a perfect candidate for nationally owned sector programmes, since it had developed a mechanism which should have allowed international funding and technical assistance agencies directly to support national sector frameworks through the Reconstruction and Development Programme (RDP). But there is little evidence that this actually happened (see King in this book). Again, in India, the development of the District Primary Education Programme (DPEP) can be looked at as a national umbrella for the co-ordination of almost all of the hitherto scattered agency initiatives in support of primary education (see Tilak in this book).

In several different contexts, it is also possible to see how the concepts of donor co-ordination, national capacity-building and local ownership translate into country-specific actions (see Kann, and Kaluba and Williams in this book). But more generally, it can be anticipated that the very process of trust in the local partner's development priorities which has led also to the United Kingdom's notion of the sector development programme may be at odds with the other tendency in the North – to specify the importance of particular subsectors, such as basic education. In other words, if a national government has the appropriate criteria for genuine partnership, then, we have seen, it is no longer necessary to insist, for example, on a basic education project. The education sector as a whole can be supported. Indeed, it could then be argued that even higher education could and should be included within the sector programme support.

Additionality, invisibility and technical assistance

Several further considerations flow from the programme support preference which has been emerging. First, there is the vexed question of whether external support is adding to or replacing the existing national support to the education sector. The presumption, on the agency side, must be that it is adding to the budget. Yet in the discussion of DPEP in India, it has been suggested that 'an immediate fallout of DPEP can be reduced domestic efforts to finance primary education' (see Tilak in this book). The same debate has surrounded the role of external assistance funds in South Africa and whether they should be integrated fully into the budget (see King in this book). More radically still, it has been argued that in situations such as the United Republic of Tanzania's, where debt servicing takes some 40 per cent of its foreign exchange earnings, true partnership might want to focus on debt relief by the North to the country in general rather than on the detailed development of specific sector development programmes (Peter Williams, personal communication).

A second result of the sector development approach is reduced visibility of the North in the South. This is quite an important change but it is too early to anticipate the readiness of the Northern public to accommodate much less visibility for its own nationals in developing country projects. There is therefore a further connection between the sector development approach and the new approach to development education, discussed earlier. If aid is less concerned with highly visible Northern volunteers, non-governmental organizations and technical assistance personnel and/or about support to ongoing government sector plans, the approach to the Northern public's participation in development may need to be revised.

A third consequence of these new mechanisms for aid delivery linked to partnership should be a rethinking of technical assistance and the use of national capacity. Clearly, the technical assistance skills required for running a self-standing British or Danish project of the older generation of bilateral projects are very different from those required to monitor an external contribution to the government's achievement of its own goals and targets. The latter, as stated in *Partnership with Africa*, must mean the adoption of the obvious: 'that African development requires African exercise of responsibility under African auspices' (Sweden. Ministry for Foreign Affairs, 1997a, p. 152). Though obvious, this must also mean a new negotiation and compromise about accountability and capacity. Technical assistance is often involved in continuing to ensure that a Southern programme continues to be run according to the annual financial years and accounting procedures of Northern countries as opposed to the requirements of a long-term investment programme.

Confidence and national capacity

These three issues underline a high degree of optimism that runs through several of the most recent statements about development from Northern countries providing international development assistance. Apart from taking quite similar positions on partnership and acknowledging the centrality of a poverty focus, development White Papers, such as the Swedish and British ones, are also confident about the task ahead. There is a strong sense of 'can-do-ism' from the very first page of *Eliminating World Poverty* (United Kingdom. DFID, 1997, p. 5). This was echoed by the Minister for Development Co-operation of the Netherlands, Jan Pronk, in a paper of March 1998 – 'I see no reason to be pessimistic' (Pronk, 1998, p. 10). The Swedish papers and reports are also optimistic, but their emphasis is slightly different. The basis for the optimism is not just the evidence of a new determination in the North to address the international development targets. It is an awareness that Africa is on the move. State Secretary for Foreign Affairs Mats Karlsson is one of many to claim: 'The African renaissance has begun. The African renaissance . . . actually is happening' (Karlsson, 1997, p. 1). Interestingly, this is what former President Nyerere of the United Republic of Tanzania claimed in Edinburgh in October 1997.[1]

The Swedish confidence has been founded on an exercise of 'listening' to Africa, and certainly as much to women as to men. This has led, in turn, to the realization that the other crucial axiom of most international funding and technical assistance agencies in the 1990s – capacity-building – is evident in the voices of African analysts. It is being recognized that capacity, like democracy, cannot be created from outside, but 'essentially it is formed by internal dynamic' (Karlsson, 1997, p. 8). What is interesting in the Swedish papers is the recognition that little is really known about what sparks 'a capacity revolution' in society. However, a key external challenge for development may be to explore how best to support this essential internal creativity and self-reliance once they become evident.

In this regard, Sweden, as the bilateral agency with the longest history of support to primary education and adult literacy, has nevertheless pinpointed the crucial role of secondary and higher education in adding value to basic education provision. It argues that the African renaissance will need a parallel academic renaissance after the crisis of the last two

---

1. 'I believe that Africa is now on the move towards a new liberation. For there are quite definite signs that the peoples of Africa have resumed the struggle against tyranny, corruption and unrepresentative government' (Nyerere, 1997, p. 7).

decades (Karlsson, 1997, p. 8). Similarly in the British White Paper, there is an emphasis on the essential targets for universal primary education and gender equity at both primary and secondary levels. But there is a recognition that countries will also need help to build capacity more comprehensively: 'Our priority is to assist partner countries to achieve the full participation of all children and adults in quality education at all levels' (United Kingdom. DFID, 1997, p. 25).

What these insights may mean for development assistance from a partnership perspective is that much more attention must be given to renewing and sustaining strategic centres of potential excellence in the developing world. Long-term higher-education partnerships could assist this process, but to do so, it may be necessary to rethink scholarships and training aid (King, 1998). In creative forms of new bilateralism, it will be important to explore how international capacity can be sustained in the North, but also deployed more actively in parallel centres in the South that have been depleted by twenty to thirty years of both internal and external brain drain. Equally, development assistance may wish much more directly to consider reverse flows of academic and entrepreneurial capacity, including using the services of Asians, Africans and Latin Americans domiciled in the North (Sweden. Ministry for Foreign Affairs, 1997a, p. 79). Behind these concerns with local capacity and creativity is a new recognition that the aim of international funds is not to train more nationals to help with the implementation of external projects and programmes, but to give space for the development of locally owned versions of democracy, pluralism and enterprise. It may well be that, despite the 1998 financial turmoil, East Asian models of development assistance should be attended to in this regard.

The missing partners – and a health warning

In all the excitement about new North–South relationships and partnerships, based on shared ideals, there must be a level of concern about those countries that, for reasons of internal armed conflict or political leadership, lie far beyond the new narrower or broader versions of partnership. In many ways, the fate of these countries may increasingly be left to the small-scale assistance of humanitarian aid via non-governmental organizations, as more and more of the regular ODA goes through the new partnership routes. In other words, in Africa (and perhaps in other continents), there is a real dilemma about 'the Africa that does not work' and that does not qualify for partnership. In many ways, this Africa – e.g. Sierra Leone and Somalia – is often also poorer than the Africa that works.

There is, finally, also one small danger in the new Northern confidence about aid strategies, new partnerships, and the rethinking of the caring and carrying capacities of the world. The very newness of the new development texts we have been discussing, and the initiatives analysed in many of the chapters that follow, may once again give the North a moral edge over the South of the sort that we have seen in the rediscovery of, for example, human rights and multi-party democracy. It would be unfortunate if, for example, the Jubilee 2000 campaign for debt relief was seen primarily as yet another example of Northern advocacy for Southern victims, or if *Partnership with Africa* or *Eliminating World Poverty* were fundamentally misread as encouragements to take up another version of the White Man's Burden. Their purpose must surely be as contributions to a more global vision of development in the North as in the South. It may well be that, despite the 1998 financial turmoil in East and South-East Asia, the Japanese model of development assistance – with its strong emphasis on local self-reliance – should be looked at more closely by other aid providers.

References

CARTON, M. 1998. Poverty, Solidarity and Globalization: A Swiss Perspective. In: K. King and M. Caddell (eds.), *Beyond the White Papers: Partnership and Poverty Challenges for International Development Policies in Europe*, pp. 71–6. Edinburgh, University of Edinburgh, Centre of African Studies.

DOWER, N. 1998. Global Values, Global Citizenship, and the White Papers. In: K. King and M. Caddell (eds.), *Beyond the White Papers: Partnership and Poverty Challenges for International Development Policies in Europe*, pp. 21–6. Edinburgh, University of Edinburgh, Centre of African Studies.

INDEPENDENT COMMISSION ON POPULATION AND QUALITY OF LIFE. 1996. *Caring for the Future: A Radical Agenda for Positive Change*. Oxford, Oxford University Press.

JAPAN. MINISTRY OF FOREIGN AFFAIRS. 1997. *Japan's Official Development Assistance: Summary 1997*. Tokyo, Association for the Promotion of International Co-operation.

KARLSSON, M. 1997. *For a Genuine Partnership with Emerging Africa*. (Mimeo.)

KING, K. 1996. Aid for Development or for Change? A Discussion of Education and Training Policies of Development Assistance Agencies with

Particular Reference to Japan. In: K. Watson, C. Modgil and S. Modgil (eds.), *Educational Dilemmas: Debate and Diversity*, pp. 112–23. London, Cassell. (Power and Responsibility in Education, Vol. 3.)

KING, K. 1998. *Aid and Higher Education in the Developing World.* Edinburgh, University of Edinburgh, Centre of African Studies. (Occasional Paper 67.)

MADSEN, H. H. 1996. Danish Policies. *NORRAG News*, No. 20, pp. 37–8.

NORRAG News. 1995. No. 17. (Special Issue on European Union Aid Guidelines on Education and Training.)

NYERERE, J. K. 1997. *Africa: The Third Liberation.* Edinburgh, Edinburgh University, Centre of African Studies. (Occasional Paper 70.)

OECD. 1996. Development Partnerships in the New Global Context. In: OECD, *Shaping the 21st Century: The Contribution of Development Co-operation.* Paris, OECD Development Assistance Committee. (Annex.)

OLUKOSHI, A. O. 1997. The Quest for a New Paradigm for Swedish Development Co-operation in Africa. In: H. Kifle, A. O. Olukoshi and L. Wohlgemuth (eds.), *A New Partnership for African Development: Issues and Parameters*, pp. 20–9. Uppsala, Nordic African Institute.

PRONK, J. 1998. *Population, Equity and the Quality of Life.* (Speech at the workshop on Caring for the Future, 5–6 March, Amsterdam.)

SWEDEN. MINISTRY FOR FOREIGN AFFAIRS. 1997a. *Partnership with Africa: Proposals for a New Swedish Policy toward sub-Saharan Africa.* Stockholm, Ministry for Foreign Affairs.

——. ——. 1997b. *The Rights of the Poor: Our Common Responsibility: Combating Poverty in Sweden's Development Co-operation.* Stockholm, Ministry for Foreign Affairs.

THEIL, R. E. 1996. The Helplessness of Development Policy: An Assessment of Aid in the Modern World. *Development and Change*, No. 6, pp. 24–6.

UNITED KINGDOM. DEPARTMENT FOR INTERNATIONAL DEVELOPMENT (DFID). 1997. *Eliminating World Poverty: A Challenge for the 21st Century.* London, HMSO.

WOHLGEMUTH, L. 1998. Partnership Africa: A New Swedish Approach. *NORRAG News*, No. 22, pp. 42–3.

WOLFENSOHN, J. 1995. *New Directions and New Partnerships.* Washington, D.C., World Bank.

WORKING GROUP FOR INTERNATIONAL CO-OPERATION IN VOCATIONAL AND TECHNICAL SKILLS DEVELOPMENT. 1997. *Donor Policies in Skills Development, London, May 1997.* Geneva/Berne, SDC/ILO/NORRAG. (Paper 2.)

Part One.
Development co-operation in the context of globalization

The new boundaries of international development co-operation
Jacques Forster

As 'development decades' go by, and particularly since the 1970s, boundaries between North and South, that is between development and underdevelopment, are becoming increasingly hazy. Actually these boundaries never rested on solid scientific foundations; they were established at the end of the Second World War as it became clear that decolonization and the emergence of the Cold War called for a new approach towards both countries and territories — most of them colonies or former colonies — in which poverty, illiteracy and poor health standards were very widespread (Myrdal, 1969).

In the field of international development co-operation,[1] the boundaries between donors and recipients of ODA have changed. The content of development co-operation has also constantly been expanded for reasons not always devoid of opportunism. More fundamentally, the sustainability of the Western economic and societal model, dominantly accepted as the goal towards which developing societies were supposed to be moving, is being increasingly challenged.

This chapter presents some consequences of this evolving situation for international development co-operation as well as for development studies.

The point of departure

In the 1960s, when, in the wake of decolonization, international development co-operation became firmly established as a new dimension of

---

1. In this chapter, international development co-operation includes ODA and all policies and measures taken by states with the declared intention to promote economic and social development in developing countries.

international relations, its official objective was fairly plain. As it was commonly accepted that countries were divided up between rich and poor – that is, developed and underdeveloped – the development of the latter was an internationally recognized objective for which the former had a special responsibility. International development co-operation – and particularly ODA – became the means to reach this objective.

The world was then also divided along ideological and geostrategic lines defined by the interests of two superpowers and their more or less influential allies. This caused international development co-operation to become an instrument used to gain or maintain influence among allied or client states and to ensure that non-aligned states would not lean too far towards the Cold War rivals.

Although the means propounded by the two competing political, economic and social systems to achieve economic development were very different, the end pursued was by and large the same: namely, to reduce the gap between rich and poor countries through economic growth and diversification (industrialization) achieved by higher rates of investment. The international transfer of resources – through ODA or otherwise – was meant to contribute to investment financing and, subsequently, growth.

Social development was not explicitly on the agenda: inequalities would eventually be reduced either as the benefits of growth trickled down to the poorest segments of society or, in the socialist model, through the public appropriation of the means of production. The relationship between environment and development, which at present plays a key role in North–South relations, only became a meaningful component of international development co-operation after the 1992 United Nations Conference on Environment and Development in Rio de Janeiro, although awareness of the significance of this issue gradually increased after the United Nations Conference on Human Development (Stockholm, 1972).

With hindsight, the most striking feature of this epoch might well have been the lack of questioning of a so-called 'developed' society; the Western type of market economy was widely accepted as a model for those not convinced by the promises of the Soviet model. This somewhat simplified picture does not do justice to individuals, institutions and schools of thought that did not adhere to the main stream and that, from the start, questioned this dominant development paradigm either because of the structurally unequal relationship between the 'centre' and the 'periphery' or because the dichotomy between 'developed' and 'developing' societies did not, in their view, rest on very solid ground.

The changing boundaries of international development co-operation

Over the past decades, the boundaries of international development co-operation have changed both because its scope has been constantly enlarged (as we shall see below) and because dramatic changes have occurred in the distribution of roles among donors and recipients of official development assistance, particularly since the beginning of this decade.

The group of recipients has been newly defined by OECD's DAC – the main donors' club – as it decided for statistical purposes to establish two separate lists of recipients (DAC, 1997), namely:
- ODA recipients, defined as developing countries.
- Official assistance recipients, defined as countries in transition.

The latter category includes two different subgroups of countries: (a) some of the former communist countries of the former USSR and of Eastern Europe; and (b) 'more advanced' developing countries which currently comprises twelve countries and territories including high-income oil-exporting countries and a few wealthy small island-states and territories. By the year 2000, this group should include four more countries and territories (Republic of Korea, the Libyan Arab Jamahiriya, Gibraltar and the Virgin Islands).

The list of developing countries receiving ODA has been expanded since the end of the Cold War by the addition of no less than nine of the fifteen republics of the former USSR and Albania.

The donors' side has also undergone profound changes:
- The former communist countries which in 1988 had disbursed some US$4.7 billion (approximately 10 per cent of what DAC countries provided) have, with the exception of the Czech Republic, completely disappeared from the donors' scene.
- The net flows of aid provided by Arab oil-exporting countries have decreased very substantially over the past decade (more than tenfold in the case of Saudi Arabia). This is due, in the first place, to the economic situation of many of these countries, which has led them to cut

public spending to reduce substantial budget deficits. It can also be explained by the low – sometimes even negative – net flows of resources resulting from debt-service obligations.

An increasing number of developing countries are both recipients and donors of foreign aid (Turkey, China, India, Israel and Brazil are but a few examples). Nevertheless, the trend of the past decade is very clearly towards a stronger concentration of ODA resources in the hands of DAC members (86 per cent of world ODA in 1988; more than 98 per cent in 1995).

As development decades have gone by, the boundaries of international development co-operation have constantly been expanded. New objectives did not replace but rather were added to the original ones. In a first phase, accelerated growth was the key objective; it was to be brought about by higher rates of capital formation made possible by the international transfer of resources (capital and know-how). This objective is still very much in the forefront, particularly for low-income countries. However, the means advocated to promote economic growth now emphasize policy and institutional reform rather than the transfer of resources *per se*.

At the end of the 1960s, there was growing awareness that the gap between rich and poor continued to widen both internationally and at the national level in many developing countries. This awoke a greater concern for distribution issues. In the wake of strategies designed to eradicate absolute poverty before the turn of the century, more attention was paid to programmes and projects specifically designed to combat poverty. This task was added to the development agenda; in the following years environment-related programmes and projects were also added progressively.

Early in the present decade, yet new dimensions were included in North–South international development co-operation. Issues such as democracy, human rights, good governance – in short, political reform – came to the forefront of the aid relationship at the end of the Cold War. Major policy statements to that effect were produced by all major Western donors between 1990 and 1992 (Stokke, 1995, p. 22). The European Bank for Reconstruction and Development (EBRD) was the first development bank to include explicitly such objectives in its statutory mission statement.

These progressive enlargements were brought about by a combination of learning from past experience and adjusting to new situations, needs and demands. This adjustment process was not devoid of opportunism, both political (the end of the Cold War made it easier to put human rights issues on the agenda) and institutional (the need to follow or appear to follow the new main stream in order to preserve the institution's access to financial resources).

An indicator of this evolution is provided by the changes in the content of ODA, in other words, the description of the projects and programmes that can be legitimately included in official DAC aid statistics. Over the years many items were added to that list:
- Assistance for democratic development.
- Development-related contributions to combat narcotics.
- Participation in United Nations peace-keeping operations (excluding purely military components).
- Assistance to demobilization efforts.
- A share of contributions to the Global Environment Facility (GEF).
- A share of disbursements related to asylum-seekers and refugees from developing countries in the host industrialized country.

At a time when aid funding stagnates or diminishes, this extension of the scope of what ODA can finance represents a reduction of resources for traditional development programmes.

The changing boundaries of development

The dichotomy dividing the world into developed and developing areas was scientifically questionable from the start as both groups always displayed a certain degree of heterogeneity. The main indicator for this dichotomy, namely per capita GNP, was too simplistic to reflect economic and social development. It was, however, widely accepted both because it reflected the expectations of many new post-colonial states to see their specific problems taken seriously in the wake of decolonization and because of a general common understanding of what development was to achieve. In fact, one could also say – somewhat provocatively – that the 'developed' countries were those that had the ambition to have other countries adopt their development model and the resources to persuade them to do so.

Things have since changed considerably but have not become simpler.

The South has become more heterogeneous

Taking as an indicator the human development index (HDI) of the United Nations Development Programme (UNDP), the group of countries displaying high human development includes sixty-four countries, of which thirty-three are developing countries (UNDP, 1997). These are, by and large, Caribbean, East Asian and Latin American countries.

At the other end of the scale one finds forty-four countries with low human development. All of them are developing countries, mostly from Asia and Africa. Their average life expectancy at birth is 25 per cent below that of industrialized countries and adult literacy only reaches half the level of the North.

The analysis of other social and economic indicators would confirm this heterogeneity and the fact that the boundaries of the so-called Third World are definitely not the same as when the concept was created in the early 1950s. Yet, the Third World still exists as many developing countries continue to face 'traditional' unresolved development problems: lack of diversification of economic activities, inadequate physical and social infrastructures, poor management of natural resources, external dependency, unequal income distribution, poverty and lack of opportunities for large segments of the population.

Former communist countries represent a complex phenomenon

Five of the former communist countries belong to the group of countries with a high HDI (Slovakia, the Czech Republic, Hungary, Poland and Belarus (the only representative of the former USSR). All others, including the Russian Federation, are in the group of countries with medium human development.

The 'transition economies', although they are not included in the list of developing countries, are difficult to characterize because they display, in a manner perhaps even more striking than developing countries, characteristics typical of both developing and industrialized countries. In areas such as education, scientific research and technology development, they reach high standards. Nevertheless, they also display many characteristics typical of developing economies, particularly as far as their international economic relations are concerned (structure of foreign trade and capital movements, including direct investment). In many of them, the use of environmentally damaging technologies and poor maintenance of industrial infrastructures and equipment account for particularly acute pollution and natural resources management problems.

The transition process in these societies has entailed particularly high social costs. In the Russian Federation, for instance, the social groups hardest hit are those that were already below the poverty threshold under the former regime: old people, large and single-parent families, the handicapped, and minority and marginal groups. Children seem to be severely affected by rampant malnutrition, declining school enrolment and the neglect of institutions designed to care for the most vulnerable of them. The most spectacular indicator of this state of social hardship is undoubtedly the sharp decline in life expectancy, particularly concerning the male population. According to UNDP, life expectancy has fallen to 59 years in the Russian Federation and is thus lower than in China (67) and India (61). The high cost of transition to the vulnerable sections of the population cannot be explained merely by economic recession. It is also, if not primarily, related to an institutional vacuum due to the erosion of the role of the state and the weakness or sheer non-existence of alternative institutions.

Western development model in jeopardy?

The perception of the West proposing a development model to the rest of the world has profoundly changed over the past quarter of a century.[2] On the one hand, countries in other areas of the world have established their own models which demonstrate an impressive ability to promote rapid economic growth, even if the 'economic miracle' proves to be fragile. On the other hand, the Western model is confronted with a set of very difficult and far-reaching questions and challenges.

The most fundamental question may be the sustainability of a development model based on economic growth for societies with high per capita incomes. It is widely admitted today that the mean Western per capita consumption of non-renewable energy cannot be sustained in the long run, far less be generalized to other regions of our planet (UNDP,

2. The West refers here to the group of high-income market economies which, besides Western Europe, the United States and Canada, also includes Japan, Australia and New Zealand.

1994). The challenge is therefore to conceive a development model capable of reconciling human development and substantially lower rates of consumption of energy and other non-renewable natural resources.

A few decades ago, the dominant perception in Western societies was that poverty and destitution were bound to disappear as the benefits of economic progress would trickle down to all segments of society. This perception no longer holds. Recent research shows that poverty in the rich countries is spreading. Today in all major Western European countries and in the United States at least 12 per cent of the population is below the poverty line (UNDP, 1997). An increasing number of people – half a million in France, close to 2 million in the United States (Bairoch, 1997, p. 541) – experience progressive exclusion from their traditional social environment as they lose their jobs and homes, and as their ties to their friends and even family are jeopardized. Since 1975, inequality has been increasing in many Western European countries and in the United States. According to Bairoch (1997, pp. 536–7), 1975 can be considered to mark a reversal of the trend towards the reduction of inequalities that started during the last quarter of the nineteenth century in Europe.

The 'development crisis' in the Western world has many other aspects. A particularly important one is the ageing of the population and uncertainty concerning future demographic trends. This, combined with sluggish economic growth and increased unemployment, has also led to the crisis of the welfare state and its dismantling. Thus, it is at the very moment of its triumph over its rival that the Western development model seems to be in jeopardy. This is not as paradoxical as it may appear at first sight.

International development co-operation: the need for a new agenda

The main tentative conclusion that can be drawn from the above presentation is that the dichotomy dividing the world according to the degree of development of countries has lost its validity – if it ever had one – and political usefulness. This conclusion would lead to the recognition that all regions of the world face unresolved development problems. This is obvious for transition economies and most developing countries; it is becoming more apparent in Western industrialized societies because of awareness that 'more of the same' will not be enough to meet current challenges. The sole pursuit of economic growth is by no means sufficient to ensure social and environmental sustainability. A different development model is needed, based on values, behavioural patterns, institutions, structures and policies capable of ensuring a safe and sustainable passage into the next millennium.

This conclusion involves important implications for international development co-operation. Our view is that it will remain an important component of international relations. It will have to deal with persistent international inequalities and cope with the problems arising from more intensive trade, economic and financial relations and trade in services among unequal partners. These problems will continue to require action to prevent and correct the unbalanced distribution of costs and benefits resulting from the new global economic order.

In its *modus operandi*, international development co-operation should no longer reflect the asymmetric nature of the world power system and serve as a means of promoting external development models. More emphasis should be placed on the exchange of experience. Adjustment is – and most probably will remain for a long time – on the agenda of every single region. This is an area in which developing and transition countries have undoubtedly more experience than the North which, until now, has managed to conduct its adjustment process at a much more leisurely pace than that imposed on other countries. For example, the adjustments imposed as a result of the Uruguay Round[3] to the textile and garment industry and to the agricultural sector give the industrialized countries far longer transition periods than those of structural adjustment programmes.

At present, international development co-operation is confronted with a paradoxical situation. As we have seen, its scope has constantly been enlarged. In other words, the tasks to be financed through ODA

3. I am referring here to adjustments under way as a consequence of the conclusion of the Uruguay Round. The Uruguay Round of multilateral trade negotiations conducted under the auspices of the General Agreement on Tariffs and Trade (GATT) – the eighth of its kind – was initiated in 1986 in Punta del Este (Uruguay) and concluded in 1994. It is undoubtedly the most important negotiation in the history of international economic relations. It led to the creation of the World Trade Organization (WTO) and the inclusion of new areas in the scope of multilateral negotiation such as trade in services and intellectual property rights. In the field of trade, it initiated a process of tariff reduction and dismantlement of other obstacles to trade for goods, such as textiles and garments and agricultural products, that the industrialized countries had managed to shelter from international competition.

increase at a time when resources are constantly being reduced. In the 1990s, the volume of resources available for development-oriented programmes and projects has furthermore been restricted by the increasing share of ODA attributed to emergency relief operations in conflict situations. In real terms, the volume of DAC official development assistance is today approximately at the same level as in 1987. This means that resources available to developing countries have clearly diminished. Indeed, in the first place the list of such countries has been lengthened by the addition of a number of former communist countries. Moreover, this period of time has witnessed the sharp reduction of ODA from non-DAC countries. The trend of declining ODA resources is not likely to change in the near future. It is due mainly to budget deficits of most DAC countries, but also to what has been called 'aid fatigue', that is an expression of disappointment resulting from the limited results achieved after half a century of international development co-operation. This is not the place to discuss the extent to which this view is justified. But the fact is that the foreign aid business is severely criticized for its lack of performance.

In this context, a new agenda for international development co-operation is a necessity both in terms of meeting new needs and of acquiring a new legitimacy in the industrialized world. Following on thoughts that have been developed during the past four years by the Office of Development Studies of UNDP, international development co-operation, in our view, should concentrate its efforts on contributing to the management of some of the world's main global development problems.

Global problems can be defined as those which combine the three following characteristics:
- They affect global security and welfare.
- Their negative effects have an impact in areas from which they did not originate.
- They can only be solved or alleviated through international co-operation.

The following problems qualify for inclusion in the list of global problems and on the agenda of international development co-operation (Griffin and McKinley, 1996):
- Environmental problems (deforestation, air and water pollution, use of non-renewable resources, management of global commons).
- Production, distribution and consumption of narcotic drugs.

- International crime.
- Spread of communicable diseases.
- International transfer of weapons.

This new agenda also needs to include traditional development objectives, giving a higher priority to low-income countries and particularly to the group of least-developed countries which, in spite of repeated declarations, have not received the attention required by their specific problems. In the poor countries, mass poverty and its many root causes are also a global problem in the sense given above.

The implementation of this agenda requires more financial and human resources than development co-operation agencies can currently muster. UNDP (1994) launched a number of proposals on new sources of financing. They are attractive, but their implementation requires strong political will, i.e. strong and active constituencies in many countries, and not only in the North. They will take time to develop. But a renewed agenda may convince large sections of the population that this is a worthwhile price to pay for global welfare and security. There are no less costly alternatives.

However, with – or even more without – additional resources, international development co-operation badly needs to increase its efficiency and effectiveness. To achieve this objective, it is not only necessary to improve ODA programmes and projects. It is also mandatory to take a broader look at North–South relations and take into account the impact of other dimensions of these relations on developing countries. This approach, advocated by DAC (1993), has been referred to as the 'policy coherence' approach.

Coherence would require that policies related to various dimensions of North–South relations all aim at achieving the same objective, that they should be complementary rather than at cross-purposes. DAC (1993) makes a distinction between interrelated policies which have for a long time been included in the development co-operation dialogue (trade, debt, tied aid and foreign direct investment) and new policy areas (environment, drug addiction, AIDS, migrations and human rights). This enumeration, to which one could also add military expenditure and transfers of weapons, indicates that, in that broader approach, the quest for greater coherence encompasses a very wide range of issues and policies involving practically every ministry and government agency.

Since 1992, some DAC members have taken steps to improve the coherence of their policies towards developing countries. They have set up mechanisms to identify and attempt to reduce possible contradictions or inconsistencies between policies. Experience shows – as common sense would indicate – that this is far from sufficient to eliminate all contradictions. It nevertheless indicates that through such processes areas can be identified where unintended incoherence prevails and corrective action be taken. By identifying areas of contradiction, the process also encourages public debate on important issues and ensures that policy decisions are made in full conscience of their impact on developing countries.[4]

Implications for development studies

Development studies have emerged in a very specific historical context very aptly defined by Myrdal (1969) as a combination of three elements: decolonization, the emergence of new power elites in many developing countries with a development-oriented agenda and the Cold War. The scene has since then considerably changed.

For a long period of time, development studies were, with important exceptions, an asymmetric business. 'Northern' social scientists were studying the South, that is, those parts of the world which were facing 'development problems'. As time went by, the South's capacity to study its own problems increased considerably. By and large, developing countries today have the expertise to study their development problems, even if in some of the least developed countries the institutions and financial resources may not yet be adequate to meet all needs for research, training and consultancy. Does this mean that development studies in the North have become obsolete?

The answer is no, both because there still are needs in the traditional areas of development studies and because new development problems in different parts of the world call for the kind of expertise developed over time by development studies.

4. An International Workshop on Policy Coherence in Development Co-operation took place at the Graduate Institute of Development Studies in Geneva in April 1997. Its objective was to compare and assess the efforts of selected industrialized countries and of the European Union to introduce more coherence into their policies towards developing countries. A book reflecting the content of this workshop will be published by Frank Cass, London, in early 1999 as No. 22 in the EADI Book Series: *Policy Coherence in Development Co-operation* (edited by J. Forster and O. Stokke).

Traditional areas

In the North there is still a continued need for expertise on developing countries and their specific development problems. The ongoing integration of the world economy intensifies and diversifies the impact of many – and sometimes new – dimensions of international relations in developing countries (as discussed above, the Uruguay Round has opened up new and important fields of interaction). In the North, decisions on aid and trade, but also on environment- or migration-related issues, have to be made in full cognizance of their impact on developing countries, even if, for reasons of national interest, the decision has adverse effects on developing countries. The need for more policy coherence calls for impact assessments. Decision-makers in the North will therefore continue to need research and expertise on developing countries.

New areas

The new areas in which development studies can provide valuable inputs derive both from the new agenda of international development co-operation and the development problems confronting the North. As far as the international development co-operation agenda is concerned, global problems – such as those listed above – need to be studied: What are their root causes? What is their impact in various parts of the world? Who are the main actors? What are the policy options in the North and the South? Development specialists cannot pretend to deal competently with all these issues which require specific, specialized expertise. They do, however, have a number of assets that enable them to participate meaningfully in research teams working on such themes:

- Experience in multidisciplinary work. This is by no means a monopoly of development studies, but development-oriented social scientists can contribute to the integration of social, economic, political and anthropological dimensions of research on global issues, which all require a multidisciplinary approach.
- Expertise in the analysis of the impact of exogenous factors in developing countries at various levels of society (national, regional, community).
- Experience in intercultural relations. This is a requirement to study any of the global issues, if only to grasp the diversity of their perception in different cultural contexts.

- Experience in co-operation (notably through participatory research) with social actors at various levels of society.

Today, the high-income industrialized countries are confronted with genuine development problems. They are in search of new development models requiring far-reaching adjustments in modes of production and consumption as well as patterns of distribution. The experience of development studies specialists can be pertinent in that context. This is the case when analysing the impact on developing countries of structural changes in the North. But it also concerns issues in which developing countries have gained experience and which, *mutatis mutandis*, could be relevant for the North, for example:

- Dealing with poverty and inequality-related issues.
- Coping with structural adjustment and its social and political feasibility.
- Providing basic social services at a time of severe financial constraints.

These are a few areas in which development studies can make a contribution in collaboration with government and academic institutions specifically concerned with these questions.

In view of the changing context of development studies in the North and the South, there is a need for development studies to adopt a new agenda based on its strengths and comparative advantages. Development studies institutions in the North have to define an enhanced relationship with sister institutions in the South based on genuine partnership and complementarity, common research agenda-setting and evaluation procedures. They should move away from the donor–recipient relationship that continues to prevail in North–South research co-operation (Maselli and Sottas, 1996).

Development studies institutions should in addition develop their co-operation with research and teaching institutions in industrialized countries that deal with global issues and new development patterns for Western societies.

In conclusion, development studies must adjust their agenda to the present world development situation. This will require far-reaching changes. It can be achieved by building on existing comparative advantages, developing a new style of co-operation with partner institutions in the South and concluding alliances with new partners in the North.

References

BAIROCH, P. 1997. *Victoires et déboires. III. Histoire économique et sociale du monde du XVIᵉ siècle à nos jours*. Paris, Gallimard.
DAC. 1993. *1992 Development Co-operation Report*. Paris, DAC/OECD.
——. 1997. *1996 Development Co-operation Report*. Paris, DAC/OECD.
GRIFFIN, K.; MCKINLEY, T. 1996. *New Approaches to Development Co-operation*. New York, UNDP, Office of Development Studies. (Discussion Papers Series, 7.)
MASELLI, D.; SOTTAS, B. (eds.). 1996. *Research Partnerships for Common Concerns*. Hamburg, LIT Verlag.
MYRDAL, G. 1969. *Asian Drama. An Inquiry into the Poverty of Nations*. New York, Twentieth Century Fund and Pantheon.
STOKKE, O. 1995. *Aid and Political Conditionality*. London, Frank Cass. (EADI Book Series, 16.)
UNDP. 1994. *Human Development Report 1994*. New York, UNDP.
——. 1997. *Human Development Report 1997*. New York, UNDP.

The future of international aid to education: a personal reflection
Aklilu Habte

Introduction

As the twenty-first century is about to dawn upon us all, we are all feverishly articulating our 'millennium' wishes. This chapter is no exception. Its central purpose is to revisit the future of aid to education and to conjoin those agencies, organizations and scholars that have discussed the issue in one form or another.[1] The future of aid to education continues to be in the realm of confusion despite the tremendous amount of experience gathered over the past several decades underpinning the centrality and, indeed, the inevitability of education for development and other desirable goals of societies.

The issue does become compounded with additional cultural, geopolitical and socio-economic global and regional developments that are bound to have an impact on the lives of ordinary people and countries. This chapter does not deal with these issues, but we need to mention some of them, albeit briefly, as reminders of the complexity and uncertainty of the future of education.

The most striking and indeed the most pivotal event or development of our era is the end of the Cold War, which politically has accelerated the emergence of an economic, military and political superpower, and in terms of the global flow of aid has put 'pressure to divert resources to so-called transitional economies particularly in Central and Eastern European countries and in the newly independent states of the former Soviet Union' (Buchert, 1995, p. 1).

1. OECD/DAC, the United Nations Children's Fund (UNICEF), UNDP, the International Working Group on Education (IWGE), UNESCO, the World Bank, NORRAG and other organizations have touched on the issue in their publications and in innumerable meetings, especially since 1990, as have several scholars and development practitioners.

Equally important and, in some futuristic sense, perhaps more important is the trend towards globalization and the economic groupings process, on one side, and the fracturing of societies, the ethnic, religious and cultural specifications and assertions, on the other, as is now being manifested in the former Yugoslavia, Ethiopia and the Lake regions of Africa. This poses the issue of the long-term role of education in nation-building and harmonization processes juxtaposed within the too frequent atmosphere of short-term conflict, violence and social turmoil.

A third and already possible consequence of the above two trends is the emphasis on the need to respect the Universal Declaration of Human Rights and, in general, the emergence of a strong role for civil society, the emphasis on democratization and the participation of people in the art and science of governance.

A fourth and powerful trend is the widespread recognition of the absolute necessity for gender equality.

In all these and others, the pivotal role of education emerges as a common factor. What is going to happen to education in general, and to the international support that education is or is not going to receive in the future, appears as a decisive factor to be reckoned with. Coincidentally felicitous, however, is the emergence of strong and compelling evidence of the importance and critical role of education in the totality of the development process, as one of the undisputed generalizations advocated in national plans and by international agencies.[2] These are major and important trends which the world needs to watch and participate in.

Another reason why these trends are critical to mention, besides showing the intricate linkage between them and education, is to alert the world community that if these are to be taken as indicators of our future, we may face stiff and legitimate resistance, since the majority of humanity did not participate in their articulation. They may not, therefore, capture the totality of the problem or aspiration faced by the majority of the earth's citizens.

We need to stop and think of the consequences of considering the future merely as a continuation of the past. We need to invent the future, a future that accommodates the majority, if not all of the peoples of the

---

2. For reference, consult, for example, the World Bank's *World Development Reports*, 1980 and following years; UNDP, *Human Development Reports* 1992–94; and UNICEF, UNESCO and other agencies' discussions on the subject.

world.[3] We need also to note that a future in which the majority of the people do not participate, either directly or through their representatives, does not represent their future, their aspirations.

How could that be? Look at the following World Bank statistics (Serageldin, 1995, pp. 8–9):

- The richest 20 per cent of the world's population receive 83 per cent of its income. The poorest 20 per cent receive 1.4 per cent.
- Over 1 billion people live on less than $1 a day.
- Over 800 million people go hungry every day.
- Over 2 billion people are suffering from either hunger or malnutrition.
- Over 40,000 hunger-related deaths occur each day.
- There are over fifteen countries in Africa whose primary-school participation rate is less than 50 per cent.

These are by any definition beneath human decency. The gap is wide and the need for continued aid clear. More importantly, the need for education aid is even strikingly evident since, in order to overcome most if not all of the above ills, education will be a necessary precondition. This we have learnt during the past thirty to forty years. Aid agencies seem to be learning these lessons, although the developed countries embraced them a long time ago. This is why the developed countries are where they are today in comparison to poorer countries.

The purpose of my remarks is not to focus merely on the abundance of knowledge, information and technological leapfrogging currently prevalent in the developed countries, but to pose the serious question: where will the world be a decade from now if such gaps are not narrowed or alternatives devised? The inescapable conclusion is that the already existing gap has prevailed because of the absence or weakness of educational capacity, and the gap will continue to widen if due importance and support are not given to education nationally and internationally in the future and in an extraordinary manner. As mentioned earlier, the future of education, and the amount, quality and nature of aid to education should not be a mere continuation of our past performance. The above statistics do not need further explanation. Visionary leapfrogging to invent a better world with better living conditions is required. Existing educational institu-

---

3. See the thoughtful contributions by Charles Handy, in particular Handy (1997).

tions in developing countries and international institutions with a mandate in education need to be dynamized. One could of course suggest the relative irrelevance of these poorer countries following the end of the Cold War? And the problem stops there. This is not harsh speculation.

But do prevailing conditions in the developed and industrialized countries favour or constrain the continued need for a dramatic support to education? There are indications that send chilling signs. Consider the following observations:

First of all, several of the developed countries are working with stringent budgetary conditions that are putting pressures on them to look more into domestic issues, turning 'inward and away from internationalism or even multilateralism' (Serageldin, 1995, p. 11).

Commercial or business considerations are increasingly being given more weight in bilateral aid formulation and allocation strategies. The latest information that seven African leaders have signed a pact of a new relationship with the President of the United States of America based on 'trade and a deepened respect for human rights' (Davies, 1998) is yet another example of a recent event. Organizationally, the twinning of aid and trade is being strengthened in ministries of foreign affairs. Multinational corporations' continued important role in bilateral relationships is, if not officially sanctioned, then unofficially condoned. The recent example of the French oil company ELF's involvement in the political struggle of the two parties in the Congo, the involvement and/or support of several companies in apartheid South Africa, the 1997 prize-awarding ceremony on 'good governance', organized by a number of corporations and the corporate council on Africa and held at the Westfields Conference Center in Chantilly (Virginia), are yet other examples.[4]

A fourth example comes from the private military companies which are growing in certain countries and providing a variety of services, including training, equipment and combat assistance to governments (Lederer, 1998). In the context of the prevailing notion of partnership among governments, multinationals and other private organizations, examples such as those mentioned above may seem ordinary. But in the circumstances of several Third World countries that manifest weakness and whose political

4. At this latter, which was attended by First Lady Hillary Clinton, there was a strong demonstration that opposed the recognition of certain heads of state as having any track record of good governance.

structure is rampant with self-serving dictators, the danger of foreign non-governmental corporations' involvement in their internal affairs without the supervision, sanction or indeed knowledge of any credible international organization is an extremely dangerous trend that needs to be nipped in the bud. At bottom, such organizations work for money and for profit. They do not possess any moral, representational or other authority to play an international role such as the awarding of prizes to young and corruptible heads of state. One may indeed ask who they are. To whom are they accountable? From where do they derive their credibility?

Given the too prevalent practice of corruption around the world, one could ask the question whether such activities do not reinforce and legitimize individual and/or party enrichment at the expense of the populace.

Education aid is further facing stiff competition from such global events and occurrences as peace-keeping (Europe), disaster relief (global), environmental protection and the collapse of governments (Somalia). Although the issue of foreign aid is a topic that rises and falls over time, and varies from country to country, by the mid-1990s there seemed to be a widespread aid fatigue together with a feeling of hopelessness and discouragement. In such circumstances, advocacy of an increase in official aid in general did not seem to be the winning election ticket in European and North American capital cities.

As mentioned earlier, what-is-there-in-it-for-me? business attitudes prevail. The classic humanitarian argument keeps flickering during emergencies and anticipated disasters. Despite the emergence of poverty alleviation or poverty eradication as a policy platform by multinationals and some bilaterals, it is as yet too early to detect the emergence of any meaningful strategy, at least in the Africa region. Yet most recognize education as having a central place in whatever strategy is suggested.

The future of aid for education: will the future look like the past?

Given the usual lethargy when it comes to introducing dramatic changes in bureaucratic practices and the general conservatism of education systems, the challenging question is how much of the future will be reflected in present-day policies and how much of the past will persist in future programmatic activities? The experiences of aid to education over the past four or so decades is instructive. The several volumes of documents produced, the regional meetings held in preparation for the World Conference on Education for All, and the national, regional and global conferences organized and held since then all indicate the generally low priority accorded to education by both governments and aid agencies.

There are of course exceptions. The successful Marshall Plan approach in Europe after the Second World War was transplanted to other developing countries. The emphasis on infrastructure, transport, power and agriculture in Europe and in other countries was perhaps legitimate and even wise. The devastation of the Second World War necessitated a massive physical reconstruction. In hindsight, the major reason for the success was, of course, the presence of an educated population with the requisite general knowledge ready to be trained in the necessary skills. This educational reservoir and motivation succeeded in rebuilding the war-torn economy.

However, a transplantation of this approach to Africa, Asia and elsewhere did not work because the educated human reservoir was not there. And the prevailing wisdom of the 1960s and subsequent decades dictated the use of technical assistance, with its twin components of study abroad and importation of technical expertise. In hindsight, the lack of concern and emphasis on endogenous capacity-building over a long period turned out to be a disaster. Until very recently, the proportion of support given to human resources development was low. A good example is the case of the World Bank. In 1996, education aid as a proportion of the overall aid budget of the World Bank was a pathetic 5 per cent, and at the time of the World Conference on Education for All (1990) it was 7.2 per cent. The situation in the World Bank and in other aid agencies is so well known and documented that further treatment is not needed here.[5]

The proportion of DAC aid to education in 1990 was less than that for agriculture and energy and less than in the 1980s. The picture is similar in other bilateral and multilateral institutions (Buchert, 1995, Table 2, p. 14).

This discussion on developing countries in general is more forcefully applicable to the situation of the sub-Saharan region, with the possible caveat that multilaterals tended to provide a disproportionate share of

5. See various World Bank *Annual Reports* and other agencies' publications.

their loans to capital expenditures, while bilaterals supported technical assistance. There is of course a reason why the aid paradigm is intensified in Africa. When taken together, (a) the preference for capital intensity, (b) foreign exchange dominance, (c) the limited choice of geographical location for such institutions as secondary schools or universities compared to the dispersed primary schools, (d) heavy reliance on the use of international expertise and (e) overseas fellowships support the strong logic and policy paradigm perpetuated during the colonial era and continued thereafter, since, initially, the same people shifted their seat from colonial offices to the offices of development agencies.

Jomtien and its promises: have agencies and countries responded positively to the World Declaration on Education for All?

Did a paradigm shift in the amount, manner and use of international aid to education occur following the 1990 Jomtien Conference? It would be extremely complex to even attempt to discuss the extent to which both countries and agencies have met the Jomtien objectives. The document of the mid-decade review indicated rather inconclusive and mixed results. Let us consider one area, that of increased resource flow. Have international funding and technical assistance agencies responded and subsequently increased their financial contribution to education in general and basic education in particular? Several observations and studies, including the interesting study recently concluded by Bennell and Furlong (1997, p. 1) seem to indicate that:

- In real terms, total aid for the education sector from bilateral agencies was lower in the mid-1990s than before the World Conference on Education for All.
- The additional external resources that have been and are likely to be forthcoming will be insufficient to meet the basic Education for All objectives by the year 2000.

Let us look at the picture of the World Bank, which has perhaps conclusively increased its resources for primary education. What does the picture look like in one of the regions of the world whose needs are clearly unmistakable – Africa? 'Whilst the overall proportion of lending for education has increased, its relative share for Africa has declined from 11.2 per cent in 1990 to 4.8 per cent in 1996.' Similarly, it declined from 11.6 per cent to 8.1 per cent in East Asia and the Pacific, remained about the same in South Asia (16.6 per cent in 1990 to 17 per cent in 1996), and from 4.1 per cent in 1990 to 0.1 per cent in 1996 in Europe and Central Asia (Bennell and Furlong, 1997, Table 4, p. 11).

Further discussion and understanding of why such a disturbing picture is happening in the African region are called for. Would it be that the international community still has serious problems and difficulties in designing and implementing primary and basic education projects in sub-Saharan Africa? Should we study more seriously than hitherto internal country circumstances that in the end are the principal determinants of any programme or project? Is the International Development Association (IDA) allocation for education in Africa facing tougher competition from other sectors, in particular the public sector? Is it likely that the IDA funding for the education sector is receiving a limited increase from the overall IDA package?

My personal observations in the sub-Saharan region, where I travel frequently,[6] are that international aid for education continues to face several problems that require attention. Although there are exceptional cases, one observes dilapidated classroom and office conditions, gloomy-looking teachers, university laboratories that do not function, and a lack of resources to improve the access issue and others. The involvement and participation of communities in the formulation and implementation of projects are not a frequent sight. I do not observe dynamism and concern around the established leadership to bring about drastic changes. The translation of educational policies into programmes and implementable activities continues to be hampered as before. The low quality of staff, the lack of educational leadership, and the excessive and frequent change in the education portfolio continue.

I wonder whether meaningful changes are actually taking place. Of course there are exceptional cases, but how long do we have to keep worrying about support for basic education? I am worried whether the quality and experience of several staff members of the international agency community will make it possible to bring about change. I am worried that too

6. In 1996 and 1997, I visited Botswana, Chad, Côte d'Ivoire, Ghana, Kenya, Malawi, Mali, Niger, Senegal, South Africa, Uganda and Zambia.

often education is excessively politicized. The views and visions of Jomtien to reduce inequality and to emphasize student learning and teaching interaction are not visible. I think we need to stop and consider why things are going the way they are or why they are not going differently. I am also excessively worried that the continued nibbling at our fingers will end up at a standstill.

The international funding community should take seriously the behaviour of governments that are 'pro-people' and shy away from dealing with those that are 'anti-people'. It may be difficult to identify certain situations, but one could at least avoid dealing with corrupt dictators and human-rights violators. Partners should be prepared to audit the level of efficiency, honesty and commitment before giving grants or loans, i.e. before indebting future generations by pouring out loans whose investment returns to the country are indeed very questionable. There could not and should not be a compromise concerning the effectiveness and efficiency of aid. We should call a spade a spade and stop officially refuting that we dialogue on economic parameters, while unofficially toeing the political line. Any attempt to separate politics from economic development is creating a false paradigm, simplistic, untrue and therefore unproductive.

Perspectives of international aid to education

The above discussions and impressions seem to indicate that:
- The future of aid in general and aid to education in particular will probably continue at the current level with a faint possibility of some increase.
- Any increase is likely to benefit those countries with a firm and innovative plan of action on primary education, including the education of girls and training of adult women.
- The financial institutions, including the international financial corporations, are likely to finance higher education and private training.
- Aid support for countries is likely to be heavily based on political, commercial and hegemonic considerations.
- The most productive and effective scenario is for countries themselves to streamline their own priorities and reallocate internal resources, including shifts from areas such as defence and security budget items to basic social services and research.

- Forceful effort is needed to do more with the level of the current aid resources. We need to address those issues or factors that are likely to increase the effectiveness and efficiency of education aid. This includes the strengthening of the democratic process and the governance of countries, both likely to nurture the increasing participation of the populace and the direct involvement of all the stakeholders in the running of states, regional and local affairs, including the running of schools.
- Most of the international aid institutions that do not have a strong and meaningful presence in the recipient countries would continue to be token historical bureaucracies. A serious debate on either strengthening or transforming existing institutions needs to take place. We need to dismantle several of them. After all, they were established decades back and, since then, dramatic changes have been and are taking place. What was relevant yesterday might well be irrelevant today.

I think that at issue is the level of commitment of the political leadership to serve its people and the strengthening of the nexus between the professional and technical elite and the people. Also at issue is the fact that education reform is not a single event but a process. It has to have a strong local root and a longer time horizon.

Capacity development and institutional capacity

We have so far observed that despite the importance of education for nation-building and development, the amount of aid might not increase in a dramatic sense in the foreseeable future. We need, therefore, to explore other avenues and alternative scenarios than the ones indicated above to increase educational opportunities. This necessitates the presence of an endogenous capacity that can be creative and innovative, that evaluates internal circumstances, and that advocates what is essential and necessary over what is frivolous and prestigious. And yet, at the turn of the twenty-first century, we are raising similar, if not identical, issues and worries on capacity development as we did in the early 1960s and thereafter. What has gone wrong? Perhaps several things. Singled out below are the issues of (a) institutional capacity development, (b) technical assistance and (c) partnership.

Institutional capacity development

This is the most serious issue and one in which the means–end consonance is severely faulty. If capacity development is the objective, the means to be used must be capacity-building, not the opposite. Goodwill notwithstanding, let us observe the following situations:

First, the World Bank recently sent a group of fourteen experts to Ethiopia to explore the feasibility of an education sector programme. This is a country where more than 100,000 professionals from the civil service, technical establishments and institutions of higher learning have been retired or expelled on political pretext, but using World Bank and IMF structural adjustment justifications. These include over fifty of the university's experienced and seasoned professionals who, from my personal knowledge of a large number of them, could do as good a job, if not better than, the World Bank in response to the country's needs (Negash, 1996, pp. 11–27).

Compare this with the significant role of the World Bank in the undertaking of the 1971–72 Education Sector Review, as a result of an agreement signed between the Government of Ethiopia and IDA (Ethiopia, 1972). A distinctive aspect of this study was that it was undertaken largely by national institutions and citizens. Of the fourteen task forces and five smaller working groups, more than 75 per cent were chaired by professors and administrators of the university in Addis Ababa. A quarter of a century later scores of technical teams are being shipped to the country in total disregard of this capacity. Should we not pause to try to understand the causes of such a disaster? Of such capacity unutilization? Of such capacity destruction? Do not international morality and human integrity require agencies to take a position? Are we not heading for a new disaster? What would prevent it from recurring?

Second, UNICEF prepared a large number of National Plans of Action following the World Summit on Children (New York, September 1990). It appears that perhaps over 75 per cent of those reports were prepared by external consultants, including expatriate UNICEF staff. The plans were completed in time. The external experts learnt a great deal in the process. There were questions of ownership, of local capacity involvement. Very few of the countries I visited talked about them.

Third, UNESCO, chairing one of the working groups of the Association for the Development of Education in Africa (ADEA), analysed the contents, procedures and manning of about 240 leading education sector studies on Africa that had been undertaken during 1990–94 (Samoff et al., 1996). This interesting review documents some useful conclusions and observations, two of which are worth noting in this connection.

- The studies had all been undertaken by an expatriate-led team with nominal representation or inclusion of local researchers, never as senior consultants or document authors (pp. 14–15).
- Having raised the issue of institutional capacity – the issue of the prevalent deficiency in education management and administration – the review commented that such issues of education management and administration have been raised since independence days; consequently a variety of courses, training, short- and longer-term scholarships and fellowships have been provided. 'Yet still those who study African education point to a deficiency of managerial and administrative skills' (p. 18).

Now some forty years after the African countries gained their independence, we are discussing the same problems, without seriously addressing what happened, why it happened and whether further repeat performances of training will change the situation. I do not know of any serious, frank and systematic study or discussion on the issue which explains past failures or inefficiencies of training efforts unless, of course, such studies are locked up in the safe-boxes of some capitals. Is it not, for instance, worth asking the question why 'Africanization' of education sector studies has not proceeded? Why does the World Bank to date use expatriates to undertake studies? Is it, therefore, an exaggeration to read the conclusion that education sector studies in Africa seem to have been written more to be accountable to the parliaments and decision-makers of Europe and North America rather than to those of Africa (Samoff et al., 1996, p. 22).

These examples indicate that there is a serious ends–means discordance. And it raises the issue of whether the purpose of education to empower people is being violated, not by what we say but by what we do. We need to discuss this issue and undertake more in-depth studies. The conclusion of this part of my discussion is to indicate the serious neglect as regards using universities and other institutions in Africa that could do the job and in the process reinforce the capacities of African institutions.

Technical assistance

Technical assistance has been used consistently for several decades by international funding and technical-assistance agencies as the main avenue or instrument for capacity-building. Much has been written on this issue as it pertains to Africa. And there is an overwhelming consensus that there is more failure than success. This is disturbing since the money involved is huge and continuing. A recent World Bank study indicates that technical assistance represents between one-quarter and one-third of all external economic assistance to African nations, and absorbs a large chunk of the resources available for development (World Bank, 1996, p. XIV). This figure is much higher than earlier estimates on the subject. The inescapable conclusion is that if even a fraction of the money were to be used to strengthen national institutions and supply the market, African capacity would be in a better shape than we now find it.

Strengthening partnerships: co-ordination and co-operation

One of the major recommendations of the Jomtien Conference was the strengthening of partnerships. It states that 'new and revitalized partnerships at all levels will be necessary' (World Conference on Education for All, 1990, Art. 7). Much effort is being exerted to improve the situation, but to date the result has not been satisfactory, either at the national or at the international level.

At the national level, the critical missing link is the presence of a buoyant and strong civil society. In much of Africa, the civil society is young, fragile and too much under the control of the political authority. Yet most thinkers on governance agree on the important role played by civil society. Non-governmental organizations are facing a variety of difficulties. Some of them are of their own making and a large proportion of them come from the prevalent authoritarian and uncompromising political frameworks and leadership. Because of the important role which civil society plays in good governance, one needs to explore ways and means of strengthening it.

The co-ordination of assistance by international funding and technical-assistance agencies has not improved as much as expected, largely owing to national political and other interest considerations. Nevertheless, ADEA is pioneering an effort that is evolving along the lines anticipated in

Jomtien – encouraging co-ordination and fostering and strengthening ownership. Yet one is observing how difficult it is to change the attitudes of both agencies and countries. But at least one is now observing a frank exchange of views, and countries are beginning to assume a more dynamic role in national co-ordination of the international agencies.

Given the changing political scene and the necessity to nurture relationships over a longer period than an average project is expected to last, it would seem that we need to strengthen the co-operation, co-ordination and networking of professional associations, non-governmental organizations and representatives of civil society.

References

BENNELL, P.; FURLONG, D. 1997. *Has Jomtien Made any Difference? Trends in Donor Funding for Education and Basic Education since the Late 1980s*. Brighton, University of Sussex, Institute of Development Studies.

BUCHERT, L. 1995. *Recent Trends in Education Aid: Towards a Classification of Policies*. Paris, UNESCO/International Institute for Educational Planning.

DAVIES, K. 1998. US-Africa Endorse Free Trade. *The Associated Press*, 26 March.

ETHIOPIA. MINISTRY OF EDUCATION AND FINE ARTS. 1972. *Report of the Education Sector Review. Education Challenge to the Nation*. Addis Ababa.

HANDY, C. 1997. Finding Sense in Uncertainty. In: R. Gibson (ed.), *Rethinking the Future*, pp. 17–23. London, Nicholas Brealey Publishing.

LEDERER, E. M. 1998. Hiring Mercenary Forms a Hot Topic. *The Associated Press*, 26 March.

NEGASH, A. 1996. *The Pillage of Ethiopia*. Los Angeles, Adey Publishing Company.

SAMOFF, J., et al. 1996. *Analyses, Agendas and Priorities for Education in Africa. A Review of Externally Initiated, Commissioned and Supported Studies of Education in Africa, 1990–1994*. Paris, UNESCO, Working Group on Education Sector Analysis/Association for the Development of Education in Africa. (Doc. ED-96/WS/12.)

SERAGELDIN, I. 1995. *Nurturing Development*. Washington, D.C., World Bank.

WORLD BANK. 1996. *Partnership for Capacity Building in Africa. A Report of the Working Party on the Impact of Bank Policies, Instruments, and Operational Practices on Capacity Building in Africa*. Washington, D.C., World Bank.

WORLD CONFERENCE ON EDUCATION FOR ALL (Jomtien, Thailand, 5–9 March 1990). 1990. *World Declaration on Education for All and Framework for Action to Meet Basic Learning Needs*. New York, Inter-Agency Commission for WCEFA. (3rd impression, Paris, UNESCO, 1994.)

Aid, international co-operation and globalization: trends in the field of education
Michel Carton

Economic globalization and education

What is the future of educational international development co-operation in the present period of accelerated globalization? As Forster rightly points out in his contribution in this book, international development co-operation is no longer what it used to be. The inclusion in official OECD/DAC aid statistics of assistance for democratic development, participation in United Nations peace-keeping operations, development-related contributions to combat narcotics, assistance to demobilization efforts, and disbursements for asylum-seekers and refugees from developing countries residing in the industrialized ones indicates that the definition and scope of ODA have been substantially enlarged during the last ten years. It is not surprising, therefore, that the meaning and importance of aid to education, in the 1970s' sense of the term, have been changing rapidly. Despite static or even declining ODA, international development co-operation has to cover new fields of concern to international agencies and to fit new objectives. Education now has to contribute explicitly to democratic development, environmental concerns, narcotic reduction and others.

Nevertheless, until recently this trend remained compatible with the paradigm of aid to education as identified by King (1991), despite the fact that it questions the long-standing project-oriented way of identifying and running activities in that field. In addition, the content and quality of messages transmitted through education have become as important as their structures. The evolutions on the aid scene are now accelerating because the globalization process has dramatically changed our perspective on international co-operation during the past ten years. If we accept the definition of globalization as a process of systematic elimination of institutional and technological obstacles to the movement and profitability of financial capital, the following impacts can, according to Vinokur (1996), be expected in the production, transmission and appropriation of knowledge:

- A strong linkage to innovation as an essential determinant of profitability on increasingly competitive markets. As the cycles of consumption are shortening owing to the rapidity of technological change, firms have to constantly innovate and update themselves or call upon new knowledge.
- Consequently, education and training are increasingly articulated both in terms of structures and processes as the efficiency of the production and utilization of knowledge is defined primarily by economic agents (enterprises, firms and corporations). In other words, the leading role exerted by the political and social constituencies of civil society – usually represented through state structures – is declining vis-à-vis the economic and financial actors whose objectives are primarily market-oriented.
- An example of this evolution is clearly confirmed in France, for instance, where the concept of 'competence' (as a sum of different types of knowledge only validated through action) is now officially used in the law ruling education and training as well as in the corporate discourses and practices for production, staff organization and evaluation.
- Nevertheless, in spite of this move towards a strong economically oriented coherence among education, training and production, the ever-accelerating change in the production sphere has led to an increasing dissociation between output flows from education and training systems and input flows in production structures and processes. Because of the reaction time of these systems, stronger pressure is put on education and training institutions and on individuals to be more productive and effective in the short term and to adapt constantly to new situations. The social price is a dramatically increasing rate of non-insertion and/or exclusion of those who cannot cope.
- In other words, the dominant ideology of entrepreneurship is colonizing the field of human resources development as it encourages individuals to assume larger responsibility for their education and

training. This 'demand-driven' approach obviously leads to basic questioning of the education and training institutions which have tended to exert some kind of monopoly on the offer of programmes and curricula and, hence, have lost contact with the economic reality. This has led some people to compare the productivity of a kolkhoz-based Soviet production unit with that of a school system, and to underline that both are totally inefficient (Perelman, 1993).

- The apparent paradox of this trend is that it goes alongside a tendency towards the standardization of school-based skills at an international level in view of an improved assessment of the potential of labour markets across the globe. 'Standards for performance of an educational system do not differ systematically between Ghana and Georgia (either the state or the country). Educational officials in Africa, Asia . . . hold to the same standards and as a result they are demanding the same knowledge of innovation and system reforms as educational leaders within the OECD countries' (Heyneman, 1995, p. 2). The International Mathematics and Science Study highlights some of the consequences of this standardization process as it compares results of country/regions/people with reference to one single scale.
- In order to stimulate and/or accompany the previous trends, the growth of powerful knowledge industries has been facilitated by the boom of new information and communication technologies (*Prospects*, 1997*a*, *b*). The development of these industries has been based on the phenomena cited above of content standardization and individualization of consumption in education and training.

From international aid to international trade in educational co-operation: a challenge for the agencies

What we are witnessing, then, is an acceleration of the multiple phenomena of innovation, deinstitutionalization, standardization, privatization and individualization of the process and organizational modes of research, education and training (Vinokur, 1996). It is the combined effects of these trends that must be confronted by aid agencies and international development co-operation in the field of education and training. Will such agencies be capable of dealing with these phenomena and propose original and constructive responses? This uncertainty is particularly obvious in the case of public bilateral and multilateral agencies, as the development concepts and strategies adopted by such agencies in the 1970s are now being strongly questioned by the acceleration of phenomena linked to globalization. In addition, the decrease in international development co-operation activity observed since the mid-1980s is now being amplified as a result of:

- Reduced public resources for development aid and the consecutive and significant drop in the number of positions available within agencies.
- Ageing of agency personnel. Staff renewal is far from being guaranteed by a new generation, since the latter is more concerned with humanitarian aid, environmental issues and international trade than with the aims of traditional development co-operation.
- Transfer of public development aid to the private sector through competitive tendering as used, for example, by the European Union. This results in: (i) the dislocation of the potential for a coherent overall vision of educational policies leading to a sort of 'capacity debuilding'; and (ii) a shift in emphasis to rapid resolution of immediate problems (relief having replaced development).
- Significant growth of economic actors for whom educational research and projects constitute new flourishing markets. Corporations (and their 'demand' linked to globalization as mentioned above) are gaining increasing influence in the fields of scientific and technical research as well as in education and training (Carton, 1996).

The way in which international development co-operation responds to these phenomena will depend on each agency's analysis of both the general trends of globalization and its consequences on the ground.

If we adopt Vinokur's analysis of globalization referred to earlier, a number of consequences may be identified for governments in the South. Traditionally, these governments constituted the main partners of international co-operation, but they are now confronted with social and political reactions resulting from the excesses and paradoxes of processes of unification inherent to globalization (exclusion and poverty). Reduced public expenditure for human and social development (education, health and others) has also given rise to alternative systems of production and dissemination of knowledge, not only through new, but also through traditional channels (linked to religion, ethnic groups, neighbourhood, age groups, networks and so forth). Although these channels were still being resisted one decade ago by governments keen to reinforce their legitimacy through state educational policies, traditional practices in the provision of education services are now being widely encouraged. Indeed, the same governments have now 'accepted' the rehabilitation of what they once considered to be 'non-rational factors such as religion, culture, tradition . . . as success components of modern economies in a global economy' (Fukuyama, 1995, p. 103). This acceptance by weakened states is dictated by the need to promote national competitiveness on a globalized investment market. Both reduced public expenditure in education and the social and financial self-management of education expenditure by individuals and groups within civil society contribute to this competitiveness.

International aid agencies consequently face a dilemma. It is true that the shift of emphasis since the beginning of the 1980s towards non-governmental organizations and civil society (often in opposition to the state) is now bearing fruit. However, the significance of this shift may be ambiguous. Civil society can be a source of innovation at the national level, but it can also be an instrument of integration into an increasingly competitive market dictated by transnational economic agents rather than by political and national representatives of a particular society. This rather pessimistic vision is not shared by Heyneman:

It is true that educational assistance by OECD-DAC countries declined between 1989 and 1994 (France 13 per cent, the United Kingdom 16 per cent, Canada 56 per cent) and the case has not been sufficiently compelling for the public to reconsider their many other important priorities and problems in order to allocate more international assistance to education (the voting public in donor countries tends to be older, hence more concerned with issues of pensions . . .). As traditional aid declines, what will happen to education? Much of the international co-operation in education has developed under the auspices of international aid. There is reason to believe that the level of international co-operation in the field of education is on the increase in spite of the fact that the level of international aid is on the decline (Heyneman, 1997, p. 522).

This last point is at the heart of the debate which cuts across bilateral and multilateral 'aid' agencies:

The decline in foreign assistance for education can be considered a tragedy. On the other hand, the elevation of education in domestic debate and the increase in trade of professional ideas on educational reform might be considered a benefit. The adjustment to these new functions on the part of development assistance agencies and international agencies familiar with the traditional rationales for education investment will be different, however, in the end, their successful adjustment will be good for the field of education (Heyneman, 1997, pp. 524–5).

This partly explains why contradictory positions and practices often develop both within the headquarters of aid agencies and within their decentralized management structures. Within the same agency they may lead to the simultaneous existence of the following perspectives:
- A resignation to the trend of reduced public development aid in general and in the education sector more particularly. The progressive privatization of international development co-operation has transformed agencies into administrative and financial intermediaries. As a result, trends towards deprofessionalization and absence of staff renewal are becoming commonplace.
- A perception of educational innovations within civil society as instruments of 'resistance', not so much against an inefficient state but against increased poverty and exclusion associated with globalization.
- A growing interest among aid agencies in training. As the training sector is seen as representing the link between educational and productive concerns, articulations between sectoral policies in technical and vocational education and training, on the one hand, and the promotion of small and micro-enterprises, on the other, is now on agency agendas (Working Group . . ., 1997*a*, *b*). These new interests reflect concerns for coherence between political, technical and technological investment policies by countries which are decreasingly seen as donors and more as partners (Forster and Stokke, 1998).

International co-operation is not solely a market product

These different strategies reflect conflicting visions and concerns about the relations among the three poles of any socio-economic system, whatever the period or the place concerned. If we accept the idea that these three poles are: the public sector (state, co-ordination, institutional property), the capitalist sector (capital, competition, individual property) and the social sector (work, co-operation, community property), then any international co-operation in the field of education can be initiated and implemented by and among any of these three poles from the local to the global level. The very fact that Heyneman still refers to an international scope indicates that his perspectives are not yet fully clear. The emerging new global socio-economic system underlines the fact that the concept of nation is beginning to be either undermined or disconnected from the public sector/state dimension. Co-operation can, therefore, develop between the three previously mentioned poles and be of many different types according to the specific combination. For example, in the field of education,

As long as there is a scarcity of public resource to finance public education demands, there will be an international trade for educational reforms. The demand can, therefore, be expected . . . to continue the process for a shift away from the traditional lines of international relations. . . . These traditional linkages may be replaced gradually with interests of partners or competitors in trade, and with interest in similar educational issues, such as higher education diversity, experience with voucher and loan systems and the like (Heyneman, 1997, p. 524).

This vision of 'international' co-operation – which is different from one of relations between nations – illustrates the challenge and fears stemming from the globalization process. Is it possible to accept that education objectives, strategies and policies are influenced by the capitalist sector as well as by the public and social sectors, and that their respective actors co-operate in different ways according to their specific views? Are we, by contrast, faced – as Vinokur (1996) expresses it – with a dominant, unique perspective strongly marked by the financial and technological dimension of a sole market-oriented globalization process? If the answer is in favour of the latter, it should be no surprise that humanitarian aid and assistance become the main answer to crisis situations. Where this unrequested duty of aid/assistance is the main answer to crisis, its rationale seems to be grounded more on moral values than on a socio-economic and political analysis.

    Questions concerning the role of education in the sudden development of the crisis and its possible future prevention of new such situations are just beginning to be posed (Tawil, 1997). It will be difficult to provide the answers as they relate to ideological, political and religious dimensions of education which cannot be traded and standardized. They will be affected by as yet unforeseen consequences of the globalization process which can, in turn, be expected to strongly influence the future of co-operation in the field of education.

References

CARTON, M. 1996. Consultancy and Research in Education and Training: From Segmentation to Globalization. In: L. Buchert and K. King (eds.), *Consultancy and Research in International Education*, pp. 35–43. Bonn, DSE.

FORSTER, J.; STOKKE, O. In press. *Policy Coherence in Development Co-operation*. London, Frank Cass Publishers. (EADI Book Series, 22.)

FUKUYAMA, F. 1995. Social Capital and the Economy. *Foreign Affairs*, Sept.–Oct.

HEYNEMAN, S. P. 1995. International Educational Cooperation in the Next Century. *CIES Newsletter*, No. 109.

——. 1997. Economic Growth and the International Trade in Educational Reform. *Prospects*, Vol. XXVII, No. 4, pp. 501–30.

KING, K. 1991. *Aid and Education in the Developing World*. London, Longman.

PERELMAN, L. J. 1993. Hyperlearning: Would You Send Your Kid to a Soviet Collective? *Wired*, No. 1.

Prospects. 1997a. Vol. XXVII, No. 2, pp. 249–307. (Open File: New Technologies in Education, I.)

——. 1997b. Vol. XXVII, No. 3, pp. 367–443. (Open File: New Technologies in Education, II.)

TAWIL, S. (ed.). 1997. *Final Report and Case Studies of the Workshop on Educational Destruction and Reconstruction in Disrupted Societies*. Geneva, International Bureau of Education (IBE), University of Geneva.

VINOKUR, A. 1996. *Mondialisation, compétitivité et sécurité humaine*. (Communication to the VIIIth General Conference of the European Association of Development Research and Training Institutes (EADI), Vienna, 11–14 September.)

WORKING GROUP FOR INTERNATIONAL CO-OPERATION IN VOCATIONAL AND TECHNICAL SKILLS DEVELOPMENT. 1997a. *Donor Policies in Skills Development, Frankfurt, November 1996*. Geneva/Berne, SDC/ILO/NORRAG. (Paper 1.)

——. 1997b. *Donor Policies in Skills Development, London, May 1997*. Geneva/Berne, SDC/ILO/NORRAG. (Paper 2.)

Education, development and assistance: the challenge of the new millennium

Simon McGrath

As the new millennium approaches, there is an increasing sense of looking both forward and backward. Whilst there is a danger in assuming that a new millennium signifies anything much,[1] it is clear that a powerful discourse is at play. This in turn builds on some of the most influential intellectual trends of the late twentieth century. The past decade in particular has seen the popularization of notions such as post-modernism, globalization and post-Fordism, which point to new paradigms of research, production and trade. In addition, this period has witnessed the precipitous decline of state socialism and the emergence of new forms of contestation of the dominant development paradigm from both intellectuals and grassroots activists.

There is a need to maintain a critical stance regarding many, if not all, of these trends. However, their combined discursive power requires a revisiting of our notions about the natures of and relationship between education and development, and the processes of aid and international co-operation that arise from these. Educational challenges cannot be wholly separated from debates about development and the changing nature of development assistance. These too will be examined, although in less depth.

Education revisited

The crisis of education

For more than two decades there has been a concerted questioning of the very purpose of education. Across the globe there has been a massive,

1. The notion of the approaching millennium is rooted in the Christian calendar and represents another example of 'globalization as Westernization'.

though uncoordinated, international re-examination of education. This review has been wide-ranging in its scope, including within its ambit: the growth of competency/outcomes-based learning; national qualifications systems, national curricula, challenges to teacher autonomy; and re-appraisal of pedagogical principles. More fundamentally, it has seen a reworking of the balance between what may be termed the vocational-instrumental and the liberal-intrinsic functions of education. The importance of the vocational-instrumental function of education has been powerfully re-emphasized in the last quarter of the twentieth century, although in ways and forms that are often radically different from those of the previous era.

Though many of the changes that have occurred in educational thinking and practice stem from national debates and considerations, development assistance and funding agencies have played a significant role in shaping the educational debate of recent years. The most visible manifestation of this has been the 1990 World Conference on Education for All in Jomtien. Thus it is worth spending some time looking at some of the key commitments made at Jomtien and what we have learnt since.

Education for All

Whereas previous international commitments to basic education typically had focused primarily on the quantity of those enrolled into school, particularly in the first grade, the Jomtien deliberations demonstrated a far more sophisticated understanding of the numbers game. Completion rates were seen as an important indicator and target. Crucially, concern was also expressed about the importance of attainment (World Conference on Education for All, 1990).

Enrolments. What has been the achievement of the Jomtien process in the past eight years? First, as was acknowledged at the Amman mid-term review meeting of the Education for All Decade, the performance on enrolments is very mixed globally (UNESCO, 1996, p. 10). Although improvements have been marked in some areas, in many of the most underenrolled countries the barriers against school attendance have not been breached and some reverses are evident in poorer African countries (Colclough, 1997). Moreover, in some relatively highly schooled countries, such as Kenya, recent data point to a pronounced decline in enrolments (K-REP, 1997). Significantly in terms of the changing face of development assistance, the former aid provider, the Russian Federation, is also reported as experiencing declining enrolments (Forster, in this volume).

It is important to note that the data on enrolments continue to be subject to severe criticisms. One of the most significant outcomes of the Amman meeting was a greater acceptance of the massive inadequacies of educational statistics. This has led to considerable commitment by the international funding and technical-assistance agencies to cross-national analyses of educational statistics and the development of national capacities.[2] Whilst the paucity of adequate statistics makes any comment on enrolments rather tentative, it does appear certain that major gender imbalances in educational access remain across large parts of the globe (World Conference on Education for All, 1990; Colclough, 1997).

Perhaps the most telling indicator of the failure to deliver on Jomtien goals is the fact that the development community was by 1995 pledging itself to the goals of 'universal primary education by 2015' and the end to gender disparities in primary and secondary education by 2005 (DAC, 1996, p. 2). Thus, five years after Jomtien, the time-scale for Education for All was to be extended from ten to twenty-five years, even in its narrower form excluding education for youths and adults.

Completion. The second element of the Jomtien stance was that completion rates needed to be addressed. Here the problems, achievements and data limitations are likely to be similar. Again, the evidence available, for instance from Kenya, often points to a decline rather than an improvement, and in several African countries less than 50 per cent of those enrolled in Grade 1 make it to Grade 5 (Colclough, 1997, p. 7). As regards reasons for drop-out, there are a number of anecdotal tales of students skipping schooling, for instance, to work in the forestry industry in western Kenya or to cross the border from southern Zimbabwe to try their hand on the farms of South Africa's Northern Province. However, there is a need for more first-class qualitative and quantitative work illustrating both the extent of the phenomenon and its logic.

Attainment. The third element of the Education for All triad is attainment. It is not hard to collect data on performance in public examin-

---

2. An example here is the Working Group on Educational Statistics under the umbrella of ADEA.

ations, given the nature of the examination process internationally. However, the reliability and validity of such data as a measure of what level of learning and understanding has been attained are highly questionable. In many countries there are widespread irregularities throughout the examination and certification processes. In other systems such as that in England and Wales, where school-based examinations are perceived widely to be exempt from such irregularities, there is an annual ritual discussion of whether continuously rising levels of attainment are a sign of lower standards rather than higher achievement. Thus, much of what passes for data on attainment is treated with suspicion by both the public and professionals.

The Jomtien conference has led to important projects such as the Joint UNESCO–UNICEF Project on Monitoring Education for All Goals: Focusing on Learning Achievement (Chinapah, 1997). This has contributed to the development of national capacity in fifteen countries to carry out criterion-referenced testing on basic learning competencies.

The use of such methodologies points towards a greater knowledge in the future of how far learning achievements are being enhanced. However, in Ghana, a non-project country, use of criterion-referenced testing in the primary school points to dramatic failings with regard to educational attainment. In the most recent round of criterion-referenced testing at the end of the first cycle of schooling, less than 10 per cent of those tested were deemed to have reached acceptable levels of attainment in English or mathematics (McGrath, 1997a). Whilst the newness of adoption of criterion-referenced testing precludes comparisons with pre-Jomtien performance, it is evident in many countries that attainment levels continue to be a source of worry. Significantly this applies to Northern countries, such as the United Kingdom, as well as those in the South.

Quality and relevance. In promoting access, completion and attainment, Jomtien also considered the importance of quality and relevance. However, in spite of long-standing critiques of whether examinations can measure educational quality and, if so, through what mechanisms, there is still an absence of a generally accepted and adequate theory or practice of the measurement of educational quality. Developments in this field, which are particularly prevalent in countries with international funding and technical-assistance agencies, include reworking of examinations to shift away from rote learning and developments of more complex league tables of schools, taking for example catchment areas into account. None the less, the picture globally is disheartening. There is a general commitment to improving educational quality but still a lack of agreement on theories and methodologies of how to do so and how to evaluate successes and failures.

Examination results represent a flawed mechanism for evaluating the intrinsic performance of education, as has been long documented (e.g. Dore, 1976). However, their validity as a measure of the potential value of education for society is even more questionable. Research that links education to economic, health or demographic benefits often does so in a disaggregated way which makes it difficult to discern what it is about education that is of importance. Where it does seek to link the acquisition of specific educational skills, knowledge or competencies to improved economic performance, it often uses measurements that are outside the mainstream examination-certification process (e.g. Adam, 1996; Obura, 1996).

Internationally, the long-standing complaints of employers about educational relevance continue. In recent years, particularly in the Old Commonwealth,[3] there has been an attempt to develop core or generic skills to provide what employers are heard to demand. However, these skills as yet are short on theoretical underpinnings or adequate mechanisms for evaluation. Moreover, much of the employer call for greater relevance may plausibly be seen as a means of deflecting criticism for economic failure on to other actors. It cannot necessarily be read as an articulation of a well-developed view of what education plausibly or appropriately should be doing in a democracy.

Implementing Education for All. As collaboration/co-ordination among agencies has increased post-Jomtien, so the pendulum has swung dramatically in favour of primary education at the level of discourse. However, recent research (Bennell and Furlong, 1997) has found that, in several cases, change is far less dramatic at the level of disbursements from the agencies. Moreover, data from the World Bank indicate that its funding has shifted away from Africa, where enrolment rates in fifteen countries at the primary level are still below 50 per cent (Habte, in this volume). It seems evident that, as so often, there is a significant gap between rhetoric

3. The historically white-settler dominated dominions of Australia, Canada, New Zealand and South Africa, along with the constituent parts of Great Britain and Northern Ireland.

and reality. To some extent this is because the forces operating with technical-assistance agencies and international financial institutions bias investments away from interventions in first-cycle enrolment (Habte, in this volume). Equally, there is an extent to which economic and educational rationales for the redistribution of resources ignore the very real political dilemmas for governments seeking to change funding to secondary and tertiary education. The activism of Kenyan university students during July 1997, for example, owed as much to threats to the financing of tertiary education as it did to electoral matters. A strategy for educational reform which ignores the effects of such factors is more likely to succeed through good luck than good judgement.

The pedagogical impasse

The limitations of our understanding of issues of educational quality and quantity are compounded by our lack of an adequate view of what is pedagogically sound. Despite considerable advances in the field of understanding learning, debates about appropriate approaches remain unsatisfactory. Theorists and politicians working from different assumptions and perspectives seem to develop recommendations that, on the surface at least, are contradictory.

Those who contend that we are embarked on a new period of economic organization, called post-Fordism, argue that the type of education needed for the future is one which encourages students to be questioners and problem-solvers (e.g. Reich, 1991). Organizing their charges so as to promote both individual discovery and teamwork, the post-Fordist teacher is a facilitator, motivator and information-broker. On the contrary, others (e.g. Nick Tate, head of the new Qualifications and Curriculum Authority in England and Wales) see the way forward in learning from the tiger economies the virtues of whole-class teaching with a heavy emphasis on memorization, frequent testing and rigid conformity.

These are generally debates of the more developed economies. In differing ways, they make use of new technologies, with the computer set to be a tool for diagnostic testing of students after whole-class teaching and/or a launch pad for discovery through surfing the internet. In richer countries too, the emergence of other new technologies such as e-mail and video conferencing greatly expand the possibilities for distance learning.

Where are less developed countries in this debate? At present there is neither a convincing account of a globally appropriate pedagogy or a sophisticated model or series of models linking pedagogies with cultures or levels and types of socio-economic development.[4] Are chalk-and-talk and whole-class chorused answers the appropriate tools for learning in less individualistic societies? Are approaches stressing a mixture of individual discovery and collaboration in teams necessary for future economic success, both individually and nationally? How can new technologies be appropriated suitably for learning in poorer countries, regions and communities? All these questions are of great and immediate importance for the development-assistance community.

Considering the curriculum

The above debates about pedagogy are intimately linked to discussion of curriculum. In many ways these debates mirror each other. Whereas some countries have rigidly enforced national curricula or syllabuses, others allow more local control. In a handful of countries, such as South Africa, a move can be seen towards a consciously post-Fordist curriculum which emphasizes a series of national learning outcomes but which purports to allow students and teachers considerable latitude to develop appropriate learning and instruction strategies.

The ongoing South African reforms highlight many of the key questions of the current curriculum debate (Republic of South Africa, 1997). Should the curriculum begin to shift away from an emphasis on bodies of knowledge arranged in subjects, focusing instead on a series of cross-curricular learning outcomes? How far should these learning outcomes, though cross-curricular, be embedded in subject context, rather than be truly generic? Is it desirable to build a national qualifications framework that can map all levels and types of learning achievement? Is such an approach far too ambitious, even for developed countries? Should the emphasis instead be on getting students to grasp thoroughly a set of basic skills and knowledge?

The last of the above questions is very prevalent in debates about education reform in the South. There has been a strong line of argu-

---

4. Heyneman's (1997) comments about the typical type of pedagogy at different levels of GNP is a very useful step in sharpening the debate on this issue.

ment, particularly from the international aid community, that education systems in Africa (and elsewhere) cannot be expected to deliver on a comprehensive curriculum.[5] Rather, it is argued, what is required is a lean curriculum, focusing on the basics of language, mathematics and science.

One country where this argument is currently being played out in policy reform is Kenya. For more than a decade Kenyan education has been clearly based on a notion of a diversified curriculum under the 8-4-4 system. However, the draft *Masterplan for Education and Training* (Republic of Kenya, 1997) has recommended a reduction in the number of subjects and a strong concentration on a core of mathematics, the sciences, English and Kiswahili.

It is important to be clear that this is not motivated out of a rejection of vocationalist and instrumentalist views about the function of education or a hankering for liberal education on the part of education planners. Rather, it is grounded in a pragmatic view of the most effective way of vocational preparation. As such, it remains firmly based upon an instrumentalist view of education.

In spite of the power of the lean curriculum, other more expansive models of education-for-work still exist. Of these, enterprise education is a particularly interesting example. For more than thirty years there has been a growing acceptance in the aid world of Foster's (1966) arguments about a vocational school fallacy.[6] This viewpoint has been particularly strongly echoed by the World Bank. However, many funding and technical-assistance agencies and governments are still attracted by the notion that schools can provide students with the necessary attitudes, skills and knowledge to become successful entrepreneurs. The presence or absence of an

5. The subjects which come under most criticism are the heavily resource-intensive practical-vocational subjects. However, the argument seems to be extended implicitly to other subjects such as the social sciences. The other donor views, of course, have an impact on the nature of the curriculum. Concerns about good governance, for example, may serve to increase pressure for a focus on social science education.

6. Just as Foster (1966) argued that the school was unlikely to be able to change attitudes and aspirations conditioned by socio-economic realities, so it seems plausible to argue that curriculum reforms designed to promote entrepreneurship are insufficient in themselves.

enterprise school fallacy is another of the blind spots in our knowledge of education and its links with development.

The South African case, mentioned above, and similar examples from other Old Commonwealth countries, also point to a reluctance in more developed countries to accept that general means academic in the above axiom. In these countries, although often in hesitant and contradictory ways, a process is under way to seek to bring the vocational and the academic into a new relationship of parity of esteem. This points to the forging of a new general education which constitutes a 'seamless system' of academic and vocational education and training.

A series of uncertainties remains. Are such 'unified' or 'integrated' systems appropriate for countries at one level of development and a concentration on the 'basics' suitable for others? Do both Southern and Northern nations need a curriculum that prepares conscientious workers or one that produces innovative thinkers? What form of explicit vocational input, if any, is appropriate? Is the general education on offer (in both the above forms) anything more than a new, improved version of vocationalism that treats education in an instrumental way and denies it any intrinsic worth? Are criticisms of instrumentalism merely elitist and unrealistic? All these questions have important resonance with debates about the future of aid to education.

Implementing educational reform

Finally, for this consideration of the state of our knowledge on education, the theory and practice of implementation of educational policies and programmes must be addressed. Recent years have seen an increased emphasis by funding and technical-assistance agencies in particular on the importance of stakeholder involvement in the development of new policies and programmes. Greater importance has also been given to the better co-ordination of activities and interventions through such tools as sectoral development plans and policies.

However, there is still much to do in turning these commitments into realities. Moreover, there are still reasons for thinking that these attempts to reorganize planning are not sufficient in themselves to deliver on improved implementation. Too often, stakeholder involvement is about bringing together the politically significant rather than including those who have a strong grasp of grass-roots realities or are genuine practitioners.

Sectoral plans, devised with international assistance, often tell us more about international best practice than about local institutional realities. As a result, policies often tend to reinforce the tradition of the centre making decisions for the periphery (whether geographic or political). Failing to take account of capacities and cultures of educational institutions, they condemn many policy interventions to a series of failures and unintended effects (McGrath, 1997b).

There is a role for the innovations in the policy process and a need for national policies to take cognizance of international experiences. However, this must be within the context of a far better understanding of institutional, cultural and political realities, and a viable theory and practice of how to build upon the existing structures.

The development dilemma

The crisis of Keynesianism and the rise of structural adjustment

The recent debates cannot be understood without consideration of what has become of development and the health of economies internationally. The global education reform movement can be seen as part of a far broader response to the crisis of the models of economic development that is conventionally timed as beginning in the period 1968–73 (Piore and Sabel, 1984; Boyer, 1989; Castells, 1996). In the Northern economies this was the period in which the post-Second World War 'golden age' of low unemployment and low inflation began to unravel, along with the mass production-consumption system and Keynesian mode of state capitalism upon which it was based.

For some economies in the South,[7] most notably in East Asia, this crisis offered niches to be exploited which allowed new players to emerge on to the stage of industrialization. For the majority of Southern nations, however, fragile economic structures were catastrophically undermined by the effects of economic contraction in the North and the double explosion of oil prices.

7. The ability of East Asian states to break into industrialization is one aspect of a breakdown in simplistic North–South divisions. None the less, in so far as the concept of the 'South' was useful, it continues to be so in the case of the sub-Saharan region, as well as some other areas of the world.

With Northern Keynesianism apparently dead,[8] the incapacity of the Southern state became all the more apparent to the development assistance community, which now started to ask more critical questions of it. The 1980s saw the emergence of a new dominant development discourse that stressed the importance of the market over the state. It was a discourse which increasingly sought to use the perceived experience of the Asian success stories as exemplars of what was needed elsewhere. The new touchstone of viable development policies became structural adjustment with its promises of revitalized markets, increased exports and a reduction in the dead weight of state regulation (World Bank, 1993).[9]

Thus, by the end of the 1980s fundamental restructuring of the dominant discourses of both education and development had been under way for a decade or more. However, as the 1990s have progressed, the validity of the replacement discourses has been increasingly challenged both by events on the ground and by continuing shifts in intellectual fashion. These challenges serve to highlight the impoverishment of our models of education and development, and point to the opportunity and necessity of using the coming millennium as a spur to rethink education, development and aid.

As Leys (1995) has argued, there is currently a lack of a convincing theory of development. In spite of its logical elegance and power, the neo-classical account of development enshrined in structural adjustment programmes has failed to deliver on its promises, at least as far as Africa is concerned. Across the continent, the reforms have frequently either fallen foul of political realities (DEUG/DEUN, 1994; Teal, 1995; Wignaraja, 1996) or have had such serious short-term costs that they have adjusted economies downwards rather than upwards (DEUG/DEUN, 1994; Castells, 1996).

8. In reality, Keynesian forms remained apparent across the North. None the less, at the ideological level, it was comprehensively defeated.
9. This is not to imply that the Northern aid-providing countries sought to impose a discourse on the South that lacked Southern adherents. It was, however, primarily generated in the North, even when it used Southern examples. Moreover, it is not to suggest that many of the basic tenets were not held to be relevant to Northern situations. However, Northern governments had more latitude to be selective in their practical adoption of the dominant discourse, none more so than the United States, which ran up its greatest ever budget deficit at the same time as preaching greater fiscal probity.

Education, development and assistance: the challenge of the new millennium
Simon McGrath

It is fashionable to argue that there is a general crisis of the African state. Certainly much state intervention in and regulation of African economies have been disastrous. However, the critique of this has often been overly crude, ignoring the many genuine success stories among parastatal bodies and elsewhere. Equally, the proffered solution has been too simplistic. If African states are weak and inefficient, so are African markets. Moreover, much of the limitation of these markets arises because of the limited reach of states rather than their excessive influence.[10] What is required is a viable approach to strengthening both states and markets to mutually reinforce each other's operation.

Empirical justification for these policies is also often derived from the 'East Asian Miracle' (World Bank, 1993). However, this is based on a rather tendentious reading of the growth paths of these economies (Amsden, 1989; Wade, 1988, 1990; White and Wade, 1988). Moreover, it is implicitly based on the assumption that the economic strategies of the past will work in the future. But if globalization and post-Fordism are realities, then such an assumption needs to be interrogated.[11] Oman (1994) argues that one aspect of globalization has been to reduce the level of offshore production, thus closing down a significant niche exploited by the tigers.[12]

Post-Fordist writing would argue for a significant catalytic role for the state as part of a neo-corporatist or stakeholder political economy (Mathews, 1989; Kraak, 1993; McGrath, 1996). Untrammelled market forces alone, it is believed, are insufficient to ensure the necessary paradigmatic shift from one regime of accumulation to another.

The rise of the globalization discourse has been used by free marketeers as confirmation of the imperative of export-led growth. However, this

10. There is, for instance, a growing micro-economic literature highlighting the effects of weak contractual enforcement mechanisms and other failures of the state to maintain the market (e.g. McCormick, 1996; Barr, 1997).
11. The tiger economies' pronounced economic downturn has been blamed on globalization and has led to concern about the appropriateness of their largely imitative technological strategy and the education and training system upon which this is based.
12. There are two principal reasons for this. First, the increasing concern with highly skilled labour, linked to the exploitation of new technologies, acts to move many productive activities back to the developed world. Second, the growing fashion of just-in-time production emphasizes the importance of location near to the best markets, i.e. those in the North.

is potentially only a half-truth. The export-led growth paradigm is based on a neoclassical system which, though no friend of state interference in the market, is predicated upon the existence and viability of the nation-state. Much of the discourse on globalization, however, emphasizes more of the transnational and supranational. Again, those interested in the practicalities of development lack a widely accepted account of how, if at all, globalization changes the debate.[13]

As noted at the outset of this chapter, there are reasons for being cautious about the current literature of globalization and post-Fordism. None the less, the weight of evidence from the most sober of social scientists (Reich, 1991; Cardoso, 1993; Castells, 1996)[14] indicates that the world is probably undergoing a paradigmatic shift from one mode of regulation to another. Radical changes in technology and work organization both drive and are shaped by societal transformations. In such a situation it becomes unclear as to how many of the old certainties still hold. The task of responding to the challenges of such a new paradigm are made far greater for those involved in development assistance owing to the uneven diffusion that such a shift can be expected to have. The challenge of building assistance on what is currently in place whilst having in mind what might develop in the future is an immense one.

Whether or not the predictions of such social scientists are correct, a series of other concerns in any case point to the fundamental weaknesses of development theory. In the more than fifty years since the creation of the International Bank for Reconstruction and Development (IBRD) ushered in the development era, theory and practice have failed to move sufficiently far away from narrow economistic understandings. Increasingly, too, development comes to be deconstructed as being infused with now questionable Enlightenment assumptions of positivism, universalism and linear history (Wallerstein, 1991).

In the face of these new challenges, any adequate methodologies for including the human, the cultural or the spiritual in development

---

13. A questioning of the future of the nation-state is of considerable significance to the development assistance community, given the centrality of nation-states to its operations.
14. As well as eminent social scientists they have been United States Secretary for Labor, the President of Brazil and the Adviser to the Prime Minister in the Russian Federation respectively.

definitions and approaches are still lacking. Despite now well-established highlighting of the issues, policy-makers continue to struggle to find ways of developing the environment in sustainable and sound ways, as the Kyoto Summit on Global Warming illustrated most profoundly. The recent return of some international agencies to a principal concern with poverty alleviation indicates that there is still a need to find an adequate response to the assertion of the Yale historian, Kennedy, that economic change and technological development, like wars and sporting tournaments, are usually not beneficial to all (Kennedy, 1993, p. 15).[15] Whether as academics or agency staff, we have an imperative to consider the truth and implications of this statement as we look at responses to globalization and post-Fordism in policies for education, development and aid.

The changing terrain of development assistance

The face of development assistance has radically changed in recent years. The end of the Cold War has changed the geopolitical context in which assistance was given as well as removing a number of aid-providing countries from the system.[16] The success of the tiger economies, the rise and demise of the Oil Producing Export Countries (OPEC) as international players and the recasting of several former communist countries as official aid recipients have also helped to transform the geography of development assistance (Forster, in this volume).

Processes have also undergone significant review. The mega-conferences such as Jomtien have done much to foster the notion of co-ordinated agency strategies. This process has also been promoted by the work of DAC and by the greater integration and co-ordination inherent in the development of the European Union (Gmelin, in this volume).

Along with these new developments comes an increasing questioning in the North of the merits of development assistance. This arises both from an isolationist populism building on the maxim that charity begins at home and from a radical critique of the paternalistic and unsound prac-

---

15. The European Union concern with social exclusion within its borders clearly stems from similar worries.
16. In fact, Soviet expenditure on development assistance had been strongly curtailed during the Brezhnev era (my thanks to Kenneth King for this point).

tices of previous development assistance. These trends have resulted in a dialectical process that sits at the heart of the current development-assistance discourse. On the one hand, the conservative backlash against aid (seen most clearly in North America) has led to the prioritization of efficiency and accountability as central touchstones of the development-assistance debate. This has been a force behind the growth of conditionalities.[17] On the other hand, progressive concerns with the morality of local ownership of development merge with pragmatic considerations of its importance in delivery. As a result, development assistance is struggling to develop a consistent and coherent view of how to move beyond these two forces.

This process is hugely complicated by the diverse range of stakeholder interests, North and South, that enter into the process and debate. As with educational policy, there is a real danger that the voices that will not be heard are those from the grass roots and from the institutions charged with delivering development: clinics and extension offices as well as schools. Here, too, the probability exists that policy will continue to have more to do with the fashionability of ideologies and discourses globally than with realities on the ground.

Development assistance is also faced with a series of other major questions. Too much in the past it has been compartmentalized within itself and inadequately articulated with trade and diplomatic programmes and policies. The potential impact of structural adjustment on enrolment is but one example of the dangers of inadequate co-ordination. Although there are recent signs of better intra-agency co-ordination (Working Group . . . , 1997), it is important that the trend towards donor co-ordination develops further in this direction.

The resources to be set aside for development assistance must also be interrogated more thoroughly. Whilst the United Kingdom has recently pledged itself to return to the target level of 0.7 per cent of GNP, the trend as a whole is towards a fall in development assistance in real terms. Yet, as King (1996) points out, the totals put into development assistance are already minuscule in comparison with the costs of either the Marshall

---

17. Naturally, conditionalities were made more possible by the end of the Cold War. No longer are the Mobutus of this world defensible, and, indeed, not open to criticism, as anti-communist bulwarks.

Plan or the reunification of Germany. If assistance is to genuinely be for development, then there would seem to be a need to rethink how and where it is spent. The need for local capacity-building, for a focus on supporting innovation and for ensuring sustainability are all talked about in the development-assistance debate. These all seem to be important emphases. However, it is debatable that they are really at the heart of current practices.

Education, development and the role of assistance

A wide range of instrumental claims have been made for education in the development era. Education reduces population growth and maternal mortality rates, enhances agricultural productivity and contributes to democratization. Crucially, it is identified as a key determinant of economic development itself (World Bank, 1993, 1995; Stewart, 1996).

Whilst it is gratifying for educationists to hear they are useful, they also have a duty to acknowledge the limitations of these claims. They are typically based on either incomplete or limited data sets. Moreover, in the quest for numbers that can explain reality, much of that reality is filtered out as unquantifiable.

Even if the flow of causality between education and development is established satisfactorily, the nature of the relationship becomes very complex. An example of the weakness of the economists' account of the relationship is evident in Stewart (1996).[18] Part of its argument involves taking two groups of countries: 'successes' and 'failures'. Their gross domestic product (GDP) and enrolment growth rates are considered and the conclusion reached that there is a significant relationship between the two. However, the data appear to show that the 'failures' – Madagascar, Peru and Zambia – had comparable primary enrolment rates to the 'successes', Malaysia and Thailand (Stewart, 1996, pp. 329–30). At secondary level the contrast works better, but even then Bolivia, Peru and Zambia appear to be comparable to Thailand.

Stewart does note the improvements in these countries and suggests that they have attained a level where potentially they might join the high-

---

18. I use this particular example as it is a rare one of an economist agreeing to put her arguments in an education journal.

flyers (Stewart, 1996, p. 330). However, countries such as Zambia need far more than increased secondary enrolments to secure new industrialized country status. Another of Stewart's failures also highlights the 'education equals development' fallacy. Sierra Leone currently suffers from low enrolments and a weak economy. However, in 1865 it boasted a level of school attendance higher than that of England or Prussia (Walls, 1997, p. 490).[19] None the less, this was not sufficient for it to enjoy economic take-off.

A large part of the reason that the economists' view about the education–development relationship is unsatisfactory relates to educationists' own theoretical failings. As this chapter has already argued, educationists lack a comprehensive picture of the educational process. Without adequate ways of measuring quality or quantity, the attempt to model relationships between education and extrinsic variables is doomed to impotency.

In the case of development too there is a lack of adequate understanding. Stewart's view of development is explicitly one of production and trade. However, many would want to retain a wider meaning for the notion of development. This is illustrated by the case of Namibia where the national university is seen as having an explicit national development role but where national development is viewed holistically and includes culture as well as economy (White, 1998). Clearly the educational and assistance implications of such a view of development are radically different from those which currently pertain.

Even if development is seen more economistically, there is a need to reflect more closely on the nature of Southern economies. For the most part, they are not dominated in employment terms by large firms.[20] Instead they are populated by huge numbers of micro- and small enterprises, often informal or hidden, and large rural populations with agriculture as their principal economic activity. Thus any consideration of education–development relationships needs to take this reality into account.

19. The figures were for the Colony of Sierra Leone, the creolized area around Freetown, rather than the whole of what now constitutes Sierra Leone.
20. In reality the Northern fascination with the mega-corporation often blinds us to the huge numbers of micro-, small and medium firms in the developed countries.

Recent German work on the competencies required for successful insertion into sustainable informal-sector livelihoods is of considerable relevance here (Adam, 1996; Institute for Scientific Co-operation, 1997). This work points to broad competencies, rather than either capital or technical skills, as the key ingredient in successful insertion. However, the evidence from research in Africa, Latin America and Asia is that schools are doing little to promote these general competencies. More generally, there are question marks about the ability of formal education structures to support informal activities. None the less, as the informal sector increasingly comes to be seen as a key battleground in the struggle both for economic growth and poverty eradication, so the ability of education to promote informal-sector activities needs to come even further to the forefront in both government and agency concerns. At the present time this remains a largely undeveloped field.[21]

Many of these German authors believe that non-formal education is of more importance in this field than formal systems. However, non-formal education and training remains at the periphery of educational, and often development, thinking. In spite of the concerns of the Education for All movement to see basic education as being for all ages, too often it has been narrowed down to the older call for universal primary education (Colclough, 1997). Whilst some agencies have put non-formal education and training at the heart of educational sectoral papers, its absence from key documents such as the most recent World Bank sectoral paper (1995) is indicative of the continuing failure to re-evaluate the relative merits of support to formal and non-formal developments.

Towards the new millennium

As the new millennium approaches it is indeed time for reflection. The mysticism of the notion of millennium is important but this is reinforced by the power of the discourses of globalization and post-Fordism. These argue that there is an urgent need to examine whether existing paradigms have relevance for the present and the future. They require a reconsideration of the extent to which 'learning from experience' is sufficient as a

21. Much of the work to date on education and training for the informal sector (e.g. Fluitman, 1989; Birks et al., 1994; McGrath et al., 1995; Kent and Mushi, 1996) has been directly supported by development agencies.

guide for new policies and practices, and the situations in which it needs to be abandoned as an irrelevance for a new era.

If indeed a paradigm shift is required in our way of viewing the world, then it is clear that this necessitates a whole range of lower level, but equally crucial, shifts in our understanding of education. There are signs that such a shift is slowly beginning at the theoretical level (Reich, 1991; ECLAC-UNESCO, 1992; McGinn, 1997[22]; McGrath and King, 1997). However, a new paradigm has not been fully developed, let alone popularized. This, of course, is a huge task and is made difficult by the very real and major questions that remain about the reality of the alleged changes at the macro-structural level.

The challenge for educationists concerned with development and assistance is a considerable one as the new millennium dawns. It is important to continue to appraise critically the lessons of experience, particularly for what they indicate about the need to link better policy development and implementation in ways that reflect and respect the importance of both. Attempts to improve our knowledge of the internal workings of the educative process and to enhance our concepts of and methodologies for analysing educational quality and quantity remain high on the educational research and policy agendas.

However, in addition there is a need to look critically and rigorously at developments beyond the discipline. Educationists must better inform themselves of what post-Fordism and globalization mean in practice and what that in turn means for education. Crucially, they must examine what these putative trends might cause development to mean.

New thinking on education and on development inevitably leads to new challenges for development assistance. Whilst this chapter has been principally concerned with the uncertainties and challenges in the substantive domain of education for development, it has touched on questions of process. These are also of vital importance as we approach the millennium. The 1990s have seen the appearance of new funding agencies and new recipients, and an ever sharper realization that the concepts of North and South are in need of revisiting. With new processes and new players comes also the need to have a fundamental look at new relationships in the field of

22. This paper is part of a *Prospects* special issue on globalization and education which makes a useful starting point for those new to these debates.

development. Fifty years on from Bretton Woods and the beginning of the development era, nothing less than a new paradigm for the relationship between education, development and assistance is required.

References

ADAM, S. 1996. *Competence Utilisation and Transfer in Informal Sector Production and Service Trades in Ibadan, Nigeria,* Hamburg, LIT Verlag.

AMSDEN, A. 1989. *Asia's Next Giant.* Oxford, Oxford University Press.

BARR, A. 1997. *Enterprise Performance and the Functional Diversity of Social Capital.* Oxford, University of Oxford, Centre for the Study of African Economies.

BENNELL, P.; FURLONG, D. 1997. *Has Jomtien Made any Difference? Trends in Donor Funding for Education and Basic Education since the late 1980s.* Brighton, University of Sussex.

BIRKS, S.; FLUITMAN, F.; OUDIN, X.; SINCLAIR, C. 1994. *Skills Acquisition in Micro-enterprises: Evidence from West Africa.* Paris, OECD.

BOYER, R. 1989. *The Regulation School.* New York, Columbia University Press.

CARDOSO, F. H. 1993. New North/South Relations in the Present Context: A New Dependency? In: M. Carnoy (ed.), *The New Global Economy in the Information Age,* pp. 149–60. University Park, Penn., Penn State University Press.

CASTELLS, M. 1996. *The Rise of the Network Society.* Oxford, Blackwell.

CHINAPAH, V. 1997. *Handbook on Monitoring Learning Achievement.* Paris, UNESCO.

COLCLOUGH, C. 1997. *Aid to Basic Education in Africa: Opportunities and Constraints.* Oslo, NORAD.

DEPARTMENT FOR INTERNATIONAL DEVELOPMENT. 1997. *Eliminating World Poverty: A Challenge for the 21st Century.* London, HMSO.

DEPARTMENT OF ECONOMICS, UNIVERSITY OF GÖTEBORG/DEPARTMENT OF ECONOMICS, UNIVERSITY OF NAIROBI (DEUG/ DEUN). 1994. *Limitations and Rewards in Kenya's Manufacturing Sector: A Study of Enterprise Development.* Washington, D.C., World Bank. (Unnumbered RPED Country Study.)

DEVELOPMENT ASSISTANCE COMMITTEE (DAC). 1996. *Shaping the 21st Century: The Contribution of Development Co-operation.* Paris, OECD.

DORE, R. 1976. *The Diploma Disease.* London, George Allen & Unwin.

ECLAC-UNESCO. 1992. *Education and Knowledge.* Santiago, ECLAC-UNESCO.

FLUITMAN, F. (ed.). 1989. *Training for Work in the Informal Sector.* Geneva, International Labour Office.

FOSTER, P. 1966. The Vocational School Fallacy in Development Planning. In: C. A. Anderson and M. Bowman (eds.), *Education and Economic Development*, pp. 142–66. Chicago, Aldine.

HEYNEMAN, S. P. 1997. Economic Growth and the International Trade in Educational Reform. *Prospects*, Vol. XXVII, No. 4, pp. 501–30.

INSTITUTE FOR SCIENTIFIC CO-OPERATION (ed.). 1997. *Education and Training for the Informal Sector.* Tübingen, ISC.

KENNEDY, P. 1993. *Preparing for the Twenty-first Century.* London, Harper-Collins.

KENT, D.; MUSHI, P. 1996. *The Education and Training of Artisans for the Informal Sector in Tanzania.* London, Overseas Development Administration. (Education Division Occasional Paper 18.)

KING, K. 1996. Aid for Development or for Change? A Discussion of Education and Training Policies of Development Assistance Agencies with Particular Reference to Japan. In: K. Watson, C. Modgil and S. Modgil (eds.), *Educational Dilemmas: Debate and Diversity*, pp. 112–23. London, Cassell. (Power and Responsibility in Education, Vol. 3.)

KRAAK, A. 1993. *Free or Coordinated Markets? Education and Training Policy Options for a Future South Africa.* Cape Town, University of the Western Cape. (Unpublished D.Phil. thesis.)

K-REP. 1997. *The Widening Gap between Theory and Practice in Kenyan Education, 1985–97.* Edinburgh, University of Edinburgh, Centre of African Studies. (Papers on Education, Training and Enterprise, 11.)

LEYS, C. 1995. *The Rise and Fall of Development Theory.* London, James Currey.

MCCORMICK, D. 1996. The Impact of Economic Reform on Entrepreneurial Activity: A Theoretical Framework for Analysing Small Enterprise. *Independent Review*, Vol. 1, No. 1, pp. 65–78.

MCGINN, N. F. 1997. The Impact of Globalisation on National Education Systems. *Prospects*, Vol. XXVII, No. 1, pp. 41–54.

MCGRATH, S. 1996. *Learning to Work? Changing Discourses on South African Education and Training, 1976–96.* Edinburgh, University of Edinburgh. (Unpublished Ph.D. thesis.)

——. 1997a. *From National Project to Sectoral Policies: Examining Ghana's 2020 Vision.* Edinburgh, University of Edinburgh, Centre of African Studies. (Papers on Education, Training and Enterprise, 9.)

——. 1997b. *Reforming South African Technical and Vocational Education and Training: Linking National Policies and Institutional Practices.* Edinburgh, University of Edinburgh, Centre of African Studies. (Papers on Education, Training and Enterprise, 3.)

McGRATH, S.; KING, K. 1997. The Future of TVET. In: W. Cummings and N. F. McGinn (eds.), *Education and Development: Preparing Schools, Students and Nations for the Twenty-First Century*, pp. 865–78. New York, Garland.

McGRATH, S.; KING, K.; LEACH, F.; CARR-HILL, R. 1995. *Education and Training for the Informal Sector*, Vol. 1. London, Overseas Development Administration. (Education Division Occasional Papers, 11.)

MATHEWS, J. 1989. *Tools of Change*. Sydney, Pluto.

MID-DECADE MEETING OF THE INTERNATIONAL CONSULTATIVE FORUM ON EDUCATION FOR ALL. *Education for All: Achieving the Goal. Working Document.* Paris, UNESCO. (Mid-Decade Meeting of the International Consultative Forum on Education for All, Amman, Jordan, 16-19 June 1996.)

OBURA, A. 1996. Skill and Technology Requirements in Kenya's Small Enterprises: Implications for Curriculum Development. In: D. McCormick and P. O. Pedersen (eds.), *Small Enterprises*, pp. 249–74. Nairobi, Longhorn Kenya.

OMAN, C. 1994. *Globalisation and Regionalisation*. Paris, OECD.

PIORE, M.; SABEL, C. 1984. *The Second Industrial Divide*. New York, Basic Books.

REICH, R. 1991. *The Work of Nations*. New York, Alfred Knopf.

REPUBLIC OF KENYA. 1997. *Draft Masterplan for Education and Training*. (Unpublished).

REPUBLIC OF SOUTH AFRICA. 1997. *Curriculum 2005*. Pretoria, Government Printer.

STEWART, F. 1996. Globalisation and Education. *International Journal of Educational Development*, Vol. 16, No. 4, pp. 327–33.

TEAL, F. 1995. *Does 'Getting Prices Right' Work? Micro Evidence from Ghana*. Washington, D.C., World Bank. (RPED Discussion Papers, 58.)

UNESCO. 1996. *Education for All: Achieving the Goal*. Amman, UNESCO.

WADE, R. 1988. State Intervention in 'Outward-looking' Development: Neoclassical Theory and Taiwanese Practice. In: G. White (ed.), *Developmental States in East Asia*, pp. 30–67. London, Macmillan.

——. 1990. *Governing the Market*. Princeton, Princeton University Press.

WALLERSTEIN, I. 1991. *Unthinking Social Science*. Cambridge, Polity.

WALLS, A. 1997. Meditations among the Tombs: Changing Patterns of Identity in Freetown, Sierra Leone. In: S. McGrath, C. Jedrej, K. King and J. Thompson (eds.), *Rethinking African History*, pp. 489–504. Edinburgh, University of Edinburgh, Centre of African Studies.

WHITE, B. 1998. *Relevance, Rhetoric and Reality: Higher Education Policy and National Development at the University of Namibia*. Edinburgh, University of Edinburgh, Centre of African Studies. (Occasional Paper, 73.)

WHITE, G.; WADE, R. 1988. Developmental States and Markets in East Asia: An Introduction. In: G. White (ed.), *Developmental States in East Asia*, pp. 1–29. London, Macmillan.

WIGNARAJA, G. 1996. *Industrial Adjustment, Technological Capabilities and Competitiveness in Africa*. (Paper to the CAS/ODA workshop: Learning to Compete. Edinburgh, October.)

WORKING GROUP FOR INTERNATIONAL CO-OPERATION IN VOCATIONAL AND TECHNICAL SKILLS DEVELOPMENT. 1997. *Donor Policies in Skills Development, Frankfurt, November 1996.* Geneva/Berne, SDC/ILO/NORRAG. (Paper 1.)

WORLD BANK. 1993. *The East Asian Miracle*. Oxford, Oxford University Press.

——. 1995. *Priorities and Strategies for Education*, Washington, D.C., World Bank.

WORLD CONFERENCE ON EDUCATION FOR ALL (Jomtien, Thailand, 5–9 March, 1990). 1990. *World Declaration on Education for All and Framework of Action to Meet Basic Learning Needs*. New York, Inter-Agency Commission for WCEFA. (3rd impression, Paris, UNESCO, 1994.)

Part Two.
New approaches to development co-operation among international funding and technical-assistance agencies

Educational multilateralism at a crossroads
Karen Mundy

Introduction: educational multilateralism in a changing world order

In the context of globalization and the rapid and dramatic changes that have unfolded in the interstate system since 1989, many political scientists have begun to reconsider the significance of multilateralism, defined as 'an institutional form which co-ordinates relations among three or more states on the basis of generalized principles of conduct' (Ruggie, 1992, p. 571). Scholars of international relations increasingly view multilateral organizations, such as the United Nations and Bretton Woods institutions, as the cornerstones of the relative political and economic stability of the post-Second World War world order. They and others – most notably the Commission on Global Governance in its report (1995*a*) – have argued that international organizations should be seen as especially important institutions today, if we hope to redirect processes of economic globalization towards more humane and equitable purposes (Commission on Global Governance, 1995*a*; Held, 1995; Rosenau, 1992; Archibugi and Held, 1995; Falk, 1995.)[1] Debates abound, but among them there has been relatively little attention paid to the work of international organizations in specialized fields – science, health, education – or to their contribution to relations of power and inequality in a changing world order.[2]

This chapter explores the role which educational multilateralism, and more specifically the educational activities of such multilateral organizations as the United Nations, UNESCO, UNICEF, the World Bank,

---

1. See also the new journal *Global Governance* (Lynne Rienner and Academic Council of the United Nations).
2. Exceptions here include Finnemore (1996); McNeely (1995).

OECD and others, have played in the construction of world order since 1945. To do so, it draws from critical and constructivist approaches used in the study of international organizations. Both approaches use a historical perspective – one which begins by asking how major shifts in the international system have shaped, and in turn been shaped by, the existence of multilateral institutions (Mundy, 1998). They regard post-Second World War multilateral institutions not simply as instruments or reflections of interstate economic and geopolitical power (as in realist and many neo-Marxist accounts), but more broadly and critically as arenas within which states and other social forces continuously construct the shape and meaning of world order itself (Ruggie, 1983, 1992; Cox, 1980, 1981, 1992; Murphy, 1994; Lee, 1995; Finnemore, 1996; Barnett, 1997). In this view, multilateral organizations hold the unique power of reflecting and shaping ideas about the 'limits of the possible' on the world stage.

In what follows, I begin by setting out a broader framework for thinking about the evolution of multilateralism over the period 1945–95. I then consider the inheritance from the period between 1945 and 1980. Final sections look at the changing shape of educational multilateralism since 1980 and explore its future prospects in a dramatically shifting world order.

The broader context

As I have explored in more detail elsewhere, three distinctive periods in the development of multilateralism can be identified and used to understand the evolution of educational multilateralism since 1945 (Mundy, 1998). An initial period, one of 'embedded liberalism', lasted roughly from 1945 to the mid-1970s. In this period, multilateral institutions such as the United Nations, IMF and the World Bank emerged, originally designed to promote and protect the Keynesian welfare states of the Western world within and through the expansion of a stable, liberal world economic and interstate system (Ruggie, 1983; Ikenberry, 1992). One aspect of this was the incorporation of ex-colonial states into the new world order, a task undertaken both through United Nations organizations and (on a larger scale) bilaterally, through the creation of large programmes of development assistance in the 1960s (Escobar, 1994; Wood, 1986).

The rise of Third World development as a major focus for multilateralism in the 1960s and 1970s had a dual impact. On the one hand, development-assistance programmes brought countries into a world order dominated by the developed world. Yet they also helped to extend notions of rights, entitlements and redistribution drawn from the societal compromises of Keynesian welfare states (Lumsdaine, 1993; Noel and Therien, 1995). Ultimately, the multilateral organizations with universal membership (mainly the United Nations and its Specialized Agencies) emerged as key political sites for contestation between North and South during the 1970s (Murphy and Aguelli, 1993; Lee, 1995). Thus a second era in post-Second World War multilateralism can be seen in the growth of Third World demands for a 'new international economic order' within multilateral forums from the late 1960s, and in the various responses to these demands made by such organizations as UNESCO, UNICEF and the World Bank during the 1970s (Mundy, 1998).

The 1970s also heralded in a period of fundamental structural change in the world economy. These changes included the displacement of 'Fordist' patterns of production and accumulation with new service and technology-based industries; the rise of transnational networks of production and of new competition from Asian economies; the rapid rise of international financial flows; and the weakening of the post-war institutional structures that had protected the domestic societal compromises embedded within the Western Keynesian welfare state (Harvey, 1989; Stubbs and Underhill, 1994). As part of these processes, many Third World countries suffered from declining raw materials' prices, an increasing inability to compete in the emergent global economy and mounting, often seemingly insurmountable, levels of international debt. In the advanced industrialized world, Keynesian economic policies were replaced with monetarist and neo-liberal approaches to public policy aimed at adjusting national economies to the globalizing world economy (Colclough and Manor, 1993). Such policies contributed to the erosion of state-provided social security and to the widening of gaps between rich and poor, both domestically and internationally (UNDP, 1992; Arrighi, 1991).

The impact of these changes on the shape of multilateral cooperation has been considerable. By the mid-1980s, the United Nations and its specialized institutions had entered a period of crisis, faced at once with the expanding demands of developing countries and declining support from the developed world. The United Nations had also become the locus for the increasingly vocal demands of transnational social movements and non-governmental organizations – helping to open up new political spaces for opposition (Weiss and Gordenker, 1996; Stienstra, 1994; Princen and Finger, 1994). At the same time, a group of 'rich country' institutions (including new regional bodies such as the European Union, as well as IMF, the World Bank, OECD and the Group of 7) grew in importance. These organizations continued to advocate the liberalization of world trade and financial markets, as well as neo-liberal approaches to economic and social development (Helleiner, 1994). They remained distant from the demands of new civil society actors and closed to the membership of developing countries. Instead, they were more closely liaised with the most powerful new actors on the international stage: representatives of multinational corporations and capital (Gill, 1994). Yet despite their growing influence, the prominence of the 'rich country' multilateralism also signalled the growing need for legitimation among Western governments, whose sovereignty and domestic societal compromises continued to be challenged by the growing strength of transnational financial capital markets and the need to compete in a globalized world economy (Castells, 1997, pp. 262–9).

Overall, globalization has transformed state sovereignty, producing new kinds of actors and levels of interaction on the international stage. It is in this context – one of large-scale social and economic transition, and of major shifts and uncertainties in the form and content of multilateralism – that the work of international organizations involved in education needs to be evaluated.

The origins and limits of redistributive forms of educational multilateralism, 1945–80

The institutionalization of educational multilateralism

In order to understand the present challenges that face forms of multilateral co-operation in education, it is necessary to look backwards at the kinds of expectations and norms for multilateral co-operation institutionalized between 1945 and 1980. In the post-Second World War world order, the consolidation of the Keynesian welfare state in the West was explicitly linked to the development of a stable, liberal world economic and interstate system. Though the central institutions of post-war multilateralism (the United Nations and Bretton Woods institutions) were intended to support the integration, stabilization and expansion of a world capitalist economy, their distinctiveness lay in the extent to which they incorporated aspects of the societal compromises reached in Western societies, including national governmental responsibility for domestic social security and welfare, and notions of citizenship based on rights, redistribution and entitlement, including the right to employment, education and health care (Lumsdaine, 1993; Noel and Therien, 1995).[3]

In this context, it was hardly surprising that education emerged as an important component of post-war multilateral arrangements. Drawing upon a widespread consensus in the Western world that compulsory mass primary education was a basic right and a responsibility of the modern state, Western governmental and non-governmental actors converged around the notion of an international organization with responsibility for promoting international educational co-operation. UNESCO was created in 1945 and became a United Nations Specialized Agency. UNESCO was to be financed through weighted subscriptions and autonomously governed by a General Conference in which member nations had equal voting rights. Its mandate included the promotion of the 'common welfare of mankind' and the 'universal right to education'. The organization was given the task of acting as an international clearing house for educational information, a norm-setting or regulatory body, a venue for non-governmental linkages and cross-national exchange, an arena for intergovernmental debate, and a provider of services and programmes to Member States.

From its inception, however, it was unclear exactly what the scope of this new institution for global educational multilateralism should be (Jones, 1988). Western members initially viewed direct involvement in educational reconstruction as among UNESCO's central tasks; non-governmental organizations emphasized its role in spreading a common cultural founda-

---

3. As evidence, see for example the Atlantic Charter, which calls for 'Enjoyment by all States . . . of access, on equal terms, to the trade of the world', and the 'fullest collaboration between all nations . . . with the object of securing . . . improved labor standards, economic advancement and social security'. Similarly, the signatories of the United Nations Charter agreed to work towards 'higher standards of living, full employment and conditions of economic and social progress and development', as well as to find co-operative solutions for 'international economic, social, health and related problems . . .' (World Peace Foundation, 1945).

tion for peace. Developing country members, on the other hand, pressed for UNESCO to play a part in international 'equalization' of educational opportunities, a position supported by the representatives of the Soviet Union and by many other Member States. Yet, though Western governments supported the broader goal of educational development in newly independent countries, they remained sceptical about committing the resources needed for a broader programme of educational 'equalization', especially to an organization increasingly marked by East-West tensions. Despite their rhetorical commitment to a redistributive form of educational multilateralism, UNESCO's budget remained smaller than that of a medium-sized university.

Western country support for 'redistributive' forms of educational co-operation did expand, however – very rapidly, as can be seen in Table 1. By the mid-1960s, educational multilateralism included not only the activities of UNESCO, but also new programmes for educational development launched by the World Bank and UNICEF (as well as growing UNDP-funded projects carried out by UNESCO).

This expansion emerged as a Western response to decolonization and was institutionalized in a way that suggested sharp limitations to foundational ideals of redistribution and common welfare embedded in the Charters of UNESCO and the United Nations. One aspect of these limitations can be seen in the fact that most Western countries decided to channel resources for educational development bilaterally rather than through the multilateral bodies created under the United Nations. When resources were channelled multilaterally, they tended to be given as 'voluntary contributions' to organizations in which the largest contributors exercised significant control, a phenomenon reflected in the rapid rise of World Bank, UNICEF and UNDP funding for education, as shown in Table 1.

A second aspect of these limitations can be seen in the content of the new educational multilateralism. Though organizations such as UNESCO continued to draw attention to issues of adult literacy and non-formal education, in practice a highly Eurocentric model of formal, graded schooling was being diffused and reinforced. In it, an ideology of state-led economic modernization was married to concepts of individual productivity and national citizenship (Ramirez and Boli, 1987; McNeely, 1995; McNeely and Cha, 1994). Furthermore, though both bilateral and

TABLE 1. The expansion of educational multilateralism, 1965–95 (millions of constant 1994 US$)[1]

	1961	1965	1970	1975	1980	1985	1990	1995
Bilateral educational aid (OECD countries)[2]	...	3 412.5	3 628.8	4 038.1	5 962.4	4 596.9	4 073.4	3 985.0
World Bank lending to education[3]	0.0	230.3	409.5	636.9	772.9	1 785.3	1 663.6	1 923.7
UNESCO								
Total regular budget[4]	228.3	298.6	401.2	483.8	532.1	721.4	423.8	417.9
Education programmes[5]	52.1	69.5	84.5	105.0	98.5	169.3	81.7	89.3
Extrabudgetary support[6] for education programmes (Primarily UNDP)	...	140.8	117.2	214.0	174.92	...	83.3	94.2
UNICEF[7]	0.0	...	51.8	71.1	60.4	62.3	63.8	78.0
OECD/DAC GDP Deflator	14.24	16.41	19.29	35.14	56.94	51.97	89.36	109.5

1. OECD/DAC Weighted GDP Deflator was used to calculate constant 1994 dollar amounts.
2. Commitments, as reported in UNESCO (1993) and OECD/DAC (1996).
3. World Bank, *Annual Report, Trends in Lending*, various years.
4. UNESCO, *Approved Programme and Budget*, various years. Figures refer to biennial budgets.
5. UNESCO, *Approved Programme and Budget*. Figures refer to biennial budgets.
6. Estimated extrabudgetary contributions as they appear in UNESCO, *Approved Programme and Budgets*. Figures refer to biennial budgets.
7. Phillips (1987); UNICEF, *Annual Report*, 1996.

Sources: OECD/DAC, *Annual Report of the Development Assistance Committee*, 1995; Phillips (1987); UNESCO (1993); UNESCO, *Approved Programme and Budget*, various years; UNICEF, *Annual Report*, various years; World Bank, *Annual Report*, various years.

multilateral development agencies considered compulsory primary schooling an essential factor in the modernization of developing countries, they saw this as a domestic responsibility. They themselves focused their aid on secondary, vocational and higher education, where assistance could be offered in the form of training and expertise tied to Western institutions and services (OECD/DAC, 1972, pp. 130–1; Weiler, 1983; Arndt, 1987, p. 66; King, 1991).

Overall, the period between 1945 and 1970 saw the promise of redistributive educational multilateralism interpreted and enacted within multilateral organizations essentially as a problem of national economic modernization, solvable through a combination of 'national political will', the diffusion of a Western model of schooling and the provision of technical, depoliticized forms of Western educational expertise. The foundational commitment to education as a basic universal right apparent in the Charters of UNESCO and the United Nations became ever more deeply embedded in the fashionable language of national planning and economic modernization, circumventing larger questions of global equality, security and redistribution (Sewell, 1975; Cox, 1968; Jones, 1988, p. 116).

Educational multilateralism and the rise of basic needs

During the 1970s, the limited approaches to redistributive multilateralism which had been institutionalized in the 1950s and 1960s were sharply challenged by a coherent Third World bloc in the United Nations. Taking up some of the broader ideals and expectations encouraged in the United Nations Charter, this bloc demanded alternatives to existing patterns of international economic and political relations, including new mechanisms of international economic regulation to ensure stable commodity prices and the access of developing-country trade to First World markets, the direct redistribution of global wealth from North to South and the transfer of global economic decision-making to the more democratic United Nations institutions. Their challenge culminated in the United Nations General Assembly resolution for a 'New International Economic Order' in 1974 (Cox, 1979; Mogami, 1990; Marchand, 1994).

Although few Western countries showed enthusiasm for these broader structural changes, Third World demands did spur support for the introduction of new redistributive and compensatory themes into development programmes, especially among 'middle-power' nations whose development co-operation budgets and domestic social welfare programmes were continuing to expand (Lumsdaine, 1993). Seeking to maintain their legitimacy and in some cases expand their reach, multilateral organizations, such as the World Bank, UNICEF and UNESCO, also began to incorporate new basic needs programmes into their work during the 1970s (Mundy, in press).

These new poverty-oriented approaches were taken up in a variety of ways in the educational work of multilateral organizations. UNESCO, the most universal and democratic of the three organizations, struggled in vain to translate majority support for a 'new international economic order' into a new common vision for educational multilateralism. Instead, it became mired in broader questions of United Nations restructuring and North–South relations, entering a period of 'turbulent non-growth' in which it steadily lost support from Western members (Haas, 1990). Ironically, UNICEF and the World Bank, both removed to some degree from direct Third World demands through their governance structures and resource base, had more success in translating the emerging consensus on poverty-focused development assistance into new programmes and resources for educational development. Yet though rhetorical support for basic and non-formal education grew in both institutions, resources channelled to education at these levels remained disappointing (Jones, 1992; World Bank, 1974, 1980; Phillips, 1987; Black, 1996).[4] The new poverty-oriented educational programmes offered short-term interventions that were targeted rather than universal and, in the case of the World Bank, were offered through loans, not grants.

Ultimately, the growing demands of Third World countries in the 1970s did contribute to the rise of alternative frames for thinking about and engaging in educational development. These changes included new attention to the poor as agents of their own development and the growth of non-governmental organizations as channels for development assistance. Yet the overall shape of educational multilateralism in the 1970s continued

4. UNICEF funding for education dropped from 27 per cent of overall programming in 1972 to 13 per cent in 1979 (Phillips, 1987); World Bank lending to education amounted to less than 5 per cent of all lending before 1980, with basic education (primary and non-formal) comprising less than one-third of this total (Jones, 1992).

to be extremely limited, reflecting an international consensus which at once incorporated the humanitarian and social democratic impulses of a large group of core countries, while setting significant limits on the South's demand for a more directly redistributive world order. These limits were further underscored by the erosion of funding by the United States for development assistance and the rise of loans from international financial institutions as the largest single source of poverty-oriented finance in the late 1970s (Wood, 1986, p. 234). Situated alongside these trends, the focus on basic education as a path to poverty alleviation in the 1970s might well be seen as an attempt to construct 'an international welfare programme to be carried out as far as possible by the poor themselves' (Cox, 1979, pp. 271, 279).

Educational multilateralism in the 1980s and early 1990s

As noted above, the years between the mid-1970s and the early 1990s mark a period of fundamental transition in both domestic and international orders. Changes in international political economy had major repercussions for post-war multilateral organizations. During the 1970s, central decision-making about the world economy became more firmly entrenched in institutions in which neither developing countries nor popular non-state actors were represented – G7, OECD, IMF (Van der Pijl, 1994; Gill, 1994). Within these predominantly Northern institutions a new vision of world order was born and steadily spread among OECD countries. It argued for limited state intervention and saw an unencumbered global market as the most efficient arbiter of resources and guarantor of growth. This ideology was further strengthened by the collapse of the Soviet Union, which marked both the end of viable alternatives to Western, capitalist development and the erosion of a central argument for development-assistance spending (Griffin, 1991).

In this context resources for what I have termed 'redistributive multilateralism' stagnated, while private financial flows dramatically increased.[5] Calls for the reform of the United Nations and of the interna-

5. Thus total official development assistance as a percentage of all resource flows to developing countries fell from 49.8 per cent in 1988 to 19.2 per cent in 1996 (OECD/DAC, 1998).

tional financial institutions mounted (OECD/DAC, 1998, pp. 68–70). At the same time, new defensive and disciplinary forms of multilateralism among OECD countries steadily increased in influence, as reflected in the work of regional and 'rich country only' multilateral institutions (Cox, 1993; Ruggie, 1992). These broader shifts in both international political economy and multilateralism precipitated major changes in international educational co-operation. It is to these changes – the erosion and reorganization of redistributive forms of educational multilateralism, the rise of defensive and disciplinary forms of educational co-operation and the transformation of the 1970s' basic needs approach to education – that I turn below.

The erosion of Northern support for redistributive forms of educational multilateralism

Among the most important changes in international political economy affecting educational multilateralism in the 1980s was the gradual withdrawal of Northern support for all kinds of 'redistributive' multilateralism. This can be seen most starkly in the decline of development-assistance funding from the United States and the United Kingdom (the earliest neo-liberal reformers), and their contentious approach to the United Nations during the 1980s (Murphy and Aguelli, 1988; Lee, 1995). It can also be observed in the overall stagnation of development-assistance flows in real terms from many OECD countries during the 1980s and the decline of aid after 1990. Official aid from the OECD countries hovered at about 0.35 per cent of GNP during the 1980s and declined even further in the 1990s to its lowest level since the early 1970s, at 0.25 per cent of GNP in 1997 (OECD/DAC, 1998). Funding for UNDP also stagnated over this period. Voluntary contributions to UNDP alone dropped 45 per cent between 1982 and 1986, and the United States and several other countries remain in substantial arrears to the United Nations (Lumsdaine, 1993; UNDP, 1992; Griffin, 1991). The acuteness of the decline in funding for development assistance is especially marked if the increasing proportion of development assistance channelled to emergencies, humanitarian relief and Eastern Europe is taken into consideration.

Educational assistance has been disproportionately affected by these declines, as shown in Table 1. Bilateral educational aid fell from 15.6 per cent of OECD development assistance in 1980–84 to 11.1 per cent in 1985–89 and finally to below 10 per cent after 1990 (UNESCO, 1993, p. 42; Bennell and Furlong, 1997, pp. 6–8). Excepting the educational lending provided by the World Bank, multilateral support for education also stagnated during the 1980s, though the percentage of multilateral resources spent on education has seen an increase in the 1990s.

One illustration of the pressures contributing to the erosion of redistributive multilateralism in the field of education can be seen in the decline of funding and support for UNESCO during the 1980s. In the early 1980s, UNESCO had already faced almost a decade of disagreement between Third World and Western members over its primary purposes and roles. UNESCO's predominantly Third World membership continued to make demands based on arguments related to the New International Economic Order – most notably through calls for a New World Information and Communications Order. These demands were fundamentally at odds with the increasingly neo-conservative agenda of the Organization's major provider, the United States (Preston et al., 1989; Weiler, 1986; Sack, 1986; Imber, 1989).[6] They also came at a time when the cohesion and power of the Third World forum within the United Nations had itself begun to fragment (Marchand, 1994, p. 294). The decision of the United States to withdraw from UNESCO in 1984 (followed by the United Kingdom[7] and Singapore in 1985) marked a further decline of the only mechanism for post-war educational co-operation founded on universality of membership and the equal participation of nation-state members in decision-making. It also signalled the beginning of a decade of attempts led by the United States to reform the United Nations around more narrow, technical tasks (Lee, 1995).

In practical terms, the withdrawal reduced UNESCO's already small budget by about one-quarter, which, combined with cuts in funding for UNDP/UNESCO education work in the 1980s, deepened the already wide gap between UNESCO's broad mandate and modest resources. For the rest of the decade, UNESCO's work in education would continue to

6. Preston et al. (1989) provide a convincing account of the role that the Heritage Foundation played in provoking the withdrawal of both the United States and the United Kingdom from UNESCO.
7. The United Kingdom rejoined UNESCO in 1997.

be highly diffuse, spanning the practical attention to planning and information-gathering set out in the 1960s and the wider, more speculative and philosophical work on education and culture established in the 1970s. UNESCO did not succeed in giving its wide-ranging education sector work the greater focus and functionality being demanded of the United Nations organizations by its Northern members. But this has clearly been attempted in three recent moves: its sponsorship of the World Conference on Education for All (WCEFA), the expansion of its work on literacy to include research on illiteracy in the North and the creation of a new flagship publication, the *World Education Report*.

The rise of defensive and disciplinary forms of educational multilateralism

As advanced capitalist countries began to slow their support for the redistributive forms of multilateralism in the 1980s, they also began to heighten their involvement in forms of multilateralism that shut out developing-country membership. Examples here include OECD, which became a steadily more prominent forum for the discussion of adjustment and reform among countries in the North during the 1980s, and the expansion of regional economic multilateralism organized to help a bloc of advanced capitalist countries adjust to a new world economy (e.g. the North Atlantic Free Trade Agreement (NAFTA) and the European Union). These forms of multilateralism can be described as 'defensive' in so far as they were developed to equip the advanced capitalist countries with educational defences suitable for heightened competition and economic globalization and 'disciplinary' in that they contributed to the diffusion of the neo-liberal approaches to public policies developed in the United States and the United Kingdom, placing particular emphasis on the use of cross-national comparison to show the relative efficiencies of down-sizing the state and reorganizing the public institutions in which the rights and entitlements of the social welfare compromise were forged.

There has been relatively little written about the educational activities of these multilateral organizations and arrangements, but they are clearly changing the overall shape of international relations in education. Especially important has been the work of OECD in education. OECD has displaced UNESCO as the central forum for educational policy co-ordination for advanced capitalist countries[8] and is now the main multilateral provider of cross-national educational statistics and research in the North. The central focus of OECD education-sector work for almost two decades has been how to adjust education to changing economic requirements in the context of stagnating budgets.[9] In recent years its work has been profoundly shaped by the emphasis of the United States on privatization, choice, standards and cross-national testing issues which reflect a much broader reordering of domestic politics in that country (Papadopoulos, 1994; Carnoy, 1995).[10]

Education for All and the neo-liberal reorganization of educational aid

The rise of neo-liberalism within the advanced capitalist world had a somewhat paradoxical impact on educational aid. As we have seen above, it contributed to a decrease in overall funding for international development assistance and especially to the destabilization of United Nations development activities, each key to redistributive forms of educational multilateralism. Yet it also contributed to the creation of much stronger, more centralized mechanisms for setting and implementing international educational policies, especially through the largest and most influential multilateral organization involved in education during the 1980s, the World Bank. It is primarily under World Bank auspices that the broad multilateral support for basic education inherited from the 1970s was reformulated to fit the neo-liberal ideology and structure of late twentieth century world order.

During the 1980s, the focus on poverty alleviation to which education had become attached in the World Bank was displaced by issues of macro-economic reform and adjustment. The overarching goals of these adjustment programmes were to free up prices and markets, increase the

8. OECD held its first ministerial level conference on education in 1978, and these have been continued at six-year intervals.
9. See also Hautecoeur (1997) on the way in which industrialized countries have reframed literacy around a 'defensive' agenda.
10. This is necessarily an oversimplified account of OECD work in education. A more complete study of OECD work in education would, I believe, show it to be the locus of much cross-national debate and contestation, not least between Ministers of Education and Ministers of Finance, between Anglo-American and European approaches to adjustment, and among these and domestic educational interests, such as teachers' unions.

export orientation of the economy, reduce the size of government and liberalize trade – each thought to be essential for creating the conditions for future economic growth and competitive advantage in an integrating world economy. For a variety of reasons, these adjustment strategies failed to raise economic growth rates during the 1980s and often had negative effects on the poorest populations. At the same time, the emphasis of these programmes on limiting public spending and imposing user fees for public services tended to further undermine the already shrinking public sector budgets of indebted countries, with negative impacts on education (Annis, 1986; Cornia et al., 1987; Carnoy, 1995, p. 665; Reimers, 1994; Woodhall, 1994; Jones, 1992, pp. 140–88). They did, however, insulate international finance from the mounting Third World debt crisis, and contributed to a heightened role for the World Bank and IMF as 'managers of the global economy' (Wood, 1986, pp. 320–2; Biersteker, 1992; George and Sabelli, 1994).

At least initially, structural adjustment programmes also inhibited World Bank lending in education and other social sectors. Yet by the second half of the 1980s, under pressure from the United Nations, middle-power countries and non-governmental organizations, the World Bank had again begun to address these sectors (Table 2). UNICEF (and later

TABLE 2. World Bank loans to education, 1970–96 (millions of current US$)

	1970–74	1975–79	1980–84	1985–89	1990–94	1995	1996
IBRD	...	1 031.2	1 950.7	2 435.6	5 723.1	1 280.6	920.8
IDA	...	579.1	992.8	1 588.9	3 973.1	816.2	784.9
Total IBRD/IDA education sector lending	876.1	1 610.3	2 943.5	4 024.5	9 696.2	2 096.8	1 705.7
Education lending as a percentage of total World Bank lending	5.1	4.3	4.4	4.5	8.8	9.3	7.9
Percentage of education lending to basic education	...	...	...	26.1	34.1	33.0	40.2

Source: Calculated from World Bank, *Annual Reports*, various years; data on basic education (which includes primary and early childhood education) provided by the World Bank.

UNDP) played a particularly important role here, rapidly developing capacities for research and advocacy, and using these to publicize the social costs of adjustment and push the World Bank towards a return to the basic needs approaches of the 1970s (Cornia et al., 1987; Jolly, 1991). UNICEF also took the lead in promoting greater attention to basic education during the 1980s, initiating the idea of a World Conference on Education for All which gained the sponsorship of UNESCO, the World Bank and UNDP (Chabbott, 1996; World Conference . . . ,1989; Black, 1996, pp. 227–40).

World Bank education sector staff were, in turn, exceptionally well prepared to take advantage of these pressures and advance their own cause, within the organization and among the wider development community (Jones, 1992). By the late 1980s, they had both a convincing rationale for expanding educational lending (supported by a decade of research showing strong links between basic education and agricultural productivity, wages, health and child welfare) and a coherent framework for financing improvements in educational quality and efficiency in line with the World Bank's neo-liberal approach to public sector reform (World Bank, 1986, 1988; Jones, 1992, pp. 244–6). None the less, it seems unlikely that the rapid expansion of the World Bank's work in education (especially basic education) after 1989 would have occurred were it not for the profound challenges to the World Bank's own role and purpose that surfaced through the rise of commercial finance for development in the early 1990s and the concurrent deterioration of international support for the IDA (OECD/DAC, 1998, pp. 67–9). Lending in basic education (and in other social sectors) provided the same kind of legitimation and role enhancement in the 1990s that the World Bank had gained through its attention to basic needs in the 1970s.

How far has the World Bank's new approach to education gone towards embedding educational multilateralism in the neo-liberal hegemony of late twentieth century world order? The World Bank's new educational prescriptions echo the marriage of populist and modernization arguments forged in the 1970 World Bank discourse: education enhances individual productivity and overall economic growth; it ensures political stability through greater equality. At the same time, these new prescriptions are remarkably close to the defensive and disciplinary approaches to educational reform being debated among the advanced capitalist countries.[11] They emphasize the more efficient use of inputs (teachers, texts and tests), the introduction of privatization and choice to increase efficiency, the greater reliance on cost-recovery through parent and community participation, and a shift of resources from higher to primary education (World Bank, 1995; Carnoy, 1995).[12] Perhaps even more importantly, the World Bank's educational prescriptions have been implemented through new, disciplinary modalities of educational multilateralism: programmes of sector-wide educational financing and adjustment, the strategic use of policy- and conditionality-based lending. This shift in some sense completes the historical displacement of grant-based forms of development co-operation delivered through multilateral organizations democratically accountable to sovereign member nations. It also raises the World Bank from being the largest single financier of international educational development to being its most powerful ideologue and regulator.

Yet World Bank efforts to lead the Education for All movement have remained fraught with contradictions, at the level both of ideology and of practice. Some of these are amplifications of earlier contradictions in educational multilateralism – the World Bank continues to emphasize economic outcomes of education rather than its intrinsic value and utilizes a top-down, expert-led, depoliticized model of educational change clearly at odds with the realities of implementing educational reform (Samoff, 1996; Henneveld and Craig, 1996). There has also been considerable debate and resistance to its educational agenda – reflected not least in the dis-ease and conflicting goals that have characterized relationships between the WCEFA partners (the World Bank, UNESCO, UNICEF and UNDP) who cling to the development alternatives of the 1970s.[13] Few United Nations

11. Additional World Bank statements of its 1990s poverty alleviation agenda can be found in its 1990 *World Development Report* and the 1989 *Sub-Saharan Africa: From Crisis to Sustainable Growth*.
12. This is not the place to review the many criticisms of the World Bank's rationale and strategy for supporting basic education. The reader is referred to the following articles which critique the conclusions of the World Bank's rate of return and production function research: Bennell (1996); Colclough (1996). See also those which argue against its emphasis on efficiency, cost-recovery and top-down planning models of educational change: Hinchcliff (1993); Samoff (1996).
13. See interviews with Ahmed and Habte in UNICEF (1997). The different perspectives on educational development held by these organizations is significant, but should not be overstated. Samoff (1995), for example, found a remarkable homogeneity among donor assessments of education in Africa.

organizations, or their academic and non-governmental supporters, miss the outstanding irony of the World Bank's efforts to marry neo-liberal policy-based lending to its bid for greater legitimacy as the mediator of 'global welfare' and 'advocate of the poor' (Ilon, 1996; World Bank, 1994; Danaher, 1994; Nelson, 1995).

Perhaps the most important rupture in the World Bank's neo-liberal framing of Education for All can be found in its failure to rally wider financial support and co-operation for its basic education agenda. This time, the failure to raise finance for educational multilateralism reflects not simply a preference among international funding and technical-assistance agencies for bilateral forms of development assistance over multilateral, but a broader disengagement of advanced capitalist countries from notions of international development and redistributive multilateralism – a disengagement ironically fuelled by the neo-liberal vision of world order that the World Bank has helped to foster. Perhaps not surprisingly, the World Bank appears to be hedging its own bets in response to the broader crisis of redistributive educational multilateralism – it is intensifying efforts to build 'partnerships' with international and domestic non-governmental organizations, and yet seems to see its own future in enhancing and selling its policy expertise to governments (Nelson, 1995; World Bank, 1995, pp. 153–4; Heyneman, 1997; Moore, 1995).[14]

The 1990s and beyond: recent shifts and future prospects

This chapter has reviewed the evolution of forms of multilateral co-operation in education from 1945 to the present. It has suggested that for the period 1945–80, educational multilateralism was organized primarily around the theme of international development. One of the outcomes of this regime was the diffusion of a Western model of schooling and of expectations and practices that viewed formal schooling as both a universal right and a state responsibility. Yet though this regime was premised on many of the redistributive goals embedded within Western Keynesian welfare states, it remained highly truncated. Resources for educational

14. These same strategies are being attempted in other United Nations organizations – both UNICEF and UNESCO have announced that they will in future focus more on policy, planning, advice-giving (and less on direct support for projects); both are seeking to enhance 'partnerships'.

multilateralism remained limited in relation to expanding needs, and the brief period of contestation and reform that materialized in the 1970s led to marginal rather than fundamental changes within the educational activities of multilateral institutions.

Much of this chapter has focused on the period of major transition in world order and in multilateralism that has been unfolding since the late 1970s. I have argued that during this period both the form and content of educational multilateralism changed dramatically. On the one hand, the resources and legitimacy of what I have termed 'redistributive multilateralism' steadily eroded. This is especially apparent in the decline of UNESCO and of bilateral and multilateral funding for educational development. Meanwhile, 'defensive' and 'disciplinary' forms of educational co-operation gained strength in the shape of closed or rich country-dominated organizations, geared towards the development of regional economic blocs or towards the broader goal of liberalizing the world economy. Many of these organizations have contributed to the elaboration and diffusion of neo-liberal approaches to public policy and to education. In the emerging landscape of educational multilateralism, many of these organizations and the professionals working within them see themselves as participating in a secure market for the 'trade' of ideas about educational reform (Heyneman, 1997).

Yet the hegemony of these organizations and the homogeneity of their approaches to education is much less secure than might first appear, as is clear from the account of changing World Bank policies. Rather than homogeneity and hegemony in the coming millennium, we should expect to see a proliferation of forms of educational multilateralism, driven by several factors. First, as regional responses to globalization deepen, different institutional models are bound to emerge. The European Union, for example, offers an example in which political and social (as well as economic) multilateralism is being attempted and in which public support for state-organized programmes of redistribution, social security and welfare remains remarkably strong. In addition, the European Union is emerging as perhaps the largest institutional player in international development (see Gmelin in this book). Though the development of educational multilateralism within the European Union has been tentative to date, education is rising in importance on the European Union agenda. Over the long term, we might reasonably expect to see new approaches and expectations for educational multilateralism emerge from the European Union as well as in other regional blocs.

A second set of factors which may drive changes in the shape and content of educational multilateralism can be found in growing demands for new institutions of global governance. These calls have been heard most powerfully from the environmental movement and within various non-governmental campaigns to extend global social rights and entitlements or increase the accountability of organizations such as the IMF, the World Bank and the World Trade Organization (WTO) (Thiele, 1993; Princen and Finger, 1994; Cavanagh et al., 1994; Archibugi and Held, 1995; Stienstra, 1994; Marchand, 1996; Weiss and Gordenker, 1996). They include demands for the democratization of multilateral institutions through the creation of a popular assembly within the United Nations, calls for new ways of financing redistributive multilateralism (such as a tax on transnational financial flows or arms sales) and for the opening up of rich-country institutions to broader membership. Though education has not emerged as an independent focus for transnational movements, the fact that gaps in educational life chances are increasing, not shrinking, globally, is certain to figure prominently in their agendas for global justice.

To summarize, it has been argued that post-war educational multilateralism drew upon the 'embedded liberalism' of post-war order – both its ideological and its material origins can be traced to the institutionalization of a purposive approach to multilateralism that envisaged the promotion of a Keynesian welfare state societal compromise within advanced capitalist countries through the expansion and consensual regulation of international economic and political relations. Over the past twenty years, the domestic and international compromises of the post-war order have been steadily displaced by economic globalization. Today, we stand in the middle of a period of profound transition, one in which traditional centres of authority and sovereignty are rapidly changing and in which no model for societal development has yet gained a similar level of popular acceptance and legitimacy. Instead, new forms and levels of integration and communication are spurring the development of new social and political actors at multiple levels of the system.

Building the social and political foundations – the societal compromise – of a more just world order in an era of globalization will surely involve the construction of more humane, democratic and effective mechanisms of global governance, particularly around issues such as education that are tightly bound into international notions of equality, social security and human welfare. For this reason, we need a more sustained and reflective debate about the place of educational multilateralism in the emergent world order.

References

ANNIS, S. 1986. The Shifting Grounds of Poverty Lending at the World Bank. In: R. Feinberg and G. K. Helleiner (eds.), *Between Two Worlds: The World Bank's Next Decade*, pp. 87–106. Oxford UK, Transaction Books.

ARCHIBUGI, D.; HELD, D. (eds.). 1995. *Cosmopolitan Democracy: An Agenda for a New World Order.* Cambridge, Mass., Polity Press.

ARNDT, H. W. 1987. *Economic Development: The History of an Idea.* Chicago, Ill., University of Chicago Press.

ARRIGHI, G. 1991. World Income Inequalities and the Future of Socialism. *New Left Review*, No. 189, pp. 39–65.

BARNETT, M. 1997. Review Article: Bringing in the New World Order: Liberalism, Legitimacy and the United Nations. *World Politics*, Vol. 49, No. 4, pp. 526–51.

BENNELL, P. 1996. Using and Abusing Rates of Return: A Critique of the World Bank's 1995 Education Sector Review. *International Journal of Education Development*, Vol. 16, No. 3, pp. 235–48.

BENNELL, P.; FURLONG, D. 1997. *Has Jomtien Made Any Difference? Trends in Donor Funding for Education and Basic Education since the late 1980s.* Brighton, University of Sussex Institute of Development Studies.

BIERSTEKER, T. 1992. The Triumph of Neoclassical Economics in the Developing World: Policy Convergence and Basis of Governance in the International Economic Order. In: J. Rosenau and E. O. Czempiel (eds.), *Governance without Government*, pp. 102–31. Cambridge, Cambridge University Press.

BLACK, M. 1996. *Children First: The Story of UNICEF, Past and Present.* New York, Oxford University Press.

CARNOY, M. 1995. Structural Adjustment and the Changing Face of Education. *International Labour Review*, Vol. 134, No. 6, pp. 653–73.

CASTELLS, M. 1997. *The Information Age: Economy, Society and Culture*, Vol. II: *The Power of Identity.* Oxford, Blackwell.

CAVANAGH, J.; WYSHAM, D.; ARRUDA, M. (eds.). 1994. *Beyond Bretton Woods: Alternatives to the Global Economic Order.* London, Pluto Press.

CHABBOTT, C. 1996. *Constructing Educational Development: International Development Organizations and the World Conference on Education for All.* Stanford University School of Education. (Ph.D. dissertation.)
COLCLOUGH, C. 1996. Education and the Market: Which Parts of the Neo-liberal Solution are Correct? *World Development,* Vol. 24, No. 4, pp. 589–610.
COLCLOUGH, C.; MANOR, J. (eds.). 1993. *States or Markets? Neo-liberalism and the Development Policy Debate.* Oxford, Clarendon Press.
COMMISSION ON GLOBAL GOVERNANCE. 1995a. *Our Global Neighborhood.* New York, Oxford University Press.
——. 1995b. *Issues in Global Governance: Papers Written for the Commission on Global Governance.* New York, Oxford University Press.
CORNIA, G.; JOLLY, R.; STEWART, F. (eds.). 1987. *Adjustment with a Human Face.* Cambridge, Oxford University Press.
COX, R. 1968. Education for Development. In: R. Gardner and M. F. Millikan (eds.), *The Global Partnership: International Agencies and Economic Development,* pp. 310–31. New York, Praeger.
——. 1979. Ideologies and the New International Economic Order. *International Organization,* Vol. 33, No. 2, pp. 257–302.
——. 1980. The Crisis of World Order and the Problem of International Organization in the 1980s. *International Journal,* Vol. 35, No. 2, pp. 370–85.
——. 1981. Social Forces, States and World Orders: Beyond International Relations Theory. *Millennium,* Vol. 10, No. 2, pp. 126–55.
——. 1992. Multilateralism and World Order. *Review of International Studies,* Vol. 18, pp. 161–80.
——. 1993. The Global Political Economy and Social Choice. In: D. Drache and M. Gertler (eds.), *The New Era of Global Competition: State Policy and Market Power,* pp. 335–50. Montreal, McGill-Queens.
DANAHER, K. (ed.). 1994. *50 Years is Enough: The Case against the World Bank and the International Monetary Fund.* Boston, Mass., South End Press.
ESCOBAR, A. 1994. *Encountering Development: The Making and Unmaking of the Third World.* Princeton, Princeton University Press.
FALK, R. 1995. *On Humane Governance: Toward a New Global Politics.* Cambridge, Mass., Polity Press.
FINNEMORE, M. 1996. *National Interests in International Society.* Ithaca, N.Y., Cornell University Press.
GEORGE, S.; SABELLI, F. 1994. *Faith and Credit: The World Bank's Secular Empire.* Boulder, Colo., Westview Press.

GILL, S. 1994. Structural Change and Global Political Economy: Globalizing Elites and the Emerging World Order. In: Y. Sakamoto (ed.), *Global Transformation: Challenges to the State System.* New York, United Nations University Press.

GRIFFIN, K. 1991. Foreign Aid after the Cold War. *Development and Change,* Vol. 22, No. 4, pp. 645–85.

HAAS, E. B. 1990. *When Knowledge is Power: Three Models of Change in International Organizations.* Berkeley, Calif., U.C. Press.

HARVEY, D. 1989. *The Condition of Postmodernity.* Oxford, Blackwell.

HAUTECOEUR, J. P. 1997. A Political Review of International Literacy Meetings in Industrialized Countries. *International Review of Education,* Vol. 43, No. 2/3, pp. 135–58.

HELD, D. 1995. *Democracy and the Global Order: From the Modern State to Cosmopolitan Governance.* Stanford, Calif., Stanford University Press.

HELLEINER, E. 1994. From Bretton Woods to Global Finance: A World Turned Upside Down. In: R. Stubbs and G. Underhill (eds.), *Political Economy and the Changing Global Order,* pp. 163–75. Toronto, McClelland & Stewart.

HENNEVELD, W.; CRAIG, H. 1996. *Schools Count: World Bank Projects Designs and the Quality of Primary Education in Sub-Saharan Africa.* Washington, D.C. (World Bank Technical Paper 303. World Bank African Technical Department.)

HEYNEMAN, S. P. 1997. Economic Growth and the International Trade in Educational Reform. *Prospects,* Vol. XXVII, No. 4, pp. 501–30.

HINCHCLIFF, K. 1993. Neo-liberal Prescriptions for Education Finance: Unfortunately Necessary or Inherently Desirable? *International Journal of Educational Development,* Vol. 13, No. 2, pp. 183–7.

IKENBERRY, G. J. 1992. A World Economy Restored: Expert Consensus and the Anglo-American Postwar Settlement. *International Organization,* Vol. 46, No. 1, pp. 289–321.

ILON, L. 1996. The Changing Role of the World Bank: Education Policy as Global Welfare. *Policy and Politics,* Vol. 24, No. 4, pp. 413–24.

IMBER, M. F. 1989. *The USA, ILO, UNESCO and IAEA. Politicization and Withdrawal in the Specialized Agencies.* London, Macmillan.

JOLLY, R. 1991. Adjustment with a Human Face: A UNICEF Record and Perspective on the 1980s. *World Development,* Vol. 19, No. 12, pp. 1807–21.

JONES, P. 1988. *International Policies for Third World Education: UNESCO, Literacy and Development.* London/New York, Routledge.

——. 1992. *World Bank Financing of Education: Lending, Learning and Development.* London, Routledge.

KING, K. 1991. *Aid and Education in the Developing World*. London, Longman UK.

LEE, K. 1995. A neo-Gramscian Approach to International Organizations: An Expanded Analysis of Current Reforms to the UN Development Activities. In: J. MacMilland and A. Linklater (eds.), *Boundaries in Question*, pp. 149–62. New York, St Martin's Press.

LUMSDAINE, D. H. 1993. *Moral Vision in International Politics: The Foreign Aid Regime 1949-1989*. Princeton, Princeton University Press.

MCNEELY, C. 1995. Prescribing National Educational Policies: The Role of International Organizations. *Comparative Education Review*, Vol. 39, No. 4, pp. 483–507.

MCNEELY, C.; CHA, Y. K. 1994. Worldwide Educational Convergence through International Organizations: Avenues for Research. *Educational Policy Analysis Archives*, Vol. 2, No. 14.

MARCHAND, M. 1994. The Political Economy of North South Relations. In: R. Stubbs and G. Underhill (eds.), *Political Economy in the Changing Global Order*, pp. 289–301. Toronto, McClelland & Stewart.

——. 1996. Reconceptualizing Gender and Development in an Era of Globalization. *Millennium*, Vol. 25, No. 3, pp. 577–603.

MOGAMI, T. 1990. The United Nations System as an Unfinished Revolution. *Alternatives*, Vol. XV, pp. 177–97.

MOORE, D. 1995. Development Discourse as Hegemony: Towards an Ideological History, 1945–1995. In: D. Moore and G. Schmitz (eds.), *Debating Development Discourse*, pp. 1–53. New York, St Martin's Press.

MUNDY, K. 1998. Educational Multilateralism and World (dis)Order. *Comparative Education Review*, Vol. 42, No. 4.

MURPHY, C. 1994. *International Organization and Industrial Change; Global Governance since 1850*. Cambridge, Mass., Polity Press.

MURPHY, C.; AGUELLI, E. 1988. *America's Quest for Supremacy and the Third World*. London, Pinter.

——. 1993. International Institutions, Decolonization, and Development. *International Political Science Review*, Vol. 14, No. 1, pp. 71–85.

NELSON, P. 1995. *The World Bank and NGOs: The Limits of Apolitical Development*. New York, St Martin's Press.

NOEL, A.; THERIEN, J. P. 1995. From Domestic to International Justice: The Welfare State and Foreign Aid. *International Organization*, Vol. 49, No. 3, pp. 523–53.

OECD/DAC. Various years. *Development Co-operation. Annual Report of the Development Assistance Committee*. Paris, OECD.

PAPADOPOULOS, G. 1994. *Education 1960–1990: The OECD Perspective.* Paris, OECD.

PHILLIPS, H. M. 1987. *UNICEF and Education: A Historical Perspective.* New York, UNICEF.

PRESTON, W.; HERMAN, E.; SCHILLER, H. 1989. *Hope and Folly: The United States and UNESCO, 1945–1985.* Minneapolis, Minn., University of Minnesota Press.

PRINCEN, T.; FINGER, M. 1994. *Environmental NGOs in World Politics.* London, ZED Press.

RAMIREZ, F.; BOLI, J. 1987. Global Patterns of Educational Institutionalization. In: J. Thomas, *Institutional Structure: Constituting the State, Society and the Individual,* pp. 150–72. Beverly Hills, Calif., Sage.

REIMERS, F. 1994. Education and Structural Adjustment in Latin America and sub-Saharan Africa. *International Journal of Educational Development,* Vol. 14, No. 2, pp. 119–29.

ROSENAU, J. 1992. *The United Nations in a Turbulent World.* Boulder, Colo., Lynne Rienner.

RUGGIE, J. 1992. Multilateralism: The Anatomy of an Institution. *International Organization,* Vol. 46, No. 3, pp. 561–97.

RUGGIE, J. G. 1983. International Regimes, Transactions and Change: Embedded Liberalism in the Postwar Economic Order. In: S. Krasner (ed.), *International Regimes,* pp. 195–231. Ithaca, N.Y., Cornell University Press.

SACK, R. 1986. UNESCO: From Inherent Contradictions to Open Crisis. *Comparative Education Review,* Vol. 30, No. 1, pp. 112–19.

SAMOFF, J. 1995. *Analyses, Agendas and Priorities in African Education. A Review of Externally Initiated, Commissioned and Supported Studies of Education in Africa, 1990–1994.* UNESCO/DAE Working Group, 11 September.

——. 1996. Which Priorities and Strategies for Education? *International Journal of Educational Development,* Vol. 16, No. 3, pp. 249–71.

SEWELL, J. P. 1975. *UNESCO and World Politics.* Princeton, N.J., Princeton University Press.

STIENSTRA, D. 1994. *Women's Movements and International Organizations.* Basingstoke, Macmillan Press.

STUBBS, R.; UNDERHILL, G. (eds.). 1994. *Political Economy in a Changing World Order.* Toronto, McClelland & Stewart.

THIELE, L. 1993. Making Democracy Safe for the World: Social Movements and Global Politics. *Alternatives,* Vol. 18, pp. 273–305.

UNDP. 1992. *Human Development Report.* New York, UNDP.

UNESCO. 1993. *World Education Report 1993.* Paris, UNESCO.
——. Various years. *Approved Programme and Budget.* Paris, UNESCO.
UNICEF. 1997. *Education News,* Vol. 6, No. 3 (February). (Special Issue: Six Years after Jomtien.)
——. Various years. *Annual Report.* New York, UNICEF.
VAN DER PIJL, K. 1994. The Cadre Class and Public Multilateralism. In: Y. Sakamot (ed.), *Global Transformation: Challenges to the State System,* pp. 100–28. New York, United Nations University Press.
WEILER, H. 1983. *Aid for Education: The Political Economy of International Co-operation in Educational Development.* Ottawa, IDRC.
——. 1986. Withdrawing from UNESCO: A Decision in Search of an Argument. *Comparative Education Review,* Vol. 34, No. 1, pp. 132–47.
WEISS, T.; GORDENKER, L. (eds.). 1996. *NGOs, the UN and Global Governance.* Boulder, Colo., Lynne Rienner.
WOOD, R. 1986. *From Marshall Plan to Debt Crisis: Foreign Aid and Development Choices in the World Economy.* Berkeley, Calif., University of California Press.
WOODHALL, M. 1994. The Effects of Austerity on Adjustment in the Allocation and Use of Resources. In: J. Samoff (ed.), *Coping with Crisis: Austerity, Adjustment and Human Resources,* pp. 175–202. London/Paris/Geneva, Cassell/UNESCO/ILO.
WORLD BANK. 1974. *Education Sector Working Paper.* Washington, D.C., World Bank.
——. 1980. *Education Sector Policy Paper.* Washington, D.C., World Bank.
——. 1986. *Financing Education in Developing Countries: An Exploration of Policy Options.* Washington, D.C., World Bank.
——. 1988. *Education in sub-Saharan Africa: Policies for Adjustment, Revitalization, and Expansion.* Washington, D.C., World Bank.
——. 1994. *The Evolving Role of the World Bank: The Challenge of Africa.* Washington, D.C., World Bank.
——. 1995. *Priorities and Strategies for Education.* Washington, D.C., World Bank.
——. Various years. *Annual Report.* Washington, D.C., World Bank.
WORLD CONFERENCE ON EDUCATION FOR ALL (Jomtien, Thailand, 5–9 March 1990). 1989. *Meeting Basic Learning Needs: A New Vision for the 1990s. Background Document.* New York, Inter-Agency Commission for WCEFA.
WORLD PEACE FOUNDATION. 1945. *United Nations in the Making: Basic Documents.* Boston, Mass., World Peace Foundation.

Education and development co-operation: a UNESCO perspective
Wyn Courtney

The role played by UNESCO in education and development co-operation is rather different from that of other agencies. UNESCO is a multilateral agency, having almost universal membership (186 Member States). But it is not an aid agency in the same way as other multilaterals, such as the World Bank and the other development banks, since it does not provide loans to developing countries. It does, however, engage in development co-operation with funding from other sources, acting in concert with a developing country or countries, on a project or programmatic basis, to enhance and/or strengthen an institution or sector. UNESCO's development co-operation involves the provision of technical and advisory services to its Member States, in the form of staff and/or consultant missions, supplies and equipment, training courses, seminars and workshops, and fellowships and study grants.

UNESCO's primary role is intellectual and ethical: to promote the exchange of ideas and experiences through conferences and meetings, studies and research, and the publication of books, periodicals, reports and documents, e.g. in the way the International Commission on the Development of Education and the International Commission on Education for the Twenty-first Century asked searching questions and explored new approaches in the educational enterprise (Faure et al., 1972; Delors et al., 1996); and to establish international norms through conventions, agreements, recommendations and declarations, such as the Recommendation concerning the Status of Teachers (1966) (UNESCO, 1998).[1]

1. See UNESCO (1998, pp. 22–5) for a discussion and illustration of the work entailed from the inter-governmental conference, joint ILO–UNESCO Committee of Experts, to reports, case studies, comparative analysis and statistical questionnaires.

The work of the Organization might almost be categorized as twofold: normative, operating in a global/international context and funded from the regular programme budget; and development activities at the country level funded from extrabudgetary sources. However, while some activities may appear to be more clearly normative or development oriented, there is not always a clear-cut distinction in reality, particularly since few staff members are confined to one mode or the other.

This chapter is concerned with UNESCO's role as a development agency and the way in which three factors affect its scope of operations in the South: its ethical mission and mandate, rephrased at each biennial General Conference as the statement of Member States' priorities; the direct and at times frequent exchanges between members of the Secretariat and officials of the Member States; and the source of its funding. The chapter furthermore reflects on the implications for UNESCO of the new patterns of development co-operation and particularly on its response and responsiveness to the concepts of partnership, donor co-ordination, national capacity-building and accountability.

UNESCO as a multilateral agency

UNESCO was established in 1945 as the intellectual body of the United Nations, with the ethical mission, according to its Constitution, of constructing 'the defences of peace in the minds of men' and a commitment to 'full and equal opportunities for education for all, in the unrestricted pursuit of objective truth and in the free exchange of ideas and knowledge' (UNESCO, 1995). It was not until the early 1960s, the start of the Second Development Decade, that UNESCO became, as a Specialized Agency of the United Nations, the educational arm of UNDP, which was then established as the funding and co-ordinating agency of the United Nations at the country level. Indeed, UNESCO was considered *the* educational body of the United Nations and entered into co-operative agreements first with the World Bank and UNICEF, and later with the United Nations Population Fund (UNFPA), the World Food Programme (WFP) and the United Nations Environment Programme (UNEP), to provide educational expertise to complement their specific technical competencies.

With a relatively small budget, about the size of a medium-sized university (see Mundy, in this volume), cut by almost one-third with the withdrawal of the United States, the United Kingdom and Singapore in 1984 and 1985,[2] and held to zero growth by its Member States through successive General Conferences since then, there are limitations as to what UNESCO can do alone; its development efforts have always therefore been undertaken with other partners. The regular budget ($544 million for the 1998/99 biennium) is comprised of assessed contributions from Member States and is spread over a wide range of activities, largely in the regional and international domains, reflecting its role in promoting exchanges of ideas and experiences. Attempts to focus on a smaller number of activities and issues are frustrated largely by the nature of the Organization.

The Organization is characterized by considerable diversity of disciplines and components. While the Education Sector is the largest[3] and perhaps best-known part of UNESCO, there are also Natural Sciences, Social and Human Sciences, Culture and Communication, Information and Informatics Sectors, a number of transdisciplinary projects and autonomous centres and institutes, such as the World Heritage Centre and IIEP, which together carry out the programme agreed at each General Conference. Attending the conference are the official delegations from each of UNESCO's Member States; they may include Ministers and other officials from several ministries or departments, as well as officials from the National Commissions for UNESCO.[4] Also attending the conference with observer status are representatives of non-Member States, other agencies and non-governmental organizations. More than 500 non-governmental organizations maintain regular relations of co-operation with UNESCO and carry out parts of the programme under contract; some of the major ones, including the International Association of Universities, the International Council of Scientific Unions and the International Council of Museums, also have offices in one of the UNESCO buildings to ensure even closer co-operation between their staff and that of the Secretariat. There are also some 5,300 UNESCO Clubs, centres and Associated

2. The United Kingdom rejoined UNESCO in 1997.
3. The Education Sector has the largest share of the budget, at $105 million of the $330 million allocated to Programme Execution; this is close to 20 per cent of the total budget of $544 million (UNESCO, 1997).
4. UNESCO is the only United Nations Specialized Agency to provide for the establishment of a National Commission by each of its Member States; the Commission is a governmental advisory body funded by the particular Member State and providing a focal point for UNESCO's regular programme actions in the country.

Schools which relay UNESCO's work in the field and promote its ideals, as well as 3,200 UNESCO Associated Schools to educate young people in a spirit of tolerance and international understanding.

This network of national officials and independent professionals is both UNESCO's constituency, to which it is answerable, and its resource base, from which it draws its expertise. UNESCO is thus not an institution of the North but given its wide and democratic membership (staffed by some 2,200 nationals from over 140 Member States) rather an important forum for North–South–East–West exchanges.

The broad range of UNESCO's programme, coupled with its small budget, limits implementation mainly to normative and global or regional activities. The exception to this are the small-scale projects carried out by the National Commissions that are funded from a special Participation Programme budget. The majority of country-level actions and activities are funded from other 'extrabudgetary' sources.

UNESCO's role in development co-operation

Being dependent on others for financial resources for major development activities, UNESCO has been very conscious of the recent decline in ODA, the drain of funds from long-term development work to short-term humanitarian and peace-keeping exercises, and in particular the diminished resources for education.

In addition, UNESCO has closely followed the debate about reform of the United Nations (and its Specialized Agencies) as it relates to development through the United Nations Economic and Social Council (ECOSOC), and particularly through participation in the Administrative Committee on Co-ordination and its Consultative Committee on Programme and Operational Questions. The debate about development has also been reflected in the priorities that are expressed at annual meetings with bilateral donors and funding partners (see, for example, *The United Nations in Development*, 1991). The rhetoric of partnership, ownership and participation has found a ready resonance in daily normative and development work.

Extrabudgetary support for education projects to be implemented by UNESCO declined towards the end of the 1980s. At the same time, the co-operative programme with the World Bank, through which UNESCO identified, appraised and to a lesser extent evaluated projects for the Bank, was terminated, in part through the generalized disaffection with UNESCO in the United States and in part through the increase in education specialists in the World Bank and differing perspectives on development co-operation. A similar but smaller arrangement continues with the African Development Bank.

Strains also appeared in the UNESCO–UNICEF co-operative programme as UNICEF moved beyond its traditional mandate of maternal and child welfare, and non-formal education into formal schooling, and recruited its own specialist education staff. Although the co-operative agreement was ended in 1997, co-operation continues in particular projects and activities, most notably the follow-up to the World Conference on Education for All, for which UNESCO provides the Secretariat with funding also from other agencies.

More substantively, UNDP at the start of its fifth programme cycle in 1992, began to effect changes to its mode of executing projects, moving from that by agencies, such as UNESCO for education, or the Food and Agriculture Organization of the United Nations (FAO) for agriculture, to that of national execution. National execution is intended to lead to national ownership of projects with national capacity to implement projects, in order to root them in the country and so avoid the establishment of expatriate-staffed 'enclave projects' which fly the agency flag (see King's comments on donor projects and sector development in the Introduction to this book) and disappear on completion without trace or without any noticeable impact.

This change in modality coincided also with the shift, starting in the mid-1980s, from stand-alone projects to the programme approach or sector development. Ideally, all 'donors' participate in the development of the sector, commit their funds to a slice of the resources needed to finance the sector's new programme, and leave the spending and implementation to the national authorities. Co-ordination of donor inputs by the national authorities and co-operation among all become necessary, but it seldom happens that way. In part to address this issue, UNDP created a facility to provide technical assistance to governments to assist them in the 'upstream' stage of this process, that of sector analysis and programme planning. The facility provides short-term technical expertise, either from an agency staff member or an international consultant, possibly from the

South, in the form of grant aid to the country. There is also a facility to assist governments with technical advice at the 'downstream' or implementation stage.

UNESCO's portfolio of UNDP projects has therefore changed markedly over the past twenty years. There are no more large-scale projects like the Experimental World Literacy Programme, launched in 1967 and covering a ten-year period in seventeen countries, with the major funding from UNDP and the participation of five other countries (UNESCO/UNDP, 1976). Nor are there projects like the Bunumbu Teacher Training Project, criticized by (among others) Elu and Banya in this book for having too many, and not always suitable, expatriate Northern staff, for providing inappropriate technology, and having to suffer from ineffectively transparent bureaucracies at both UNESCO and the country level. There are now more small-scale studies, sector analyses and thematic evaluations that are intended to assist the national authorities in determining *their* priorities, and to provide them with information and arguments for their dialogue with other partners. For this type of work, there are usually more national experts than international ones, thereby encouraging national ownership, national capacity-building and the development of national expertise.

As the volume of UNDP funds has decreased, there has been an increase in UNESCO projects funded from other sources, including the European Union, and particularly from bilateral agencies that provide funds for specific areas and projects to be implemented by UNESCO on their behalf. Thus, the contributions by UNDP and other United Nations sources – which accounted for 58 per cent of the $82 million provided for extrabudgetary activities in 1990 – declined to 27 per cent of the total of $88.7 million in 1997 (budgetary status reports, various years). There are currently more than 1,500 projects, one-third of them in the Education Sector, included in the estimated extrabudgetary resources for the 1998/99 biennium of $265 million (UNESCO, 1997).

These bilaterally funded projects typically are identified as a priority by the particular country and UNESCO's role is first to secure the resources and then to assist in implementing the project, usually through a national project director or team. As an intermediary, UNESCO sometimes has the disagreeable task of informing a country that no matter how high a priority the project is for them, resources cannot be mobilized,

Education and development co-operation: A UNESCO perspective
Wyn Courtney

either because the topic is outside UNESCO's mandate or because a donor cannot be found who is willing to finance the activity. For even the most open and generous bilateral agency that does not insist on vetting each project proposal, specifies its own set of criteria that must be met in using its funds. For example, they may be used only for the poorest countries, those with a per capita GNP less than $X, with the exception of Countries A and B whose record on human rights is rather blemished. And although UNESCO is not obliged to use the donor country's goods and services in implementing the project, it may be obliged to report each year on what goods and services from that country have been used.

So why would non-United Nations agencies channel funds through UNESCO? What is the perceived comparative advantage or the value-added for UNESCO implementation? For many bilateral agencies, education is still sufficiently important to be included in their funding of multilateral agencies. UNESCO can also undertake work of a regional or sub-regional and international nature that bilateral agencies cannot. It can put together a team of experts from as many nationalities as there are expert posts. This aspect may be less appreciated by the bilateral donor than by the 'recipient', who may look to UNESCO for independent advice, with no strings attached and no conditionalities since UNESCO has no funds, no trade connections and no goods to sell.

In addition, the shift of emphasis since the World Summit for Social Development (Copenhagen, 1995) towards the alleviation of poverty calls for non-traditional types of technical assistance, most usually of an interdisciplinary nature. Ostensibly, UNESCO is better placed than most bilateral agencies to undertake activities of this kind, as well as inter-agency ones in the United Nations system, not least because education, particularly non-formal education, is an enabling condition for almost all poverty reduction strategies.

Without funds of its own for development co-operation projects, without a particular perspective to promote, without a particular sphere of influence to protect or enhance, UNESCO may be viewed as only a bit player, using other agencies' chips to stay in the game. However, it may also be viewed as an honest broker, providing technical unflavoured advice, to be used by rich and poor, but particularly by the poor to co-ordinate the inputs of the rich. It is to this end that UNESCO has, since 1990, allocated between 5 and 10 per cent of its programme budget to a specific Co-operation for Development Fund to enable it to respond as broker or intermediary to requests for this kind of assistance and to mobilize resources for projects in the UNESCO priority areas of women, youth, Africa and the least-developed countries.

Thus the type of development co-operation activities has changed, from implementing relatively large-scale projects identified and funded by UNDP, and co-operative arrangements to provide educational expertise for other United Nations agencies and funds, to upstream work, largely for UNDP, and resource mobilization among bilateral donors for projects identified for and with the developing country. The role that UNESCO plays now is therefore less directly a supplier of technical assistance and more that of intermediary, facilitator and technical adviser. How this changed role affects UNESCO's response to the calls for new patterns of development co-operation is examined below.

UNESCO and the new patterns of co-operation

It is uncertain whether there is a 'new paradigm' for international aid to education (see King in the Introduction to this book), or a fundamental change in the relationships between the North and the South. What is clear is that there are fewer financial resources available and that the ways in which aid is provided for education in poor countries has been re-examined. The change in relationships has been associated with 'people-centred' and 'participatory' development, with policies, plans and programmes (of donors and recipients) that are 'comprehensive', 'integrated', 'coherent' and 'consistent', and that promote 'donor co-ordination', 'national ownership' and 'national capacity'. To move from rhetoric to reality is not easy. UNESCO, like other agencies, is grappling with the problem, and in particular with the implications of 'partnerships', 'donor co-ordination', 'national capacity' and 'accountability'.

Partnership

To move from discussing the nature of 'partnership' to establishing more equal and reciprocal relationships requires at least a code of conduct, such as that being developed in a number of agencies and referred to elsewhere in this book. More importantly, it requires certain changes in patterns of behaviour which are more difficult to achieve, given the nature and staffing patterns of most aid agencies. The inherently unequal and asymmetric donor–recipient relationship can only begin to approach that of a partnership when there is almost daily contact, frank and honest exchanges of opinions and ideas, and recognition that sovereignty is absolute.

The parties to the aid-to-education partnership seldom have daily contact; more usually, the financing party pays a visit to 'his/her' country once a year; the delegation may have several programmes and thus partners to meet in several ministries; there may or may not be an educator in the embassy/country office who can provide a detailed informal view of the state of the partnership. With the reduction, if not elimination, of expatriate project staff, there are few outsiders who know the internal workings, the strengths and the weaknesses of, for example, the Ministry of Education and few to provide on-the-job training and so assist in national capacity-building. There are also fewer specialists at agency headquarters with long working experience in a particular country or region; there are more generalists and accountants. The amounts offered from the diminishing ODA are often marginal to the priority and often tied to conditionalities. Partnership thus remains at the level of formalities and diplomatic niceties, whereas direct questions or recriminations about obligations, from either side, are avoided.

In order to better listen to the needs and priorities of the Member States, UNESCO has, over the past ten years, decentralized both staff and resources to establish new country offices in addition to the previous regional and subregional offices. There are now UNESCO offices in over seventy countries. This decentralization, which accounts for 25 per cent of the total professional staff posts and about 37 per cent of the regular programme budget, has stretched the zero-growth budget resources both at headquarters and at field level. As all field offices need to have multidisciplinary competencies, small offices with one or two professionals often find it difficult to engage actively in specific development activities or to provide the specific expertise needed, for example to engage in upstream work, such as education sector analyses.

Donor co-ordination

In principle, moving towards a programme approach and sector development should promote greater symmetry in the North–South relationships provided that all donors/agencies act in concert and put their funding into a common pot. However, there are difficulties in determining when is the appropriate moment to engage in a new sector development. It is more likely to be the World Bank than the national authorities that decides and it is more likely to be predicated on the Bank's lending programme than on the needs of the education system. Each donor or agency has its own budget, programme cycle and timetable, and few are willing or able to adjust them for the sake of one recipient country. United Nations agencies are no different from the World Bank or bilateral agencies although there are currently major efforts, as part of the United Nations system reforms, to co-ordinate the timing and content of their programme cycles. This is more likely to succeed in countries where agencies share common premises, which is now being negotiated in a number of countries.

In addition, often when a sector programme has been developed, assessed for feasibility and costed, there are not sufficient funds available to meet the total costs. External partners slip back easily into committing funds for those parts with which they are more familiar and/or prefer, instead of allowing the national authorities to handle the shortfall in their own way and to determine which of their priorities they wish to maintain.

The monthly donor meetings in the recipient countries on education, or education sector meetings including donors and Ministry officials and non-governmental organizations, initiated in many cases by the United Nations Resident Co-ordinator and chaired by different agencies, sometimes UNICEF, sometimes even UNESCO, are an attempt to make for better co-ordination and co-operation. UNESCO's growing strength and understanding of 'upstream' work has been important, but has not always been used by UNDP or the national authorities to co-ordinate donor inputs. Even the development of Master Plans for Education, as in Guinea and the Dominican Republic, which led to round-table meetings, have been only partially successful since neither UNDP-sponsored education sector round tables nor the World Bank's Consultative Group meetings seemed to be able to ensure sufficient external resources to cover the needs identified in the Master Plan or Sector Investment Programme.

National capacity

After so many development decades and development cycles, one might expect that there would be ample national capacity in all countries. However, those competent and able persons who have not already joined the staff of aid agencies, including UNESCO, are likely to be over-extended, being sought after by each agency, sometimes simultaneously. Since the donors/agencies are more likely to fund projects than to provide budgetary support to institutions such as ministries, colleges or universities, which have a long-term training mission or national capacity-building function, there is an internal as well as external brain and talent drain, with the fees of a 'national consultant' often being considerably higher than his/her salary.

In this situation, to be able to listen more carefully, agencies should consider using expatriates who are experts from the South. This would compensate in the long run for the national brain-drain and would double the national capacity-building efforts. Technical co-operation among developing countries has been in practice in UNESCO since its formulation in the 1980s (Hallak, 1990, pp. 294–5), especially but not only in literacy programmes. One of UNESCO's advantages is that it is not bound to identify competent persons from any particular country, and that South–South co-operation is considered fundamental in both its normative and development work.

Accountability

While donors/agencies are accountable to their parliaments/governing bodies, their obligations to the recipients are unclear. The type of co-ordination – of funding cycles, budgets and country inputs – needed to support an education sector programme is long term: ten to fifteen years. Are donors/agencies prepared to make such a commitment and to be held accountable for this support from their partners, the recipients? This is a major dilemma for all agencies, including UNESCO, since budgets are mostly measured in annual doses.

Should the rich countries be held accountable for the obligation made in 1969 (Pearson, 1969) to increase the transfer of resources to poor countries by reaching the target of 0.7 per cent of GNP as ODA? This is a target which few countries have yet attained including those with strong economies such as the United States (Buchert, 1995, pp. 6–7). However, without resolution of the debt-relief question, even an increase in ODA, in the form of long-term support and untied aid, would contribute little to solving the fundamental problems in most of sub-Saharan Africa and other least developed countries.

Accountability should also be brought to bear on the evaluation of the costs and benefits of the relationship based on agreed measures of efficiency and effectiveness. The World Bank is not alone in judging the proficiency of its staff and the efficiency of its operations largely by the rate of disbursements. There are other measures that are more important. Some agencies are now attempting to set poverty reduction indicators in all its aid programmes, with success to be measured by their attainment in five or ten years' time.[5] Much work is being undertaken or planned in the United Nations, the World Bank, OECD and UNESCO to improve statistics in developing countries and to work towards an agreed set of basic indicators of development progress in the fields of health, education, governance, environment and poverty. There is a danger, however, that in trying to improve data and indicators, we may lose sight of the main objective: does aid really benefit the people for whom it is intended? Only they can really answer that.

Conclusions

In this chapter, I have identified the particular role of UNESCO in education development endeavours: the way in which its broad constituency is both a strength and a weakness, providing feedback from its members, but also spreading its resources too thinly over large areas and subject matter; and the way, despite or maybe even because it is not a funding agency, UNESCO is able to act as an impartial intermediary, with the potential to hold the ring between donors and recipients. Being answerable to a different kind of governing body than a national parliament, UNESCO is struggling, both through the General Conference of its Member States and through its daily work, with the issues of partnership, co-ordination, national capacity-building and accountability that would make for changes in the development co-operation relationship.

Unless more resources are allocated for education and human resource development, the prospects for these changes seem slim. If more funds were channelled through UNESCO, both for upstream education policy definition and downstream programme implementation, UNESCO

5. Stated by a Swedish delegate at the Forum on Key Elements for Poverty Reduction Strategies, jointly organized by DAC and the Development Centre, OECD, 4-5 December 1997.

would be better able to assist national authorities in co-ordinating donor inputs thereby 'using the multilateral system to help mitigate inconsistencies in national policies among donors, and thereby advance a common framework for co-operation' as argued in the recent DAC report (Development Co-operation Committee, 1998). To be successful, UNESCO also needs to strengthen its financial and human resources and consolidate its outreach field office structure in order to make for real dialogue and partnerships at the country level.

References

BUCHERT, L. 1995. *Recent Trends in Education Aid: Towards a Classification of Policies. A Report from the IWGE.* Paris, UNESCO–IIEP.

Budgetary status reports on extrabudgetary operational projects as at 31 December, Paris, UNESCO (various years). (Mimeo.)

DELORS, J. et al. 1996. *Learning: The Treasure Within. Report to UNESCO of the International Commission on Education for the Twenty-first Century.* Paris, UNESCO Publishing.

DEVELOPMENT CO-OPERATION COMMITTEE. 1998. *Developing Co-operation: Efforts and Policies of the Members of the Development Assistance Committee. DAC Report 1997.* Paris, OECD.

FAURE, E. et al. 1972. *Learning to Be: The World of Education Today and Tomorrow. Report to UNESCO of the International Commission on the Development of Education.* Paris, UNESCO Publishing.

HALLAK, J. 1990. *Investing in the Future: Setting Educational Priorities in the Developing World.* Paris/Oxford, UNESCO-IIEP/Pergamon Press.

PEARSON, L. B. 1969. *Partners in Development: Report of the Commission on International Development.* New York, Praeger Publishers.

UNESCO. 1995. *UNESCO 1945–1995: A Fact Sheet.* Paris, UNESCO. (Unesco doc. ARC. 95/WS.1.)

——. 1997. *Approved Programme and Budget for 1998/1999. 29C/5.* Paris, UNESCO.

——. 1998. *World Education Report 1998: Teachers and Teaching in a Changing World.* Paris, UNESCO Publishing.

UNESCO/UNDP. 1976. *The Experimental World Literacy Programme: A Critical Assessment.* Paris, UNESCO/UNDP.

The United Nations in Development. Reform Issues in the Economic and Social Fields. A Nordic Perspective. 1991. Stockholm, Almqvist & Wiksell. (Final report of the Nordic United Nations Project.)

Development aid in education: a personal view

Stephen P. Heyneman[1]

I have been fortunate to witness many intriguing and occasionally dramatic shifts in the philosophy of education assistance over the last several decades. A true history will include observations about the personalities involved and institutional circumstances which helped determine those changes. That history will come on another occasion. Instead, I try to present a feeling for the personal odyssey, its stages, a few words of explanation and a brief prediction.

Because the discussion cannot be understood in isolation from its context, several points might be useful by way of background. The context is official development assistance. It is 'assistance' because donors in one part of the world and recipients in another part of the world believe it to be a benefit otherwise not available.[2] It is 'official' because it is provided by institutions obligated to operate within an administrative mandate officially created by countries. Multilateral development banks must lend rather than grant. Organizations within the United Nations family must adhere to multilateral ownership and control. The principles and purposes of United Nations agencies differ from those of bilateral assistance agencies responsible to the executive and parliamentary branches of one government alone. Groups outside of ODA that represent research and other special interests – gender, tribal peoples, the environment, specific curricula and mechanisms of delivery such as distance education – all have principles, purposes and administrative mandates which allow them the luxury (or force them) to concentrate on a single issue.

1. The views are those of the author alone and do not necessarily represent those of the World Bank or any of its affiliated institutions.
2. Arguments that ODA is not beneficial or not in the best domestic interest of the donor or the recipient have been present from the beginning, but cannot be addressed here.

In the case of the World Bank, there are a few relevant background points in addition. First, the relationship between the philosophy of education and the mechanism for educational lending is established through the World Bank's official point for approval, in most instances, through a country's ministry of finance. Because it is the final macro-economic arbiter for a country's programme, this contact influences the nature of educational dialogue and the purposes of educational programmes. Technical rationales — that it is good for education — are not enough. Rationales in an environment of resource scarcity must meet criteria of a different kind — why good education is a higher priority than a good hospital or a good road. This distinguishes education in the World Bank from education in agencies with a more specialized focus.

Second, one purpose of World Bank loans is to help stimulate constructive change. Loans are approved by a board of directors representing all member countries. That board frequently debates not only whether loan money is needed but whether the change which it stimulates is sufficient. Will it stimulate sufficient efficiency? Sufficient attention to equity? Sufficient products and services of higher quality? Will it stimulate more changes than would loans to other sectors of the economy? The conditions of lending therefore constitute a normal part of the established administrative mandate. One might notice that there are 'mistakes' in those policies and ask why they were recommended. When asked, I respond that judgements and resulting policies within both donor and recipient institutions are designed by individuals equipped with less than perfect knowledge of what will work. Development education is no science. To question whether a recommended policy is correct constitutes legitimate and constructive debate; to ask that the World Bank have no education policy and no condition for education lending is to ask the unattainable and is not helpful.

Third, it is worth remembering that the World Bank is just that: a single institution where demand for education borrowing emanates from six different regions and from more than a hundred countries. Though attempts to individually tailor-make programmes are frequent, and truly felt, no one who has studied Max Weber could believe that any rational organization would not seek economies of scale and efficiencies in design (Weber, 1967). There are natural and inescapable incentives (for both donors and recipients) to seek programme ideas tried elsewhere. This is no more true of assistance in education than in banking and agriculture. Nor is it necessarily more true of the World Bank than of other United Nations agencies, bilaterals and certainly non-governmental organizations. Each agency utilizes experience in a way it believes appropriate. That there is a tendency to 'engineer' is not to suggest that this transfer of experience is bad or good, but only to establish the context. It is legitimate to ask if a programme is appropriate and effective, but it is not constructive to assume that a programme is not appropriate or effective because its purposes were drawn from experience elsewhere.

It must also be appreciated that, at least since 1980, educational policy is not analogous to administrative decree;[3] policy is not an operational directive. Policy ideas and rationales take the form of suggestions and these in turn require adaptation to local circumstances. In reality, ideas spread from one country or one region to another. Therefore the interpretation of 'adaptation' varies widely. Watching for a shift in rationale is therefore an important indicator on its own. Within the academic community, 'Bankology', like 'Kremlinology', is not altogether a waste of effort or time.

Philosophies of World Bank lending in education

There have been many small shifts in purposes and rationales, but in my experience these can be categorized into three overall stages: a first when the dominant rationale was that of manpower planning (1963–80); a second (1980–96) when the rationale included earning functions and empirical relationships with other benefits, health and family-planning behaviour and the like; and a third (1996 onwards) in which the rationale may diverge from education's effects on individuals towards its effects on the society at large and, in particular, on social cohesion.

Period one: 1963–80

When I joined the staff in 1977, the general rationale for World Bank educational operations was as a means to fill gaps in 'manpower'.[4] A country's economic development required products and services. Products and ser-

3. The World Bank 1980 *Education Policy Paper* opened up the possibility for wide latitude of assistance, yet left priorities more or less up to demand.
4. As I recall, equity and efficiency always figured prominently as well. To suggest that manpower plans were the predominant rationale is not to suggest that they constituted the sole rationale.

vices required factories, farms and companies.[5] In turn, these required managers, engineers, machinists and mechanics. The number of individuals equipped with these categories of training by comparison to the number 'required' (either by historical or by international comparison) was the predominant means by which educational issues could find their way on to a country's economic agenda. For staff who believed in education, the mechanism by which one could generate educational assistance was to employ the language of discourse popular in that era. That was manpower forecasting.

With a few exceptions, operational staff were divided into 'educational planners', 'educators' (usually vocational) or 'architects'. The function of the planner was to answer the question of how many (institutions) were necessary and at what level. The function of the educator was to answer the question of what specializations were necessary. The function of the architect was to answer the question of how institutions should be constructed and at what cost. These three types of questions constituted the main demands on staff for the first fifteen years of educational operations.

Originally publicized by the work of Mary Jean Bowman, C. Arnold Anderson and others at the University of Chicago, shortcomings to manpower forecasting techniques were well known in comparative education and in academia generally.[6] Costs of one specialization versus another were ignored; benefits were not monetized; important parts of the education sector – general higher education, primary education, general secondary education, pre-school education and issues of educational quality – remained unaddressed because they could not be empirically accommodated within a typical manpower plan. In spite of the fact that these other areas constituted legitimate parts of a country's education sector and were frequently the subject of questions and requests for information and advice from local officials, the analytic techniques treated them as out of bounds.

5. In this first era, country economics often included assumptions about the role of the state in production which generally would not be common today. Improving enterprises owned and operated by the state was a common objective of development assistance, hence the role of the state in providing 'manpower' was assumed to be more prominent than it might today.
6. The classic challenge to manpower forecasting and vocational education in development policy was published by Anderson and Bowman, and Foster in the early 1960s, but took almost two decades to be incorporated into official development assistance (see Anderson and Bowman, 1968; Foster, 1965).

The techniques, in effect, created distortions in education policies and, hence, in World Bank education operations themselves.

Loans tended to emphasize areas that could be identified by forecasting techniques, namely in vocational and technical specializations. Other areas were de-emphasized. Programmes were approved for universities, but assistance to the social sciences, liberal arts or humanities could not be justified. Libraries for general use were not discussed; textbooks and other teaching materials were categorized as 'recurrent' costs, hence inappropriate for lending. General secondary education was considered legitimate only if equipped with 'practical' subjects – agriculture, woodshop, metalshop and domestic science (for girls). Most problematic were the unwritten assumptions: academic subjects were assumed to be impractical and vocational subjects practical; pedagogy was characterized as 'overly literary' and hence useless in 'the world of work', i.e. the world where employment could be categorized into specific vocations – plumbing, carpentry, engineering (Heyneman, 1986a).

Several personal recollections stand out from this era. One is my memory of an economist in a position of authority informing more junior staff that the World Bank would have no role in primary education in sub-Saharan Africa. Another is of an education manager refusing to believe that a debate even existed over whether vocational education was 'more practical'.[7]

Challenges to this reasoning were probably inevitable, but in my experience emerged from two separate sources.[8] One source was an external advisory panel on education which included, among others, Mary Jean

---

7. This latter incident is a reminder that senior managerial staff (in any organization) without academic background in education may be unaware of even a minimum level of professional substance in the sector. It is analogous to a senior manager of health operations being unaware of a common medical practice.
8. A third challenge came from the 'Marxist' academic community. It was argued that the World Bank should not loan for education because education primarily benefits the wealthy and powerful; that children of the wealthy outperformed others on selection examinations; and that investments in formal schooling reinforces rather than ameliorates the rigidity of social stratification. This line of argument was countered from within the World Bank by presenting evidence that patterns of educational performance differed in developing countries from that of industrialized countries (see Heyneman, 1980a; Heyneman and Loxley, 1983; Heyneman, 1986c).

Bowman and staff from the Ford Foundation with strong backgrounds in the social sciences and humanities and clear understanding of their role in development policy.[9] Their perspectives differed significantly from those common within the World Bank, and their report laid the groundwork for the 1980 *Education Policy Paper* in which basic education, research, capacity-building and equality of educational opportunity were suggested as principles for future operations. On a more micro level, however, there were heated internal debates and challenges both to the assumptions of the manpower techniques and to the operational distortions created by its effects (see, for instance, Habte and Heyneman, 1983; Heyneman, 1983*b*). Some of these debates were made available for public scrutiny, for instance, the challenge to the assumption that a vocational curriculum was 'more practical' (Heyneman, 1984, 1986*b*, 1987*a*); that textbooks and examinations were inappropriate issues for World Bank loans (Heyneman, Farrell and Sepulveda-Stuardo, 1978; Heyneman and Jamison, 1980; Heyneman, Jamison, Searle and Galda, 1981; Heyneman, Jamison and Montenegro, 1984; Heyneman and Farrell, 1988; Heyneman and Fägerlind, 1988; Heyneman, 1987*b*, 1990*a*, 1990*b*); that mass literacy campaigns were effective (Heyneman, 1992); that mother-tongue instruction was feasible (Heyneman, 1980*c*); that analyses of earning differences were impractical (Heyneman, 1980*b*, 1980*d*); that since it could not be measured, the quality of education had little use in economic debate (Heyneman and White, 1986; Heyneman, 1990*c*).

Period two: 1980–96

Following the 1980 *Education Policy Paper*, analytic techniques based on earning differentials and new areas of assistance in basic education were discussed openly and quickly emerged as educational priorities. By chance, however, these new techniques and areas of lending coincided with the debt crisis, particularly severe in Africa and Latin America. The crisis was a genuine emergency, for the economies at large and for the education sector specifically. The effect of the reduction in public expenditures

---

9. *Report of the External Advisory Panel on Education*, World Bank, 31 October 1978. The panel was chaired by David E. Bell, executive Vice-President of the Ford Foundation.

became an educational preoccupation (Heyneman and Fuller, 1989; Heyneman, 1983b, 1991, 1993b).

What was not anticipated but deeply important was the fact that the macro-economic crisis gave rise to new lending mechanisms and adjustment programmes of rapid disbursement. Because of the emergency's severity, it seemed necessary to place higher priority on policies of public finance and lower priority on problems of long-term educational institution-building. The newly infused analytic techniques were particularly important in providing an easily understood rationale: from the results of rates of return by educational level one could conclude that the poor could be protected by shifting public resources away from higher to basic education and from vocational to the (more generalizable) academic education. These points could be quickly incorporated into discussions with economic ministries in the context of larger adjustment issues and reassessments concerning the role of the state.[10] From my experience, this second period was also the birthplace for other assumptions: the virtues of decentralization, private education, private provision and financing, targeting public expenditures to the poor and programmes for student loans.

Like the precedents of manpower planning within the first era, the virtues of these initiatives were many, but so too were the problems and dilemmas which they raised. The health of any sector – whether agriculture, health or banking – requires attention to long-term issues – the interdependence of the quality and efficiency of its various subsectors – research, professional development, pedagogical materials and the like. Central functions require attention as well as school-based functions; higher and vocational as well as basic education; new areas of concern – professionalization of teachers, the quality of education statistics, postgraduate education, research capacity, pre-school education and education technology policy. Since the new analytic techniques were not able to incorporate these problems in the models, however, I came to believe that the techniques themselves once again would have to be reviewed and, once again, improved (Heyneman, 1995b).

10. The second era was also a period in which it seemed more efficient to use staff whose responsibilities could easily be transferred across sectors. This became particularly important following the merger of the education sector with health, population and nutrition (and later social protection) after 1987.

Perhaps nothing more profound occurred during this second era than the collapse of party/state and the introduction into the World Bank of twenty-seven members with new constitutions, new assumptions about democracy, economics, freedom of information, travel, trade and nation-building. Development debates and priorities originating from earlier experiences over access to basic education, textbook availability and gender equality, and shifting resources towards basic education were confronted with a new reality: universal access and gender parity (even in higher education) had already been achieved; expenditures on pre-primary and basic education were higher than on university education; reading materials were universally available and academic excellence was a local tradition. I recall one instance in which a senior manager remarked that the situation in the Russian Federation was not a 'real' development challenge; that real development challenges were located in Africa, Asia and the Middle East.

Were there educational problems in these new countries that justified donor attention? Some had a difficult time accepting that the educational problems justified attention. Others saw educational problems as having a single solution analogous to that of agriculture, railroads and banking – as a service better delivered privately. The new borrowers challenged attitudes as well as the content of donor programmes. The countries were not aid-dependent in the traditional sense; hence they demanded status as intellectual and professional equals. Responding to these demands turned out to be easier to claim than to practise.[11] The new countries demanded information and ideas on policy reforms not from other 'developing' countries but from industrialized countries, the implications being that much of the traditional development literature was irrelevant to them. For the most part, the experience of donor staff was limited to 'development', and did not include the policy experience of industrialized countries. This implied that to be effective in these new countries previous experience was inadequate and explanations of previously developed educational strategies and priorities stood the danger of being counter-productive.

The educational problems of these new borrowers were not the familiar ones and consequently they required questioning of assumptions.

11. I recall several instances in which operational staff with no professional record within either the academic or the administrative community were sent to discuss policy with education ministers whose professional reputations were well known outside of their government positions.

Contrary to my own past arguments, I had to revisit the question of whether parental choice of schools was more efficient and socially constructive (Heyneman, 1997b). Was public investment in vocational education really less viable or, as in the case of the Russian Federation, more viable (Heyneman, 1997e)? The experience required an understanding of new problems and new issues: the structural distortions attendant on central economic planning, the pernicious effects of the party/state in terms of pedagogy and instruction, the segmentation of research from teaching and professional training from general higher education (World Bank, 1995; Heyneman, 1994a, 1994b, 1998b). The effect on the development community of these new members was to create the most profound shock yet and has led to a new and so far uncharted era of rationales and purposes in development education.

Period three: 1996 and beyond

The new era seems to have affected development education in two ways. One derives from having the experience in OECD countries suddenly grow in demand as a point of reference for policy reforms in developing countries. This requires new functions for traditional donor institutions, including the World Bank. It requires staff with new experiences and it requires a new set of assumptions about career paths and institutional tenure (Heyneman, 1993a, 1997c, 1997d). I believe that the purposes and underlying philosophy of development education will be increasingly influenced by the worldwide trade in ideas for education reform. The geographical origins of these ideas have less relevance – whether from countries in the East or West, North or South. This may be no less true of education than for natural resources, banking or health. For sure, global economic competition is not the only paradigm for justifying a change in policies and programmes. But it is also true that it is a profoundly important source of justification.

Perhaps the most important source of change and the most profound influence on me have been the post-Soviet requirements for social stability and social cohesion. I have been an accidental witness to the precipitous educational decentralization in the former Soviet Union, Yugoslavia and Central Europe, and the subsequent concern within the foreign policy and defence communities about civil unrest among literate but deeply repressed ethnic groups. This led me to rediscover the traditional role of public education. In my academic training decades ago, I learned that the traditional purpose of public education was not reasons of human capital, but reasons of social capital and nation-building. As important as human capital skills may be for individuals, these skills become less relevant in an environment of social instability, unrest and civil conflict (Heyneman, 1995a, 1995c, 1997d, 1998a). Although the issue of how and by what mechanism education might contribute to social cohesion was an important line of inquiry in the 1960s, for several reasons attention diminished in the 1970s.[12] These questions are again rising to the fore. They include how to define and identify the mechanisms for education's influence, how to measure their efficacy and compare the efficacy of social cohesion mechanisms in one country to that in another. Because of the concerns over social cohesion, new institutions are becoming involved with development education. These may include the Open Society Institute, the Office of the United Nations High Commissioner for Refugees (UNHCR), the European Union, the Council of Europe, and many foundations and bilateral agencies aside from the traditional aid agencies. Clearly the importance of development education has been once again expanded and developed in a new and unique way.

Summary

This has been quite a journey, with many lessons. One is derived from World Bank operations. Operations mean experience on the ground as opposed to theoretical models. This operational experience has become vast and vastly varied. As some staff are engaged in a justification for why universal education is important in Mali, others are engaged in why a market economy requires new nuclear engineering curricula in the Russian Federation. While some staff are struggling with the rigidities of traditional administration in China, others are struggling with the breakdown of all administrative traditions in Bosnia and Herzegovina, and Liberia. The variability of experience within the same organization has reinforced a quiet little secret.

12. One reason had to do with the over-expectations for the results of survey research. In spite of their sophistication, neither the work of Inkeles and Smith on modernity nor of Meyer on democracy was able to isolate educational factors which made significant differences. Similar disappointments about obtaining managerial insight characterized the work in the 1980s on education production functions (see Inkeles and Smith, 1975; Meyer and Hannan, 1979; Meyer, 1972).

Some believe that good research leads to well-informed policy and that well-informed policy leads to well-designed operations. In my experience the influence has been in the opposite direction. The demand for new areas of educational advice and assistance has revealed the inadequacies of analytic models currently in place, and has required that they be challenged and discarded. Key to having good operations, in my experience, is the ability to question analytic models when they outlive their utility. To some this might constitute heresy. To me, the models themselves are only useful when they inform rather than handicap flexibility in responding to professional questions. To me, the driving force is the professional questions. Rather than a science, the models are solely a vocabulary of discourse.[13]

When closely analysed, the progress itself has hardly been revolutionary. To an experienced educator, assistance to basic education is far from profound; Ph.D. programmes, focused research and assessments, etc. – the justification for these was well known thirty years ago. What is different today is that there is no longer such a thing as a 'developed country'. There is no part of the world which does not need to modernize in the field of education. All countries, mine included, are deeply concerned with difficult, controversial education-policy reforms and are willing to learn from wherever insightful experience might emerge. In my opinion, this spells the end to development education as we know it. It represents a new era in which all countries are borrowers and all are donors. This is a refreshing change.

For me the most important lessons derived from essential principles instilled long ago but perhaps worth repeating. There is nothing so useful as a good theory. Every culture hopes to educate 'up but not away'. In some ways each person and each nation behaves like all others. At the same time, each behaves like some others. At the same time, each is

13. In comparative education, there are many 'true believers' whose point of view is determined by *ex ante* assumptions. They fall into different categories. There are 'irredentists' who believe that the only virtue derives from local non-Western culture. There are 'the single-solutionists' – education for adults, girls or at a distance, mass literacy campaigns, etc. – who view all questions through the lens of their chosen priority. There are the 'empiricists' who believe that managerial policy is only intelligent when determined by social science research. Development agencies have a sprinkling of each category, but the latter two have been particularly common in the World Bank (Heyneman, 1993*a*).

unique and behaves like no other. All three statements are simultaneously true. Insight on any sector requires a marriage between those whose professional devotion is without question with those whose analytic techniques are profound. If either partner is absent, results can prove dysfunctional. No matter how compelling the evidence, new policies breed their own distortions and will require adjustments. These have been the influences which helped determine the results in each of the three educational eras in the World Bank thus far. I see little reason to doubt their relevance in the eras to come.

One final point. Each category of development institution has a unique function – development banks, bilaterals, foundations and non-governmental organizations. A lion cannot be expected to fly. Flying is not necessary to be honourable, nor to be useful is it necessary to roar. While the academic community may be impatient with World Bank educational policies and programmes, in my experience these policies and programmes have demonstrated a surprising consistency: their intentions have been honourable and their purposes honest. Future success will depend on whether challenges to models currently in fashion continue to be encouraged and whether internal debate and self-criticism continue to prove as lively in the future as they have by tradition.

References

ANDERSON, C. A.; BOWMAN, M. J. 1968. Theoretical Considerations in Educational Planning. In: M. Blaug (ed.), *The Economics of Education: Selected Readings*, pp. 351–83. London/Baltimore, Penguin Editions.

FOSTER, J. 1965. Vocational Fallacy in Development Planning. In: C. A. Anderson and M. J. Bowman (eds.), *Education and Economic Development*, pp. 142–67. Chicago, Aldine Publishing Company.

HABTE, A.; HEYNEMAN, S. 1983. Education for National Development: Activities of the World Bank. *Prospects*, Vol. XIII, No. 4, pp. 471–9.

HEYNEMAN, S. P. 1980a. Differences between Developed and Developing Countries: Comment on Simmons and Alexander's Determinants of School Achievement. *Economic Development and Cultural Change*, Vol. 28, No. 2, pp. 403–6.

——. 1980b. *The Evaluation of Human Capital in Malawi*. Washington, D.C., World Bank. (Staff Working Paper, 420.)

——. 1980c. Instruction in the Mother Tongue: The Question of Logistics. *Journal of Canadian and International Education*, Vol. 9, No. 2, pp. 88–94.

HEYNEMAN, S. P. 1980*d*. Investment in Indian Education: Uneconomic? *World Development*, No. 4, pp. 145–63.
——. (ed.). 1983*a*. Education and the World Bank. *Canadian and International Education*, Vol. 12, No. 1. (Special issue.)
——. 1983*b*. Education during a Period of Austerity: Uganda, 1971–1981. *Comparative Education Review*, Vol. 27, No. 3, pp. 403–13.
——. 1984. Diversifying Secondary School Curricula in Developing Countries: An Implementation History and Some Policy Options. *International Journal of Educational Development*, Vol. 5, No. 4, pp. 283–8.
——. 1986*a*. *Investing in Education: A Quarter Century of World Bank Experience.* Washington, D.C., World Bank, Economic Development Institute. (Seminar Paper, 30.)
——. 1986*b*. The Nature of a Practical Curriculum. *Education with Production* (East Africa), Vol. 4, No. 2, pp. 91–104.
——. 1986*c*. *The Search for School Effects in Developing Countries 1966–1986.* Washington, D.C., World Bank, Economic Development Institute. (Seminar Paper, 33.)
——. 1987*a*. Curriculum Economics in Secondary Education: An Emerging Crisis in Developing Countries. *Prospects*, Vol. 18, No. 1, pp. 63–74.
——. 1987*b*. Uses of Examinations in Developing Countries: Selection, Research and Education Sector Management. *International Journal of Educational Development*, Vol. 7, No. 4, pp. 241–63.
——. 1990*a*. The Textbook Industry in Developing Countries. *Finance and Development*, pp. 28–9.
——. 1990*b*. Uses of Examinations to Improve the Quality of Education. *International Journal of Educational Development*, Vol. 10, No. 2/3, pp. 115–29.
——. 1990*c*. The World Economic Crisis and the Quality of Education. *Journal of Education Finance*, Vol. 15, pp. 456–69.
——. 1991. Economic Crisis and Its Effect on Equity in Education: An International Perspective. In: D. A. Verstegn (ed.), *Spheres of Justice in American Education 1990, Yearbook of the American Education Finance Association*. New York, Harper & Row.
——. 1992. Universal Adult Literacy: Policy Myths and Realities. In: D. Wagner (ed.), *Annals of the American Academy of Political Science*, No. 520.
——. 1993*a*. Comparative Education: Issues of Quantity, Quality and Source. *Comparative Education Review*, Vol. 37, pp. 372–88.
——. 1993*b*. Educational Quality and the Crisis of Educational Research. *International Review of Education*, Vol. 39, No. 6, pp. 511–17.

——. 1994a. *Education in the Europe and Central Asia Region: Policies of Adjustment and Excellence*. Washington, D.C., World Bank Europe and Central Asia Region. (IPD 145.)
——. 1994b. *Issues of Education Finance and Management in ECA and OECD Countries*. Washington, D.C., World Bank. (HRO Working Paper, 26.)
——. 1995a. America's Most Precious Export. *American School Board Journal*, pp. 23–6.
——. 1995b. Economics of Education: Disappointments and Potential. *Prospects*, Vol. XXV, No. 4, pp. 559–83.
——. 1995c. *Thoughts on Social Stabilization*. Prague, CIVITAS.
——. 1997a. Economic Growth and the International Trade in Education Reform. *Prospects*, Vol. XXVII, No. 4, pp. 501–30.
——. 1997b. Educational Choice in Eastern Europe and the Former Soviet Union. *Educational Economics*, Vol. 5, No. 3, pp. 333–9.
——. 1997c. Educational Co-operation between Nations in the Next Century. In: C. Kodron et al. (eds.), *Comparative Education: Challenges and Intermediation: Essays in Honour of Wolfgang Mitter*, pp. 219–34. Cologne, Bohlau Verlag GmbH & Cie.
——. 1997d. Educational Development and Social Stabilization in Russia. *Compare*, Vol. 27, No. 1, pp. 5–8.
——. 1997e. Russian Vocational and Technical Education in the Transition: Tradition, Adaptation, Unresolved Problems. Institute for the Study of Russian Education *Newsletter*, pp. 22–34.
——. 1998a. *From the Party/State to Multi-Ethnic Democracy: Education and Its Influence on Social Cohesion in the Europe and Central Asia Region*. Florence, UNICEF/International Child Development Center.
——. 1998b. Transition from Party/State to Open Democracy: The Role of Education. *International Journal of Educational Development*, Vol. 18, No. 1, pp. 21–40.
HEYNEMAN, S. P.; FÄGERLIND, I. (eds.). 1988. *University Examinations and Standardized Testing*. Washington, D.C., The World Bank. (Technical Paper, 78.)
HEYNEMAN, S. P.; FARRELL, J. 1988. Textbooks in Developing Countries: Economic and Pedagogical Choices. In: P. G. Altbach and G. P. Kelly (eds.), *Textbooks in the Third World: Policy, Content and Context*, pp. 19–45. New York/London, Garland Publishing Company.
HEYNEMAN, S. P.; FARRELL, J.; SEPULVEDA-STUARDO, M. 1978. *Textbooks and Achievement: What We Know*. Washington, D.C., World Bank. (Staff Working Paper, 298.)

HEYNEMAN, S. P.; FULLER, B. 1989. Third World School Quality: Current Collapse, Future Potential. *Educational Researcher*, Vol. 18, No. 2, pp. 12–19.

HEYNEMAN, S. P.; JAMISON, D. 1980. Student Learning in Uganda: Textbook Availability and Other Determinants. *Comparative Education Review*, Vol. 24, No. 2, pp. 108–18.

HEYNEMAN, S. P.; JAMISON, D.; MONTENEGRO, X. 1984. Textbooks in the Philippines: Evaluation of the Pedagogical Impact of a Nation-wide Investment. *Educational Evaluation and Policy Analysis*, Vol. 6, No. 2, pp. 139–50.

HEYNEMAN, S. P.; JAMISON, D.; SEARLE, B.; GALDA, K. 1981. Improving Elementary Mathematics Education in Nicaragua: An Experimental Study of the Impact of Textbooks and Radio on Achievement. *Journal of Educational Psychology*, Vol. 73, No. 4, pp. 556–67.

HEYNEMAN, S. P.; LOXLEY, W. 1983. The Effect of Primary School Quality on Academic Achievement across 29 High and Low-Income Countries. *American Journal of Sociology*, Vol. 88, No. 6, pp. 1162–94.

HEYNEMAN, S. P.; WHITE, D. S. (eds.). 1986. *The Quality of Education and Economic Development*. Washington, D.C., World Bank.

INKELES, A.; SMITH, D. H. 1975. *Becoming Modern: Individual Change in Six Developing Countries*. London, Heinemann.

MEYER, J. W. 1972. *Theories of the Effects of Education on Civic Participation in Developing Societies*. New York, Asia Society.

MEYER, J. W.; HANNAN, M. T. (eds.). 1979. *National Development and the World System: Political Change 1950–1970*. Chicago, University of Chicago Press.

WEBER, Max. 1967. *The Theory of Social and Economic Organization*. New York, The Free Press.

WORLD BANK. 1995. *Education in the Transition*. Washington, D.C., World Bank, Europe and Central Asia Country Department III.

The Europeanization of aid
Wolfgang Gmelin

The focus of this chapter is aid and development co-operation in the European context.[1] Although aid is viewed as part of the wider concept of international politics and co-operation, the argument presented here is that European aid needs to be better rooted in the professional development communities of the member states.

From bilateral to multilateral forms of co-operation

With the end of the Cold War and the bipolar hegemony, smaller and less influential countries have lost political leverage in their efforts to secure development aid. At the same time, the chances for truly development-oriented co-operation based upon common values shared by a majority of funding and technical-assistance agencies stand a better chance of succeeding. In principle, this should favour development co-operation that is multilateral and more coherently co-ordinated internationally.

In the Maastricht Treaty, a common European foreign and security policy is foreseen comprising traditional foreign, security and defence policy as well as trade and development policy. Whereas the weighty foreign trade policy is widely accepted by member states as a common affair, development policy – which is considered of much less importance – is still lacking this status, despite the fact that the European Union has managed to establish itself as a successful model for integrated monitoring that has transcended bilateral co-operation in many spheres. In

1. The ideas of this chapter were originally presented in the special issue of *NORRAG News* (No. 17, 1995), on 'European Union Aid: Guidelines on Education and Training'.

addition, through the Lomé Convention, the community disposes of an innovative mechanism for development co-operation based on multi-dimensional policy dialogue.

In spite of the magnitude of European development assistance – the European Union and its member states account for more than 50 per cent of global development assistance[2] – its international political weight is relatively small. It has a number of co-ordination mechanisms including the regular working contacts between experts of the Commission and the national development administrations, co-operation at the country level in the associated countries between the representatives of the member states and the European Union delegations, and regular meetings in the granting committees. There are also biennial council meetings of development ministers which, in May 1994, led to resolutions on health (AIDS) and family planning and, in November 1994, on education and training. However, there is still a need for more encompassing co-ordination within the European Union because of a lack of a common frame of reference in the form of a European Union global strategy and because the jointly elaborated guidelines and sector concepts are not widely acknowledged by the member states.

Co-ordination of development co-operation

With its *Green Paper* (European Commission, 1996), the Commission launched an initiative for such wider co-ordination. It seeks to lay the foundation for a new development co-operation and 'sets out key themes identified by the Commission in the debate over what should replace the Lomé Convention when it expires at the end of the decade' (*Courier*, 1997, p. 7). It accords high priority to the future relations with the associated Asian, Caribbean and Pacific countries and clearly stresses the political dimension of co-operation. It criticizes previous co-operation with politically doubtful partners and admits that there has been insufficient insistence on performance and endeavours for transformation.

It is, however, still rather reserved concerning support for reforms. It puts a high premium on 'structural stability' almost as an end in itself but

2. According to OECD/DAC (1998, Statistical Annex 8), in 1996 the total ODA of all DAC member countries was $55,485 million and of its European members $31,293 million.

overlooks the fact that democratization is often accompanied by profound social change and, possibly, instability. It does not explicitly recognize that there is no universally valid development model and that, therefore, reforms may originate in different sectors. It puts too much priority on one all-encompassing conditionality rather than acknowledging the need for specific and differentiated criteria beyond simply good governance. It is to be hoped that, instead of the formal consultation processes established under the Lomé Convention, room will be given for broad-based and well-informed policy dialogue with interested stakeholders from different fields.

In the *Green Paper,* the question is posed whether the European Union should play a more active role in institutional development and become involved with other international funding and technical-assistance agencies in these matters. It sees compelling reasons for the European Union to step up its activities in this area, both because the European Union has no national interest and no prototype to force upon other countries and because the experience of reform which the Union has gained from the process of European integration gives it a special know-how. Concerning the European Union capacity- and institution-building efforts, it is recommended in the *Green Paper* to re-examine ways of mobilizing local and Community expertise for transfers of know-how, for example by establishing a specialist network for analysis and technical assistance that could provide ongoing support and build up genuine experience and know-how. It sees capacity-building as one of the main influences in the practical arrangements for aid (European Commission, 1996, pp. 62–3).

In spite of many convincing arguments in favour of the multilateralization of development co-operation within the European Union framework, there is a strong movement in favour of bilateral co-operation, or even renationalization of aid, in many member countries and within technical-assistance agencies. Bilateral co-operation is claimed to be more strongly rooted in the respective countries and their policies, more transparent and therefore more easily controlled, more flexible in combining various government and non-government instruments and highly recognized in the partner countries for its professionalism. Bilateral co-operation is supported by broad segments within a pluralistic society who identify highly with the public and with professionals within ministries, non-governmental organizations and research institutions. They reflect the professional competence needed and have familiarity with the issues and countries of concern in the respective country's development co-operation.

Even though nobody denies the comparative strength of European development co-operation when it comes to large-scale and politically sensitive programmes, it still has to live up to the record of bilateral co-operation. So far, it has not been rooted in the civil and professional communities in the same way as in countries with bilateral co-operation. It could, however, become a different form of multilateralism given the existing political framework and co-operation machinery. There is a sufficient common core of development thinking and criteria among the member states for a common frame of reference to be established. There is a convincing case for European Union competence in conceptual and policy matters which could enhance Europe's role in global, regional, national and sectoral policy dialogues. This is an asset that could be used to gain support from national interests in the member states, be they political or economic.

Some key concerns

So far, the trade-offs from more Europeanization in the field of development co-operation have not been systematically put forward and bargained. There are still strong and well-entrenched special relationships with the Lomé countries. However, based on a common policy there could, gradually, be more joint action-building of the professional competencies of the member states' co-operation institutions and their professional relationships in the overseas countries. The European Union can mobilize this committed expertise and mediate a division of labour based on a common policy and comparative competency strengths. Through dialogue with partner countries and member states, the European Union can draw solid information on the specific needs in the countries, the various bilateral co-operation activities and the competencies in the individual countries.

The capacity of the European Union Commission for conceptualizing, planning and monitoring development co-operation has improved during recent years. The *Green Paper* and various sector co-ordination exercises, for example in education and training, bear witness to this. However, this capacity is still inadequate given the importance and magnitude of European development co-operation, and when one compares it with that of other large funding agencies, for example the World Bank, and with bilateral co-operation agencies.

As stated above, European development co-operation is multilateral. It has a special quality by being multilateral and bilateral at the same time. It therefore has much the same potential as bilateral co-operation. Europeanization could mean combining the better parts of bilateral and multilateral co-operation. An important prerequisite would be that European development co-operation be rooted in the public opinion of the member states and in the professional competence of its development constituencies, including research and practice as well as government and non-government organizations. This means going beyond the kind of formalized exchange of information and decision-making that exist at the level of the Council of Ministers and the various committees for project review and approval.

The proposals in the *Green Paper* for enhanced information, control and co-ordination with the implicit reform of the European Development Fund (EDF) committee and the strengthening of the Commission are necessary steps. Strengthening the Commission is unavoidable because, unlike its counterparts in bilateral organizations who rely on professional infrastructures for analysis, research and implementation, the Commission depends to a much greater extent on external consultants. The rooting of European development co-operation has to go further in terms of creating public acceptance and legitimacy. One dimension would be to strengthen the role of the European Parliament even though it is not yet a democratic representation of a European electorate.

More directly, the professional development communities in the member states could be tied together in a kind of 'European Council for Development Co-operation' in which government and quasi-government agencies, non-governmental and private organizations, research institutes of the member states and eventually the Lomé countries would be represented. Such a body could be a professional dialogue partner for the Commission, the Council of Ministers and the European Parliament. Composed of development professionals, it could gradually enhance the understanding of competencies and procedures. This would be a more formal way of involving the national development constituencies of the member states in European development co-operation than the ad hoc co-operation of consulting companies from different member countries that secure contracts from the Commission. There is a need for intermediate European bodies that bring together the interested professionals from the member countries.

References

Courier [Brussels, European Commission]. 1997. No. 162, March–April.

EUROPEAN COMMISSION. 1996. *Green Paper on Relations between the European Union and the ACP Countries on the Eve of the 21st Century*. Brussels, European Commission.

OECD/DAC. 1998. *Development Assistance Committee Report 1997*. Paris, OECD.

Education and geopolitical change in Africa: a case for partnership
Lennart Wohlgemuth

Background

Development is a multifaceted phenomenon. Since the beginning of the era of independence in Africa much research has been devoted to and much has been written about both the causes of underdevelopment and how development can be brought about. The basic criteria are that development should be sustainable and should take into account cultural and other features of the respective countries and people. Moreover, the fruits of development should be reasonably equally distributed among classes, regions and sexes, and democratic forms of government are necessary.

In this chapter, I will focus on one of many crucial factors for development, namely human resource development. Human resource development concerns how people develop through new knowledge, skills and attitudes. The concept includes all types of activities that prompt a change of knowledge, such as education, both formal and non-formal, different kinds of training, competence-building in different forms and institutional development, including the development of organizations.

The statement that people and their propensity for change are a central factor in development can hardly be opposed. It is, however, surprising that both in development theory and also in its practical application questions concerning human resource development are often overshadowed or completely ignored. It is my sincere conviction that human resource development in different forms, such as strong, independent institutions, is an essential precondition for a country's ability to attain long-term financial sustainability (Wohlgemuth, 1996).

The point of departure for this discussion is the present global situation which has been well described by many (Hallak, 1998). The situation can be summarized as global interdependence to an extent not previously known, combined, in many places, with a fragmentation of the nation-state for ethnic, religious or other reasons. At the same time, in the majority of the countries in Africa, economic and political reform programmes are being carried out. A rapid increase in population with environmental degradation and urbanization in its wake are other important basic features that provide the framework for the analysis. This is the environment in which development in general, and therefore also human resource development, is to take place. This environment differs from country to country and is therefore not easily understood or analysed. The disparities between countries are particularly great in Africa, with South Africa as the economic giant with a potential to lift the rest of the region at one extreme, and Somalia, Rwanda, Mozambique or Angola, which have been ravaged by war and underdevelopment, at the other (Wohlgemuth, 1996).

It is interesting to observe the many attempts at regional co-operation which have taken place during the last decades. A good example is southern Africa (Odén, 1996). The increasing tendency towards fragmentation affecting Africa (and other continents) must, however, also be recognized. Having been virtually taboo for a very long period of time, it has become increasingly common to discuss how conflicts between groups, and especially minorities within a society, should be dealt with democratically. Having resisted or totally ignored opposition and differences between groups in the name of 'nation-building', there is today an emphasis by researchers and other outside observers on paying attention to and appreciating differences of an ethnic, religious or cultural character. How these questions are dealt with, within the framework of a process of democratization, will determine both the fundamental stability of the respective countries and regions and of Africa as a whole (Olukoshi and Laakso, 1996; Osaghae, 1995).

The purpose of this chapter is to describe the developments that have taken place in Africa over the past decades and to discuss the external response to these developments, with particular emphasis on the recent discussion on partnership between African countries and countries in the North, using Sweden as an example.

Education and geopolitical change in Africa: a case for partnership
Lennart Wohlgemuth

Optimism and pessimism

The 1950s, 1960s and early 1970s must be recognized as an era of optimism in the world. All trends pointed upwards and the sky was the only limit to what could be achieved. For the newly liberated countries in Africa, there was no limit to their expectations and plans for reaching the set targets. Then President Julius Nyerere of the United Republic of Tanzania expressed the aspirations very well when stating that 'we must run, while others walk' (Rydström, 1996). In the area of human resources development, this was the period of manpower planning and an enormous emphasis on primary education and adult literacy.

The external response to this self-confident and optimistic view was very positive. This was the period when most funding and technical-assistance agencies introduced 'country programming' as their methodology for assistance. This concept built, at least in theory and as regards Sweden also in practice, on respect for the recipients' views and plans, aiming at a relationship between equals. This was also the time when ideas such as a New World Order and a New Information Order were launched. The Swedish viewpoints during this period of time have been summarized in Wohlgemuth (1976). Apart from country planning, this period also gave birth to the concept of sector programmes as an aid methodology, a device which also had far-reaching effects on aid to education.

This very optimistic era ended with the oil shocks in the early and mid-1970s, which, in turn, led to continued crises throughout the 1980s. The origin of this crisis was external but it was exacerbated through often totally inadequate internal responses. Many countries tried to borrow themselves out of the crises, thereby digging themselves deeper and deeper into the problems. The result was an unhealthy dependence on creditors and external agencies. The external response to the crisis was, at first, 'concerned participation', a term coined by the then Foreign Minister of the United Republic of Tanzania, Ibrahim Kaduma, at a meeting with the Board of Sida in Dodoma, 1976, and later what one could call 'donor dictatorship'.

During the 1980s, aid in the form of inputs into defined projects predominated. In those cases where sector support to programmes for the development of a specific sector occurred, it often consisted of a range of projects collected within an overall framework. Within a decade, the pendulum had in practice swung from country to project programming, even if the country programme still existed in the planning cycle. In extreme cases, project aid went so far as to consciously plan projects as a *bypass*, simply to avoid the public sector in the recipient country. In a bypass, aid funds were controlled from start to finish by the funding or technical-assistance agency, or at least by companies that were the direct agents of the agency (Valdelin, 1998).

In the mid-1980s, structural adjustment programmes were well established as a recipe for the economic crises and macro-economic conditions for support had become the rule within the international community. The economic and social impact of the stabilization and structural adjustment policies which countries have pursued over the past two decades has been a source of considerable controversy, extensively researched and debated during the past ten years, including at the Nordic Africa Institute (Gibbon et al., 1992; Gibbon, 1993; Gibbon and Olukoshi, 1996; Mkandawire and Olukoshi, 1996).

At present, the Institute is examining a number of the important socio-economic and political trends and processes associated with the dynamics of economic crisis and structural adjustment, one of which relates to 'popular forms of social provisioning'. Public health, education and other services have clearly become inaccessible to a great number of people who must now seek to satisfy their needs in non-conventional ways. A substantial literature has emerged in recent years on popular household survival strategies, emphasizing the increasing adoption of 'multiple livelihood modes'. The Institute is undertaking parallel studies of public consumption forms and survival strategies vis-à-vis social provisioning which, so far, have been noticeably absent.

A second research theme relates to the 'decomposition and recomposition of popular political identities'. The crisis of the postcolonial state in Africa during the 1980s and 1990s has been seen mainly in terms of the state's institutional capacity to implement effectively economic and social policies. However, a much more profound crisis is that of political identities. To build a secular, non-racial, non-ethnic nation-state characterized by common territorial politics no longer appears viable in many places. Most African states have ethnic, regional or religious groups deeply alienated from existing structures and actively rejecting the nation-state concept. In this context, the nature and variety of new emerging political identities are being examined (Nordiska Afrikainstitutet, 1997).

Era of realism

Where do we stand today? I have called this period an era of realism (Lopes, 1994; Wohlgemuth, 1997), but it would be more to the point to call the 1990s an era of political and economic reforms in Africa. At no time since the end of colonialism in Africa has popular support for political and economic reform in the majority of countries been stronger than in the past few years. The peoples of the continent have openly and with varying degrees of success asked their leaders for far-reaching reforms whose full repercussions are still unfolding.

There is no longer any question that political reform has come to stay in most parts of Africa. In the period 1994–97, a great number of elections took place on the continent. Although pressure for political reform has emanated from outside, there is also evidence of strong forces for democratization from within the countries. In some cases, the reform initiatives of governments have actually been contested by the people for either being too top-down in orientation or not being radical enough. However, the experience gained from the peaceful transitions to majority rule in South Africa and Malawi, and from the situations of Angola, Burundi and Rwanda, makes it clear that multi-party elections are not sufficient in themselves. To achieve political legitimacy, the state has to protect minority rights and ensure transparency, accountability, openness and the rule of law in its operation (Olukoshi, 1998; Olukoshi and Wohlgemuth, 1998).

The process of political reform is a very delicate one requiring time and care. If not painstakingly dealt with, ethnic and other potential divisions can be exacerbated rather than resolved. It is also important that the process genuinely promotes democratic conditions before, during and after multi-party elections have taken place (Luckham and White, 1998; Olukoshi and Wohlgemuth, 1995). Ethnic, religious, clan and other rivalries seem at present to be coming to the fore in many parts of Africa as well as in the world at large. It seems easier for such conflicts to appear when, for example, economic crises lead to increased competition over scarce resources. This is by no means an argument against pressing for increased democracy, but instead shows that it is even more important to ensure that all groups are fully involved in the political process (Olukoshi and Laakso, 1996).

Economic reform builds on what was discussed above: the economic decline in most states in Africa and the programmes of economic reform that have been implemented in most of the affected countries. However, concealed behind all the official statistics on poor economic performance, ordinary people in different parts of the continent are devising survival strategies by promoting informal trade and production among themselves. Where formal economic activities are declining, informal production and exchanges are generally more vibrant.

During a decade and a half after structural adjustment was introduced into the African economic policy landscape, the controversy that has accompanied its design, philosophy, implementation and consequences has still not abated. Many mistakes have been made and will continue to be made in the future. The programmes have, however, now become better tailored to meet each country's specific needs and are also to a higher degree based on the priorities of the people who are expected to implement them. The lessons learned are that if economic reform programmes are to work and be sustainable in the long run, they have to be discussed, prepared and owned by the people who will be responsible for their success or failure.

The inclusion of education in the reforms is well researched and discussed (Hallak, 1990; Samoff, 1994; Buchert, 1997; Wohlgemuth et al., 1998). This discussion has also been extensively introduced into training materials for educational planners produced by the International Institute for Educational Planning (IIEP) in Paris (Sanyal, 1995; Carron and Ta-Ngoc, 1996; Caillods et al., 1997). Furthermore, work has been done on 'the minimum requirements' to run universities during severe economic crisis. A major finding in this work, as in many other studies, is that the availability of local resources to meet the most basic requirements, e.g. living wages, remains a prerequisite for any kind of relevant training and research (Wohlgemuth, 1996).

Partnership Africa

As elaborated above, the pendulum has swung back and we are today in an era of realism. Problems are being assessed and identified in a balanced manner and, more importantly, being accepted as such. Reforms are being implemented not only as a result of outside pressure and intervention, and conditionalities by international funding and technical-assistance agencies. There is ample evidence of the internal struggles for democratic reforms and changes (Kiondo, 1995) – contemporary Kenya being a case in point.

External actors' policies are also being revisited and changed. The time of 'donor' conditionalities and interventions is, if not over, at least increasingly questioned – if only as a result of the poor records in implementing programmes and projects supported from outside. The concept of 'ownership' has been on the agenda for quite some time and is, at least in the Nordic countries, taken seriously.

'Real-politicking' is of course still very much in evidence, but even the superpowers of today consider it to be advantageous that countries or regions take responsibility for the problems in their own vicinity – if only to avoid having to send their own troops to trouble-spots around the world. The Democratic Republic of the Congo (ex-Zaire) in late 1996 is a good example.

In a number of countries in the North, the present policy towards the South in general and Africa in particular is being looked into. In the remaining part of the chapter, I will refer to the recent exercise in Sweden which seems to be typical for today's discourse.

A Swedish perspective

The Government of Sweden has stressed that the relationship between Sweden and Africa has to be revised. Two major reasons have been cited:
- The successful policy of supporting the struggle for liberation and against apartheid, which has dominated Swedish foreign and development policies during a period of more than thirty years, has come to an end.
- Studies, research and evaluations underline that a paradigm shift is necessary in the relations between countries in the North and in Africa if aid to Africa is to become effective.

A study on *Partnership Africa* was, thus, commissioned by the Government of Sweden to analyse and make recommendations on Swedish overall policy towards Africa. As a background to the main study, the Nordic Africa Institute carried out a state-of-the-art study on different policy areas, such as aid, trade, capital flows, European Union policies towards

Africa and capacity-building, and a great number of specific studies were commissioned, mainly from African representatives of academia, non-governmental organizations, governments, the private sector and others. Two major conferences were held: one in Abidjan, in collaboration with the African Development Bank, with thirty outspoken Africans, mainly researchers, and one in Saltsjöbaden (south-east of Stockholm) on a more political level. The results of the seminars have been published in two anthologies (Kifle et al., 1997; Olukoshi and Wohlgemuth, 1998), in a report by the working group itself (Sweden, 1997) and, finally, in a Government White Paper (Government of Sweden, 1998).

The process built on a close dialogue with a great number of Africans, but also with interested parties in Swedish society. The process, therefore, included a number of reference groups and seminars of different kinds. The dialogue with Africans mainly took place in the two conferences referred to above. The question posed to the African participants was what they saw as the role for a small country in Europe vis-à-vis Africa in the next century. The response was most revealing and refreshing. Its spirit is well captured in the following comments presented by Angela Ofori-Atta, a lecturer in clinical psychology from Ghana, in the form of a letter to her little brother Sweden:

My dear little brother Sweden,
    Thank you for your very caring message. I have been told that after years of helping me out, you are reviewing your policies. I appreciate this very much. You may sometimes feel that not much has been accomplished after millions of dollars of aid and expertise have been sent towards my needs. This is only partly true. I am glad that you have not given up entirely but are preparing to renew your efforts.
    I shall begin with expectations. Brother Sweden, your people for the most part, know little about my peoples. They probably think of a small continent, with everybody in small villages tucked away into oases, forests, or beaches, where everybody stands around idle all day, smiling at the next white photographer. These are supposedly simple, happy people. Like children. So your people are eager to teach them, humour them, guide them, help them, just as they do with their own children. And therefore your expectations of my people are what your people would expect of young children; not very much. The yardstick by which the progress of my people is measured is different from that used to measure yours.

Education and geopolitical change in Africa: a case for partnership
Lennart Wohlgemuth

Now you ask how best to rethink your policies. I say to that, please change your expectations of my people. Expect more from my misguided leaders, not less. Expect the same level of accountability and transparency you would demand for European Union membership in your dealings. When you find yourself thinking if you are being too tough, remember that my people are as good as your people, they understand right and wrong, they can stick to arrangements and contracts they have made, if this is expected of them, just like your people can.

Once you feel comfortable about these intangibles and can translate them into your policy statement, I would like you to consider a different entry strategy for each country you wish to forge partnership with. However, it is imperative that when you enter these countries, you speak with everybody whom you are asked not to speak with, insist on hearing alternative voices . . . Secondly, if you do decide to stay, include as many local African consultants as you possibly can so that the aid money goes further, and my people's expertise may also be built up. Foremost and finally, do not only come with aid, but with trade. . . . And more importantly, little brother, I would like you to use your European Union membership to advance these intangibles of which I speak, to your other brethren in the European Union so you can all act in concert and treat my people with the firm respect demanded of equals (Olukoshi and Wohlgemuth, 1998).

So what will the new partnership actually lead to in practice? The discussions centred around that question, as did the papers presented and also the final reports. The African representatives were very clear on their desire and demand for a 'substantial' change in the relationship between the countries in the North and Africa – regarding major geopolitical questions as well as behaviour in the day-to-day relationship concerning bilateral affairs. The discussion concentrated on the latter and some concrete proposals were made. The major point made is self-evident but very difficult to implement in practice, namely that all agreements should be preceded by a real negotiation where both parties give and take instead of one dictating to the other. This is a new but more concrete way of expressing ownership. After all the discussions and confrontations during the period of the study, it is my strong opinion that Africans will not accept being treated in the future as they are being treated at present in their bilateral relationships. Adebayo Olukoshi expressed this very succinctly in his synthesis of the presentation made on partnership at the Abidjan conference:

As the 20th century draws to a close, there is a new generation which is emerging out of the ashes of crisis and decline in Africa. It is a self-assured generation that is prepared to engage the world on equal terms. Its faith in the continent is deep-rooted and its determination to make Africa a home of which Africans can be proud is clear. That generation consists of people who are confident of themselves and are driven by a zeal to transform Africa both internally and in terms of its relationship with the rest of the world. . . . Under the leadership of this new generation, I envisage a situation where support from the international community will be welcome in the task of rebuilding Africa but not on any terms or at any cost, least of all on conditions drawn up and imposed from outside in a one-sided manner. If need be, this generation is prepared to go it alone and the world should be willing to let it be – if the international community is not prepared to listen to and respect the self-articulated hopes and aspirations of these Africans, then it should, at least, not obstruct them. In a sense, that was a central message that flowed out of the formal and informal discussions that took place in Abidjan; donors will do well to heed it (Kifle et al., 1997).

In summing up the many suggestions made during the conference in Abidjan the Swedish Secretary of State, Mats Karlsson, expressed the hope that the Swedish Government would see the quality of partnership as involving the following seven characteristics:

1. A subject-to-subject attitude. There is need for a real change of attitude.
2. Being explicit about values. You cannot engage in a partnership without sharing values and sincerity in the relationship – a major element that has certainly often been lacking.
3. Transparency of interests. Even if interests diverge – and interests may conflict without this being malevolent – it is possible to strike deals and find common ground. In a partnership, negotiations are best when interests are placed squarely on the table.
4. Clear standards. The new contractual relationship should focus on the critical success factors and avoid the plethora of conditionalities that now bedevil the politics of co-operation.
5. Stick to the agreements. A clear contractual standard must be upheld by both parties. Backtracking by the African partner must not be dealt with by misplaced acceptance. If real problems arise, they should be faced jointly, but there should be no room for an essen-

tially paternalistic and humiliating attitude in the face of unwarranted backtracking on an agreement.
6. Equality of capacity. In entering a fair contract, both parties need to be in equal command of all the issues included in the contract. The aid relationship may be inherently unequal – one side has money, the other does not – but equality in terms of capacity to analyse and judge the conditions of a contract is essential and has to be broadly exercised in society.
7. A code of conduct. The qualitative aspects should perhaps be made more explicit in order to provide a basis for and further develop the modalities of partnership (Olukoshi and Wohlgemuth, 1998).

I have deliberately confined my attention to only one, although important, question in the new Swedish policy towards Africa. Many others could be brought up for discussion, in particular the fact that this is the first comprehensive policy statement on Africa directed to Parliament by a Swedish government. This is an important indication of the increased importance of Africa in Swedish domestic as well as foreign policy. Furthermore, it should be noted that this is one of the first attempts at developing a coherent and all-encompassing policy towards another part of the world. However, the emphasis on the new ideas about the relationship between Sweden and African societies, i.e. not only government-to-government relations, is the most important issue, taking into account the above discussions on the response by the external community to new developments taking place in Africa.

Will Sweden, or for that matter any other country in the North, act in line with the important message conveyed by Adebayo Olukoshi and replied to so eloquently by Mats Karlsson? I genuinely hope so, and at least the people in Sweden who requested the report are sincere in their quest for change. But, unfortunately, when other interests compete, it is often too easy to forget even the best of intentions.

References

BUCHERT, L. 1997. *Education Policy Formulation in Tanzania: Coordination between the Government and International Aid Agencies. Report from IWGE.* Paris, UNESCO/IIEP.

CAILLODS, F.; GÖTTELMANN-DURET, G.; LEWIN, K. 1997. *Science Education and Development: Planning and Policy Issues at Secondary Level.* Paris, UNESCO/IIEP.

CARRON, G.; TA-NGOC, C. 1996. *The Quality of Primary Schools in Different Development Contexts*. Paris, UNESCO/IIEP.

GIBBON, P. (ed.). 1993. *Social Change and Economic Reform in Africa*. Uppsala, Nordiska Afrikainstitutet. (Research Report, 102.)

GIBBON, P.; BANGURA, Y.; OFSTAD, A. (eds.). 1992. *Authoritarianism, Democracy and Adjustment. The Politics of Economic Reform in Africa*. Uppsala, Nordiska Afrikainstitutet/UNRISD/C. Michelsen Institute. (Seminar Proceedings, 26.)

GIBBON, P.; OLUKOSHI, A. O. 1996. *Structural Adjustment and Socio-economic Change in Sub-Saharan Africa. Some Conceptual, Methodological and Research Issues*. Uppsala, Nordiska Afrikainstitutet.

GOVERNMENT OF SWEDEN. 1998. *En förnyad svensk Afrikapolitik inför 2000-talet*. (Government White Paper.)

HALLAK, J. 1990. *Investing in the Future: Setting Educational Priorities in the Developing World*. Paris/Oxford, UNESCO/IIEP/Pergamon Press.

——. 1998. *Education and Globalization*. Paris, UNESCO/IIEP. (IIEP Contributions, 26.)

KIFLE, H.; OLUKOSHI, A. O.; WOHLGEMUTH, L. 1997. *A New Partnership for African Development. Issues and Parameters*. Uppsala/Abidjan/Stockholm, Nordiska Afrikainstitutet/African Development Institute (ADB)/Partnership Africa. (Swedish Ministry for Foreign Affairs.)

KIONDO, A. 1995. Africa in the 21st Century. Democratization and Development from People's Initiatives. In: A. O. Olukoshi and L. Wohlgemuth (eds.), *A Road to Development. Africa in the 21st Century*, pp. 38–44. Uppsala, Nordiska Afrikainstitutet.

LOPES, C. 1994. *For an Alternative Diagnosis of the African Crisis*. Uppsala, Nordiska Afrikainstitutet. (Discussion Paper, 5.)

LUCKHAM, R.; WHITE, G. (eds.). 1996. *Democratization in the South: The Jagged Wave*. Manchester, Manchester University Press.

MKANDAWIRE, T.; OLUKOSHI, A. O. (eds.). 1996. *Between Liberalisation and Repression*. Dakar, CODESRIA.

NORDISKA AFRIKAINSTITUTET. 1997. *The Political and Social Context of Structural Adjustment in Sub-Saharan Africa*. Uppsala, Nordiska Afrikainstitutet. (Brochure on the Institute's programme.)

ODÉN, B. 1996. Critical Factors for Regional Development in Southern Africa in a Twenty Year Perspective. In: Sida, *Southern Africa – Regional Studies*, pp. 137–62. Stockholm, Sida. (Sida Project 2015.)

OLUKOSHI, A. O. (ed.). 1998. *The Politics of Opposition in Contemporary Africa*. Uppsala, Nordiska Afrikainstitutet.

OLUKOSHI, A. O.; LAAKSO, L. (eds.). 1996. *Challenges to the Nation-State in Africa.* Uppsala/Helsinki, Nordiska Afrikainstitutet/Institute of Development Studies, University of Helsinki.

OLUKOSHI, A. O.; WOHLGEMUTH, L. (eds.). 1995. *A Road to Development. Africa in the 21st Century.* Uppsala, Nordiska Afrikainstitutet.

OLUKOSHI, A. O.; WOHLGEMUTH, L. 1998. *Towards a New Partnership with Africa: Challenges and Opportunities.* Uppsala, Nordiska Afrikainstitutet.

OSAGHAE, E. E. 1995. *Structural Adjustment and Ethnicity in Nigeria.* Uppsala, Nordiska Afrikainstitutet. (Research Report, 98.)

RYDSTRÖM, G. (ed.). 1996. *Adult Education in Tanzania. Swedish Contributions in Perspectives.* Linköping University, Centre for Adult Educators.

SAMOFF, J. (ed.). 1994. *Coping with Crisis: Austerity, Adjustment and Human Resources.* London/Paris/Geneva, Cassell/UNESCO/ILO.

SANYAL, B. 1995. *Innovations in University Management.* Paris, UNESCO/IIEP.

SWEDEN. MINISTRY FOR FOREIGN AFFAIRS. 1997. *Partnership with Africa: Proposals for a New Swedish Policy towards Sub-Saharan Africa.* Stockholm, Ministry for Foreign Affairs.

VALDELIN, J. 1998. Aid Management. In: L. Wohlgemuth, J. Carlsson and H. Kifle, *Institution Building and Leadership in Africa*, pp. 203–13. Uppsala, Nordiska Afrikainstitutet.

WOHLGEMUTH, L. (ed.). 1976. *Bistånd på mottagarens villkor – filosofi och teknik.* Stockholm, Sida.

——. 1996. Southern Africa: A Perspective for the Future with Competence Building in Focus. In: Sida, *Southern Africa – Regional Studies*, pp. 163–83. Stockholm, Sida. (Sida Project 2015.)

——. 1997. *Bistånd på utvecklingens villkor.* Uppsala, Nordiska Afrikainstitutet.

WOHLGEMUTH, L.; CARLSSON, J.; KIFLE, H. (eds.). 1998. *Institution Building and Leadership in Africa.* Uppsala, Nordiska Afrikainstitutet.

Changing frameworks and practices: the new Department for International Development of the United Kingdom

Myra Harrison[1]

The expansion of human capabilities has both 'direct' and 'indirect' importance in the achievement of development. The *indirect* role works through the contribution of capability expansion in enhancing productivity, raising economic growth, broadening development priorities and bringing demographic changes more within reasoned control. The *direct* importance of human capability expansion lies in its intrinsic value and its constitutive role in human freedom, well-being and quality of life (Sen, 1997).

This clear statement by Amartya Sen of the twin purposes and benefits of education underpinned the thinking of the Department of International Development (DFID) in the latter part of 1997. This department was established from the former Overseas Development Administration following the general election in the United Kingdom on 1 May 1997. The separate establishment and new identity are more than symbolic – DFID is no longer an 'administration' but a department, with a focus on international rather than 'overseas' development. The department is headed by a Cabinet Minister, who is Secretary of State for International Development, assisted by a Parliamentary Under-Secretary of State.

The Secretary of State made clear in a number of speeches and statements the framework within which DFID would work and the ambitious aims which she has outlined for it. In June 1997, addressing the Commonwealth Institute, she talked about the 'single greatest challenge the world faces – eliminating poverty'. This is an ambitious aim, but affordable and

1. This chapter has been adapted from a panel presentation at the Oxford International Education Conference, September 1997, predating publication of the *White Paper on International Development* (DFID, 1997).

Changing frameworks and practices:
the new Department for International Development
of the United Kingdom
Myra Harrison

achievable. In education, she wrote, 'I should like us all to make it an article of faith that every child, girl or boy, born in 1997 . . . will have an opportunity to go to school in the twenty-first century. We can do it if we can mobilize the political will' (Short, 1997, p. 16).

The framework within which these statements were to be given life was the *White Paper* on international development, published on 5 November 1997 (DFID, 1997). This *White Paper*, the first on international development in the United Kingdom for over twenty years, provides an enabling and empowering framework for future policy and action.

The British Government has made a commitment to begin reversing the decline of development assistance per capita – for which the international target is 0.7 per cent of GNP – in contrast to many countries of the world where aid budgets are diminishing. There are many challenges to the developed world in supporting those countries that are less fortunate: in particular in human development, environmental protection and economic growth. The framework provided by DFID and the *White Paper* gives a clear direction to work in education. First of all, the focus is on poverty elimination, on universalizing primary education, to include especially girls. Secondly, gender discrimination in primary and secondary education must be eliminated.

New framework

A number of frameworks and conventions inform DFID's policy. Most important for future practice is the set of international targets, agreed initially in 1996 by OECD's DAC, but now more widely accepted, including by developing countries themselves. The first and overriding target is that of reducing by 50 per cent those living in abject poverty by 2015. A complementary target is that of universal primary education by 2015. The two are inextricably linked, though causal connections are not always totally clear. There are correlations between basic education and health, agricultural productivity, participation in the economic sector, maternal health and child survival.

Removing gender discrimination from education by 2005 is particularly pertinent in those countries with low female enrolment rates, but this may not hold universally: in South Africa, for example, after the first year of primary school, boys' drop-out rates are higher than those of girls. This target will augment progress towards universal primary education, which remains an international goal, with the original Jomtien target date (Education for All by the year 2000), set in 1990, now superseded by the still challenging 2015. At a mid-decade meeting of the Education for All Consultative Forum in 1996, Richard Jolly (Special Adviser to the UNDP Administrator) acknowledged the move: 'The goals of Jomtien have proved their worth. Let us build on the achievements of the last six years and accelerate them over the next five, and over the next fifteen. For that is what it will take' (Carron, 1996, p. 2).

A second framework likely to be given more prominence than before is the Commonwealth, linked by a common language, common ideals, and shared history and tradition in education. DFID has extended its support for the Commonwealth of Learning, which is becoming a vital force for the promotion and take-up of distance learning throughout the Commonwealth. The Commonwealth Scholarship and Fellowship Plan (CSFP) is regarded by Commonwealth education ministers as a flagship of cooperation on a pan-Commonwealth basis. The Chair of the Commonwealth Scholarship Commission in the United Kingdom has put forward plans for flexibility within CSFP in terms of length and type of courses of study, to make the possibility of study in the United Kingdom more accessible to those who are busy and committed in terms of time, demonstrating the evolving maturity of this long-standing scholarship programme.

The United Kingdom also re-entered UNESCO in July 1997 after some twelve years of absence. DFID took the lead in seeking to re-enter and providing the resources for our contribution. UNESCO is an important forum for support for Education for All, for the eradication of illiteracy and for fostering international relationships in the field of education. DFID has supported its commitment to re-entering UNESCO by appointing a full Ambassador to UNESCO based in Paris; the Secretary of State attended the General Conference, and both DFID and the Department for Education and Employment were represented throughout. A number of UNESCO activities that take place internationally have also been supported: the Fifth International Conference on Adult Education in Hamburg, 1997, International Literacy Day (8 September) and a Conference on Human Rights in Education. The roles and responsibilities of a UNESCO Member State will continue to be explored.

The newest frameworks described in DFID's White Paper are 'partnerships'. The role of government in providing universals such as primary

Changing frameworks and practices: the new Department for International Development of the United Kingdom
Myra Harrison

education, primary health care and clean water, which cannot be provided to citizens otherwise, is well accepted. It is therefore crucial for DFID to develop relationships with our developing-country partners based on clear devotion to the international targets and policies towards attaining them. But other partnerships will also be needed – with funding agencies and donor nations; with institutions in the United Kingdom and in partner countries; with areas of civil society, academic and research institutes; and with other United Kingdom Government departments. The *White Paper on International Development* spells out this approach, and it is clear that the move away from conceptualizing what the department does as 'aid' towards international co-operation and partnerships, in a policy framework, will change the nature of DFID's practice. How exactly partnerships will evolve will not be clear for some time, but it is apparent that 'partnership' is not about a single-event agreement so much as the longer-term, more symmetrical relationship between the United Kingdom and its 'partners' that will follow from such policy agreement.

A complex shifting framework that must be increasingly acknowledged is the globalization of knowledge, commerce and communications; information and communication technologies have the capacity to link us all more closely in the world; conversely their applications and access to them have the capacity to enlarge divisions between those who have access and those who do not. At the 13th Commonwealth Education Ministers' Conference in Botswana, Malcolm Skillbeck in his keynote address put the problem graphically: 'The world-wide advance of economic globalisation and of the new information and communication technologies might . . . seem like storm waves battering the shores of countries which often lack the infrastructure or the resources to cope' (Skillbeck, 1997, p. 5).

It will be crucial for those countries with low levels of resources in this area to adopt for themselves selective and helpful policies, which take into account the basic needs of their populations, as well as the technological needs of modernizing societies. We cannot stop evolution or advances in knowledge; if we want to see the gaps in development closing, then it will be important to work with partner governments to develop these policies in ways which are affordable, and also work with the grain of their developing education systems. The dichotomy between open access to information via the new technology and access to education in its multifarious forms must form part of DFID thinking.

Changing practices

What does this all mean in practice? First of all, it means a commitment to the twin roles of education laid out by Amartya Sen. The direct importance of – even the human right to – education means that its intrinsic value is recognized for all. The indirect role, summarized as health, wealth and well-being, is well documented. There is an agreed set of targets against which DFID will measure itself and its impact; the indicators for achieving significant reductions in absolute poverty and universal primary education are being developed in a number of forums including UNESCO and DAC. It will be important for DFID to pay rigorous attention to the agreed indicators in order to measure progress in a meaningful (and internationally recognized) way.

There are also political imperatives set for DFID. In 1997, the Prime Minister committed the United Kingdom to greater support for Africa; he said that we would increase by 50 per cent over the next three years our commitment of bilateral aid to basic education, basic health care and the provision of safe drinking water. This kind of commitment gives DFID an important milestone. There is a need to take stock of what DFID has achieved and committed in these basic human areas over the past few years. Then there is a need to plan, within the partnership framework described above, greater efforts and greater commitments for the future, and to commit and spend these extra resources for Africa's development.

DFID must search for partnerships based on shared commitment to both the international targets and to policies towards achieving them. Some countries have already moved a long way: Malawi announced a policy of free universal primary education and the numbers enrolling almost doubled virtually overnight. Uganda is providing education for up to four children from each family. South Africa has removed apartheid barriers to enrolment in schools; India has developed policies specifically to include scheduled caste and scheduled tribe children in primary education, and in particular girls. DFID is already supporting these countries in their efforts and, in the light of the White Paper, will be seeking to develop further the partnership role we have and looking to ensure that these and other important policy ventures continue successfully.

One of the ways in which this can be done is by linking with other major funding agencies or countries such as the World Bank, the Euro-

Changing frameworks and practices:
the new Department for International Development
of the United Kingdom
Myra Harrison

pean Union and others to support these major initiatives. DFID has already agreed in principle with the World Bank to support a number of investigations into removing barriers to girls' education in some countries and is actively pursuing education sector development programmes with a number of co-funding agencies in Ghana, Ethiopia, Uganda and the United Republic of Tanzania.

There is a growing consensus that an essential step on the route out of poverty is to provide primary education for all. Countries in sub-Saharan Africa in particular are suffering from falling gross and net enrolment rates, high drop-out and low quality. It is not altogether explicable by expenditure rates: Colclough (1997, p. 13) shows that a higher proportion of GNP is allocated to education in sub-Saharan Africa than typically in other regions (except the Arab States). However, real resources per person have fallen by almost 20 per cent since 1980, resulting in what he describes as a 'fairly catastrophic reduction' in the resources available. Low quality is an area that must be addressed simultaneously with enrolment and retention rates. The policy decisions made by DFID, its agency partners and partner countries must therefore embrace the quality strengthening as well as the expansion of the primary education system. This should lead to greater efficiency and therefore less wastage of resources, as well as higher levels of cognitive development and greater efficiency benefits at secondary and tertiary level. However, neither achievement of universal primary education nor of higher quality in education is an easy challenge.

DFID will not shirk from facing the challenge of education; part of the answer lies in the higher-level skills and training that are required for better education systems, better teacher training, materials production, and policy and planning. Education is an essential tool of empowerment for the poor, and especially for excluded or hard-to-reach children. Poverty has many manifestations, and the role education plays in reducing ill-health or fertility, and increasing employment skills and income levels, is well documented. Where possible the education and health sectors should work side by side, and within an enabling economic framework to bring synergy to 'separate' sectors.

The emphasis on literacy and numeracy in the United Kingdom has a parallel in the needs of developing countries. Research commissioned by DFID into reading levels in Zambia and Malawi proved to be seminal:

children learned their initial literacy better in their mother tongue; subsequent acknowledgement of the problems has led to policy changes in Zambian education, in partnership with DFID. DFID supports pilot projects in books provision in Africa – readers in Swaziland and Botswana; dictionaries in Zambia; libraries to supplement primary education in South Africa. DFID has also put together with the assistance of John Smiths Booksellers a bibliography of low-priced student editions (available in all DFID offices and Missions overseas, and electronically via DFID and John Smiths' websites). This is part of a policy to foster literacy and effective reading skills in schools in partner countries.

Conclusion

Education is a key element of human and other forms of development. The changing frameworks and practices described above are akin to the shifting tectonic plates redrawing the globe. The intention of DFID is to get closer to poverty and work with those who would eliminate it; to get closer to developing-country partners and help them to eliminate poverty and to provide education for all their children; to get closer to lending agencies and donor partners and other organizations and work together to this end. About 1.3 billion people or nearly a quarter of the world's population live on less than US$1 a day. It is remarkable that they survive, and it is DFID's stated intention to work with them and for them in pursuit of sustainable development.

References

CARRON, G. 1996. Six Years After Jomtien, Where Do We Stand? *IIEP Newsletter*, Vol. XIV, No. 3, pp. 1–2.

COLCLOUGH, C. 1997. *Aid to Basic Education in Africa – Opportunities and Constraints*. Oslo, NORAD.

DFID. 1997. *Eliminating World Poverty: A Challenge for the 21st Century. White Paper on International Development*. London, The Stationery Office Limited. (Cm 3789.)

SEN, A. 1997. *Development Thinking at the Beginning of the 21st Century*. (Paper presented at the London School of Economics.)

SHORT, C. 1997. Five Years to Lay Down the Foundations. *Times Educational Supplement*, 29 August, p. 16.

SKILLBECK, M. 1997. *Educating For, With and About Technology*. (Paper presented at 13th Conference of Commonwealth Education Ministers, Botswana.)

Redefining strategies of assistance: recent trends in Japanese assistance to education in Africa
Yumiko Yokozeki and Nobuhide Sawamura

Introduction

Japan has expanded its international aid rapidly and has become one of the world's major aid-providing countries. It has also attempted to increase its assistance for the expansion of quality education in developing countries, in line with the declaration adopted in Jomtien in 1990 (World Conference on Education for All, 1990). At the World Summit for Social Development (Copenhagen, March 1995), the Government of Japan stressed that its international co-operation would place great emphasis on social development. This has also influenced the Japan International Co-operation Agency (JICA). Moreover, the 1990s have witnessed the increased importance of Africa for Japanese international aid. There has been an expressed political will to assist Africa in the promotion of basic education, which is a new challenge for Japan.

In 1997, the Government of Japan made a commitment to co-operate as part of the global partnership spelt out in the DAC (1996) report. Partnership is described in the report as a development strategy to realize by the year 2015 a number of social development objectives, including universal primary education. The Government of Japan took the initiative to set forth these development goals, unusual in the light of its previous engagements.

Japan's involvement in international aid started in Asia in 1954, when Japan was still reconstructing its own economy and still receiving aid from the World Bank and other agencies. The number of recipient countries and the volume of aid grew rapidly with the further economic growth of Japan. During the 1960s, Japanese ODA to Asia accounted for more than 90 per cent of all Japanese aid. In the late 1970s, this figure was down to 70 per cent, and in 1995 only 54 per cent of Japanese aid went to countries in Asia (JICA, 1997b).

In the fiscal year 1995, Japanese ODA to Africa amounted to $1.3 billion out of a total of $10 billion, which represents 13 per cent of all Japanese ODA. JICA's technical co-operation provided training for 1,170 participants from Africa, dispatched 242 experts and assigned 339 volunteers to Africa (JICA, 1997b).

In the field of education, there has been a tendency to concentrate activities in tertiary education as well as vocational education. For the fiscal year 1995, 27 per cent of JICA's educational co-operation was in tertiary education and 36 per cent in technical, vocational and industrial education. In comparison, primary and general secondary education comprised only 17 per cent and non-formal education 10 per cent. Other assistance (10 per cent) included special education and educational administration. The proportional allocations within the sector are the same in Africa and Asia (JICA, 1997b).

Although the total aid budget for the fiscal year 1998 has been cut by 10 per cent for the first time in years, JICA's budget decreased by only 1.8 per cent (JICA, 1998b). As Japanese aid is distributed to different ministries according to the nature of their activities and as JICA is responsible for technical assistance but does not make decisions on grant aid or loans, this indicates that the Japanese Ministry of Finance places a higher priority on technical assistance than grant aid or loans. As JICA has not suffered any significant cutback, technical assistance in the field of education should not be greatly affected.

Japanese ODA in basic education in Africa is now at a critical juncture. It has begun to receive considerable attention and interest within and outside JICA. The first international seminar on basic education in Africa was held in Tokyo in March 1997 and was well attended by JICA staff and interested people from outside. This is a reflection of JICA's keen interest in education in Africa and its desire to know how activities in the field can be effectively increased (JICA, 1998c).

JICA and education in the 1990s

The Government of Japan was for a long time reluctant to provide aid to education. Education, especially basic education, was considered a domestic matter and Japanese intervention was considered interference in domestic affairs. However, as mentioned earlier, the Jomtien Conference, the Social Summit and the DAC report contributed to a significant, if slow, attitudinal change.

Japanese educational aid has accelerated in recent years (King, 1996). After participating in the 1990 Jomtien Conference, JICA initiated a *Study on Development Assistance for Development and Education* carried out between 1992 and 1993 (JICA, 1994). The study was entrusted to a number of experts and was the first JICA study in the field of education. It highlighted some problems and issues in education and development and can be characterized as an educational policy study. It has three – somewhat contradictory – main recommendations: (1) to increase the volume of educational aid to 15 per cent of the total ODA budget (in 1993, 5.8 per cent of total Japanese ODA was spent on education (DAC, 1995); (2) to assign the highest aid priority to basic education; and (3) to employ demand-driven and country-specific strategies.

In other words, the Government of Japan intends to provide aid to any subsector of education if there are actual needs in developing countries. Japanese aid previously tended to focus on tertiary education and vocational training in Asia, but it is now clear that Japan places a higher priority on aid to basic education than to other subsectors of education, reflecting a Japanese appreciation of the value of basic education. This is the most obvious change in Japanese aid policy since the late 1980s.

With respect to Japanese priorities, four aspects of education are emphasized: (1) strengthening educational administration; (2) training and upgrading of teaching staff; (3) development of curriculum, textbook and teaching materials; and (4) improvement of school facilities. Whereas the fourth aspect concerns school buildings, the other three relate to structures and systems which improve educational capacity. The significance of the order of priorities cannot be overemphasized. Improvement of facilities used to be the major focus of Japanese aid but is now the last mentioned. Highest priority is given to the promotion of educational administration, one of the key areas in educational improvement that Japan had earlier hesitated to provide with bilateral aid. This suggests a significant shift in Japanese policy. However, in practice the construction of classrooms is still the most common co-operation activity, particularly in Africa.

In 1995, in order to translate the policy into action, a Task Force on Expansion of Educational Aid was formed in the Planning Department of JICA (JICA, 1995). In 1997/98, a number of research studies were carried out. JICA co-operation has been compared with that of other agencies and non-governmental organizations (JICA, 1997*b*). The recommendations included more integrated and flexible approaches. Research currently carried out by the Research and Development Division based on an overview of the education system and situation analysis of a number of countries has highlighted several issues in basic education in Africa, such as medium of instruction, stakeholders in education, and education and democracy (JICA, 1998*d*). The past experience of JICA co-operation in technical and vocational education and training has also been reviewed (JICA, 1998*a*), as has basic education in sub-Saharan Africa (Kann, 1995).

Earlier on JICA produced a huge number of reports on individual projects, but reports on sectors and countries did not appear until the late 1980s. In education, there was effectively no aid policy before 1994 except for the bald statement that human resource development had to be the basis for development. Arguably, Japan did not set great value on policy issues and instead gave priority to each particular project.

Japan is now planning to use its own knowledge and experience in education to contribute to future policy formulation. It is, at the moment, analysing its own educational expertise and comparative advantage. The Centre for the Study of International Co-operation in Education (CICE), Hiroshima University, is planning to conduct a research study on Japanese experience in education and development and its applicability to current situations in developing countries which is expected to contribute to future policy planning.

Japanese aid to education and sub-Saharan Africa

In the Japanese aid policy, attention is now paid to its role in African development or, as indicated in the annual report, 'to work out a development strategy for Africa, learning from successful experiences in Asia, is an important task for Japan' (Japan. Ministry of Foreign Affairs, 1997, p. 68).

Redefining strategies of assistance: recent trends in Japanese assistance to education in Africa
Yumiko Yokozeki and Nobuhide Sawamura

The Tokyo International Conference on African Development (TICAD) was held in 1993 and some prominent heads of state from Africa were invited. The conference's resolution encouraged self-help effort and ownership by African countries of their own development and emphasized the importance of strengthening the partnership of the international community.

In April 1996, at the United Nations Conference on Trade and Development (UNCTAD) meeting in South Africa, the Japanese Foreign Minister announced a Japanese initiative on assistance to Africa. He stressed the importance of primary education and pledged that Japan would support efforts towards primary schooling for all children in Africa in accordance with the target spelled out in the DAC report, then about to be released. He promised that $100 million would be spent on basic education during 1996–99, 3,000 technical training participants would be invited to Japan, and $2 million from UNDP's Human Resources Development Fund would be used to promote South–South co-operation, mainly through transfer of Asian experience to Africa (Japan. Ministry of Foreign Affairs, 1997). To date, a majority of these funds have been utilized for construction of primary-school classrooms. In addition, co-operation in mathematics and science education in countries such as Kenya, South Africa and Ghana has begun to be prepared.

In 1996, a DAC long-term strategy for development with specific development objectives was announced (DAC, 1996). It emphasizes global partnerships and ownership and is of prime importance in Japanese ODA at the moment. To put the policy into action, six countries – in which Japanese efforts are concentrated – have been selected as case-study countries. Four are in Africa, signifying the importance of Africa in the strategy: Ethiopia, the United Republic of Tanzania, Ghana and Zimbabwe. The other two are Peru and Cambodia.

In October 1998, TICAD II took place. This conference will continued to honour the spirit of ownership and partnership expressed in the new DAC development strategy, and human resources development was, therefore, an important aspect in the conference. Within JICA and also outside, a very strong commitment has been made to co-operation in Africa.

JICA's technical assistance has traditionally been in the form of technology transfer to specific countries. This has ensured that most of the aid activities have been confined to tertiary and vocational and technical education. One of these activities has been the co-operation with Jomo Kenyatta University of Agriculture and Technology (JKUAT) in Kenya. The project started in 1980 and the current co-operation agreement continues until April 2000. To date, grant aid provision, mainly for upgrading facilities, has amounted to $75 million (JICA, 1997a). The cumulative number of Japanese experts sent to JKUAT is 309. Currently, JKUAT serves as an agricultural and engineering research and educational institute. In the future, the project is expected to expand its scope in development to set an example for African universities as active agents bridging field experience and theory.

JICA activities have been in the form of 'projects'. The term is used to cover a form of co-operation which includes: (a) technical training of counterpart personnel in Japan; (b) dispatch of Japanese experts to provide guidance to counterpart personnel within their own country; and (c) provision of necessary equipment and materials as well as a small amount of funding. The programme approach taken by other agencies, under which assistance is extended throughout the education sector, has been logistically difficult under the current Japanese system, as discussed below, although the need for this kind of approach is recognized. One attempt is a sector-wide approach in mathematics and science education in Africa using experience from the project on secondary-school mathematics and science education in the Philippines.

Issues in organization and structure of JICA

The encouraging trends at the policy level described above may not be translated at the implementation level because of the JICA co-operation system. Unlike other bilateral and multilateral agencies in which basically all departments are categorized into geographical areas and subject matter, such as education, health or industry, JICA's structure is more complex and departments are divided according to forms of co-operation. For example, the Training Affairs Department implements various training programmes and the Experts Assignment Department dispatches Japanese experts. It is, therefore, difficult to identify one specific department that is responsible for education in Africa as, generally, more than one department would be involved, depending on the nature of the activity.

The complex structure of the organization often creates difficulties in co-ordinating activities with other agencies and, in fact, even in co-ordination within JICA. There have been concerns about and criticisms of this both inside and outside JICA. Currently, the task force for organizational restructuring is working on the matter and is scheduled to make recommendations on an improved JICA structure in 1998, to be provisionally implemented in April 1999. However, this might encounter obstacles because of JICA's relationship with Japanese ministries. The operation of Japan's aid administration has been characterized as 'a wide diversification of programme responsibilities and budget allocations' (Rix, 1993, p. 73). A number of ministries are involved in ODA according to the nature of the assistance and a division of responsibilities between ministries over different aspects of the aid programme. In principle, JICA is an implementing agency of the Japanese aid programmes in technical assistance and is not allowed to formulate aid policy. According to Rix (1993, p. 73) there is 'a lack of unified political responsibility for aid' – in fact, no one seems to be responsible for aid policy in Japan.

Future prospects

The Japanese aid system traditionally provided aid for developing economic infrastructure in Asia. Japan is now in need of a new strategy to assist social development, such as education and health, in Africa. In order to be involved in basic education, JICA needs more expertise in education and more people on the ground. The Government of Japan has encouraged the adoption of specific development targets. The question is the extent to which JICA is willing to make the necessary change. This is a major challenge for JICA and the work of the task force on formulating a new institutional structure is of great interest to many. JICA is currently organized according to forms of co-operation, but should be organized according to geographical areas and subject matter.

An important task for JICA is its involvement in Sector Investment Programmes (SIP) which aim at a common funding pool and harmonizing aid procedures among funding and technical-assistance agencies. They were originally initiated by the World Bank, supported by a number of recipient countries. Currently, SIPs have been implemented in a relatively small number of countries but are likely to be extended to a greater number of African states. If Japan is serious about being involved in SIPs, organizational changes as well as changes in perspectives must be made. In addition, the operation of the current Japanese aid system, now characterized by a very rigid bureaucracy, must become more flexible.

Another challenge concerns the content of co-operation. A number of studies suggest that funding and technical-assistance agencies must support policy reform (World Bank, 1988; King, 1991; Buchert, 1995). As was mentioned earlier, the Government of Japan has, until now, been reluctant to allocate aid to basic education as well as to educational policy matters. There is a need for a change of this view. Although Japanese experience in policy reform in social sectors in Africa is limited, some of our experiences in Asia might be relevant.

Japan experienced a budget cut in international development co-operation for the first time in 1998. At the same time the task is becoming greater. Japan has made a commitment to support social sector development in line with the DAC report. At first glance, the situation seems impossible. However, it might be time for Japan to formulate a new strategy. Clearly, the negative impact on the total volume of foreign aid and the shift to the social sector as well as the larger agenda require a more efficient aid system and 'policy coherence', as Forster (1998) indicates. Having once been a recipient of foreign aid, Japan has become one of the major aid providers. The change Japan is now required to make might be even more significant than the shift from aid recipient to aid provider.

References

BUCHERT, L. 1995. *Recent Trends in Education Aid: Towards a Classification of Policies. A Report from the IWGE.* Paris, UNESCO/IIEP.

DAC. 1995. *Development Cooperation: Efforts and Policies of the Members of the Development Assistance Committee.* Paris, OECD.

——. 1996. *Shaping the 21st Century: The Contribution of Development Co-operation.* Paris, OECD.

FORSTER, J. 1998. A New Agenda for International Development Co-operation. *NORRAG News*, No. 22, pp. 1–2.

JAPAN. Ministry of Foreign Affairs. 1997. *Japan's ODA. Annual Report.* Tokyo.

JICA. 1994. *Study on Development Assistance for Development and Education: The Study Group on Development Assistance for Education and Development.* Tokyo, JICA.

——. 1995. *Kyoiku enjo kakuju no tame no teian: Task Force Hokokusho* [Recommendations on Expansion of Educational Aid: Report of the Task Force]. Tokyo, JICA.

——. 1997a. *Kokusai kyoryoku jigyodan nenpo* [JICA Annual Report 1997]. Tokyo, JICA.
——. 1997b. *Kyoiku enjo kiso kenkyu* [Educational Aid Strategies]. Tokyo, JICA.
——. 1998a. *Jigyo taikeika kenkyu-shokugyokunren shokugyokyoiku* [Integration of Japanese Aid Experience in TVET]. Tokyo, JICA.
——. 1998b. *News*, No. 289. (In Japanese.)
——. 1998c. *Report on the Seminar on Basic Education in Sub-Saharan Africa*. Tokyo, JICA.
——. 1998d. *Sabu sahara ahurika shokoku ni okeru kisokyoiku no genjo to nihon no kyoikuenjo no kanosei* [The Status of Basic Education in Sub-Saharan Africa and the Possibility of Japanese Aid]. Tokyo, JICA.
KANN, U. 1995. *The Status of Basic Education in Sub-Saharan Africa: The Case of Lesotho, Malawi, Swaziland, South Africa, Tanzania and Uganda*. London, JICA/Commonwealth Secretariat.
KING, K. 1991. *Aid and Education in the Developing World. The Role of the Donor Agencies in Educational Analysis*. Harlow, Longman.
——. 1996. Aid for Development or for Change? A Discussion of Education and Training Policies of Development Assistance Agencies with Particular Reference to Japan. In: K. Watson, C. Modgil and S. Modgil, *Educational Dilemmas: Debate and Diversity*, pp. 112–23. London, Cassell. (Power and Responsibility in Education, Vol. 3.)
RIX, A. 1993. *Japan's Foreign Aid Challenge: Policy Reform and Aid Leadership*. London, Routledge.
WORLD BANK. 1988. *Education in Sub-Saharan Africa: Policies for Adjustment, Revitalization and Expansion*. Washington, D.C., World Bank.
WORLD CONFERENCE ON EDUCATION FOR ALL (Jomtien, Thailand, 5–9 March 1990). 1990. *World Declaration of Education for All and Framework for Action to Meet Basic Learning Needs*. New York, Inter-Agency Commission for WCEFA. (3rd impression, Paris, UNESCO, 1994.)

Non-governmental organizations as partners in Africa: a cultural analysis of North–South relations

Juliet Elu and Kingsley Banya

Introduction

Some thirty-odd years after formal independence, African countries have still not achieved the economic, social and political self-sufficiency that the pioneers of decolonization had anticipated. In many parts of the continent, the initial gains made after colonial rule have disappeared, resulting in economic and social stagnation and, in extreme cases, disintegration (e.g. in Liberia, Congo and Sierra Leone). The persistent poverty of many countries in Africa is debilitating and dehumanizing.

As reported by the World Bank, poverty in developing countries is on the rise; over 730 million with inadequate diets, declining life expectancy, per capita calorie supply and real wages in the 1980s (World Bank, 1988b). The countries of sub-Saharan Africa experienced an annual decline of 2.9 per cent in per capita income from 1980 to 1987. Declines in real per capita incomes were also experienced during this period by oil-exporting and heavily indebted countries (World Bank, 1988b). This situation is no better in the 1990s. All sub-Saharan African countries fall in the 'Low Human Development Category' and in many of these countries (e.g. Mali, Sierra Leone and Burkina Faso), the annual per capita incomes have declined to as low as 1.5 per cent (World Bank, 1996).

It has also become apparent that governments alone cannot achieve meaningful development; the involvement of both citizens and foreign assistance are necessary. The nature of this involvement has included external non-governmental organizations and indigenous volunteer development organizations. The nomenclature used in this chapter reflects changes since the June 1987 meeting of African organizations in Dakar. Before this date,

International Private Voluntary Organization was the terminology used by the United Nations and in other international arenas, including Africa. Thus, for the purpose of this chapter, non-governmental organizations will refer to both Northern and Southern voluntary organizations.

Development

Development is based on the premise that certain peoples and societies are less developed than others and that those who are more developed (i.e. more modern) have the expertise (knowledge) to help the less developed achieve modernity. This concept is a linear Western definition of modernity and the rationale for the development enterprise since the 1940s (Parpart and Marchand, 1995). This definition of development has recently been challenged by scholars using post-modern critiques of modernity, Western universalism and dualist/binary thinking. Indeed some scholars are taking the development debate in a new direction (Crush, 1994; Dubois, 1991; Edwards, 1989; Escobar, 1992; Ferguson, 1990; Goetz, 1991; Johnston, 1991; Mathur, 1989; Pieterse, 1992). Recognizing the relationship between language and power, they have questioned the language/discourse of development, particularly the (re)presentation of the South/Third World as the impoverished, backward 'other' in need of salvation from the developed North/First World. This dualist construction, they point out, has reinforced the authority of Northern development agencies and specialists, whether mainstream or alternative, and provided the rationale for development policies and practices that are designed to incorporate the Southern nations into a Northern-dominated world. This approach, they argue, is no longer appropriate in an increasingly complex and interrelated world. Indeed, similar thoughts had already emerged from the 'impoverished' South (Bratton, 1988).

With increased diversity and complexity of activities, substantial levels of financing and growing levels of external support and internal legitimacy, the proliferation of external non-governmental organizations and Southern volunteer development organizations has become one of the key new factors on the African development scene. A growing number of aid agencies and national governments (e.g. the United Kingdom and Norway) have turned to non-governmental organizations as potential instruments for enacting official development projects, especially those intended to channel public resources to the poor. Some reasons for this include the growing interest among agencies and national governments in strengthening the developmental roles of institutions outside the public sector and the demonstrated capacity of some non-governmental organizations to reach the poor more effectively than public agencies. In addition, a sharp decline in public development resources has necessitated a search by governments for more cost-effective alternatives to conventional public services and development programmes. Because non-governmental organizations based in the industrial countries mobilize US$3 billion a year in development resources from private sources and manage another US$1.5 billion from official aid agencies (OECD, 1986), their role in development efforts has become critical. It has also been realized that some non-governmental organizations are sophisticated and influential organizations able to carry out programmes on a national scale, and to influence national policies and institutions. The growth of the power, external support and legitimacy for non-governmental organization involvement makes them worthy of being understood in their complexity and diversity. Major development financial institutions, such as the World Bank, IMF, the African Development Bank and host governments, are increasingly focusing on the issue of involvement of Northern and Southern non-governmental organizations in development.

The relationship between the two kinds of organizations is critically examined in this chapter, followed by a discussion of factors having an impact on their collaboration.

What are non-governmental organizations?

There is a tremendous variation in the use of the term non-governmental organization. A broad definition would include every organization in civil society that is *not* part of government – for example, political groups, labour and trade unions, and religious bodies. A narrower and perhaps more precise definition, derived from everyday usage, 'refers to a specific type of organization working in the field of "development" – one which works with people to help them improve their social and economic situation and prospects' (Commonwealth Foundation, 1995, p. 24). The World Bank (1989) seems to use a narrower definition when it defines non-governmental organizations as 'private organizations that pursue activities to relieve suffering, promote the interest of the poor, protect the environment or undertake community development' (p. 1). In this chapter, non-governmental organizations are defined by their key characteristics: voluntary, independent, not-for-profit and altruistic.

Voluntary: non-governmental organizations are formed voluntarily; there is nothing in the legal or statutory framework of any country which requires them to be formed or which prevents them from being formed. There is an element of voluntary participation in the organization, whether in the form of small numbers of board members or large numbers of members or beneficiaries giving their time voluntarily (Commonwealth Foundation, 1991).

Independent: Within the laws of society, they are controlled by those who have formed them or by boards of management responsible for control and management (UNDP, 1993).

Not-for-profit: They are not for personal, private profit or gain although they may have employees, like other enterprises, who are paid for what they do. But in non-governmental organizations the employers or members of boards of management are not paid for the work they perform on boards, except for reimbursement for expenses they incur in the course of performing their duties. They can engage in revenue-generating activities but do not, however, distribute profits or surplus or dividends to shareholders or members like other corporations.

Altruistic in aims and related values: The aims of non-governmental organizations are to improve the circumstances and prospects of disadvantaged people who are unable to realize their potential or achieve their full rights in society, whether through direct or indirect forms of actions. They are to act on concerns and issues which are detrimental to the well-being, circumstances or prospects of people or society as a whole (Tandon, 1989).

These four characteristics are the litmus test for any non-governmental organization, irrespective of location. Some examples of non-governmental organizations include: non-profit consulting firms, health committees, squatters' associations, peasant leagues, village water associations, women's associations, mosque committees, environmental advocacy groups, human rights groups, youth clubs, legal aid societies, service clubs (such as Rotary), and local development associations. There are various reasons for the formation of non-governmental organizations. Some exist to serve those who cannot help themselves. Some provide services. Others offer mutual support, engage in public education and advocacy or provide charity. Some are concerned only with local issues. Others are oriented to national or international concerns. Some, such as Amnesty International and the American Civil Liberties Union, perform watchdog functions.

Non-governmental organizations perform diverse activities such as: housing provisions, health services, agricultural services, transport and communication services, credit and financial services, research, consciousness-raising, campaigning and advocacy, information, education (formal and non-formal) and skills training. Beneficiaries of non-governmental organization activities can include: children, women, young people, refugees, offenders and ex-offenders, people with disabilities, the hungry, the elderly and the sick. Non-governmental organizations are also active in communities affected by any of the following factors: change in the physical environment, natural disasters, epidemics, marginalization due to remoteness, poor access to resources and large-scale infrastructure projects.

Northern non-governmental organizations

Originally, the idea was that non-governmental organizations were to play a significant role in development activities of the governments providing international funding and technical assistance. The expertise of non-governmental organizations continues to be seen as essential to the development enterprise as development policies and programmes are largely predicated on the assumption that development problems can be reduced to technical (i.e. 'solvable') problems that involve the transfer of Western technical expertise to the developing world (Escobar, 1992; Johnston, 1991; Manzo, 1991, Nindi, 1990).

The development business, with its ever larger bureaucracies, has been largely built on this assumption, and the transfer of expertise from developed to developing countries has been the underlying rationale and practice of development agencies and practitioners. Internal criticisms, such as those levelled by Edward Jaycox, the then World Bank Vice-President, Africa Region, focused on particular problems, such as the deleterious impact on professionalism in developing countries caused by 'the tendency to use expatriate resident technical assistance to solve all kinds of problems' (Jaycox, 1993, p. 6). Jaycox called for the creation of a 'demand for professionalism in Africa', but never questioned the authority of the North over the definition and transmission of that professional/expert knowledge.

Non-governmental organizations as partners in Africa: a cultural analysis of North–South relations
Juliet Elu and Kingsley Banya

Non-governmental organizations have often been used to attempt to transfer cultural awareness and to promote values, social contacts and political alignments centred on and patterned after countries that provide funding and technical assistance. There are widely held beliefs that Northern non-governmental organizations are fomenters of revolution or destabilizing forces (Dubois, 1991). Although these organizations in their own public pronouncements and self-image belie the claim of fomenters of revolution, over a period of time, with their diverse political and social origins, they have accommodated this role. Whatever political persuasion, whether of the left or the right, the non-governmental organizations are generally alike, and at home and abroad they are often handmaidens of the governments they presumably seek to change or redirect in the longer run. For example, Johnson (1990, p. 3) notes that

there is a contrast between their manifest objectives of development promotion and disaster relief and their latent objectives of fundamental social and political change. While it is important in itself, and not a new insight to note this, it is important to highlight the power of the manifest ones, which allow for the preservation of the nexus between the various actors. They honor the manifest ones enough, and these connect powerfully to public values.

By highlighting their manifest objectives, the non-governmental organizations can count on the goodwill and a reservoir of public sympathy and support in helping poor people and societies respond to crisis, adjust to or recover from disaster. However, they either do not stay long enough or provide adequate resources to sustain longer-term assistance that makes lasting structural changes. Thus, in the public credo and debate, both governments and non-governmental organizations have to continue to stress the short-term relief functions, which leaves intact perceptions of people in developing countries – especially in Africa – as marginal and pitiful, rather than the longer-term development aspects which would promote Africa's emergence into real actor status in the world, a status which Western societies in general are not ready to promote (Nindi, 1990). Despite the foregoing observations, however, one cannot overlook the role Northern non-governmental organizations play as a nexus between local and global actors and as carriers of new values and skills.

As part of the developmental and political change scene in Africa, Northern non-governmental organizations, Johnson (1990) notes, have an acknowledged record of good performance in delivering services and mobilizing people for self-help. They have undertaken projects which governments were financially and technically unable or unwilling to perform. Given the financial and technical know-how that Northern non-governmental organizations bring to the South, for the foreseeable future they will continue to function in the development business. However, the role and type of visibility the North will have are continuously being defined.

African voluntary development organizations

A perusal of African self-help activities illustrates that African countries have not been just recipients of Northern largesse. They have been and continue to be major players in their own development. The notion that Africa has not taken an active part in its own development is not true; hence, the so-called 'assistantial model' in which there are only Northern providers and African recipients is increasingly being challenged (Ferguson, 1990; Grischow, 1993; Nindi, 1990; Roe, 1991). Long before the end of colonization, Africans had pooled their resources to meet challenges and to make their lives better. In many villages and towns, people volunteered to build roads, bridges and even clinics to meet their own needs. On a smaller scale, two or three women sometimes got together to raise chickens and/or sheep which they sold to pay school fees and buy books and uniforms for their children. It was from such beginnings that coalitions were formed which amalgamated into the large *national* non-governmental organizations or the continent-wide Forum of African Development Organizations (FAVDO). In the rural areas in particular, such organizations were quite influential in development work. However, because of a lack of resources and proper organization, the full potential of such voluntarism was not realized. What makes a real difference in the national non-governmental organizations today is that organizations have come together to respond to problems that are of significance to the entire country, rather than to only a few individuals. The realization that African development depended on Africans themselves led to the eventual creation of FAVDO.

Over the years, the roles of non-governmental organizations have changed. The present roles are more complex and are now promoting development and longer-term structural changes. A special meeting of the Non-Governmental Liaison Service (NGLS) of the United Nations was held in Geneva in November 1985. As an offshoot of this meeting, an

African non-governmental organization steering committee convened in Nairobi in April 1986. At the Nairobi meeting, held in conjunction with the United Nations special session on Africa, the African non-governmental organization steering committee prepared a position paper on the economic and social crisis in Africa and proposed possible solutions. The formal document stated:

The term '[non-governmental organization]' was really a misnomer in the context of Africa, when many of them were traditional, village-based associations which frequently had no official status. Strengthening the capacity of these locally based non-governmental organizations, however, posed problems in terms of relationships with Northern donors, as most funding was given to projects. This posed serious difficulties for African non-governmental organizations. Participatory development projects involved a number of expenses which would not fit under the heading of project costs (Wangoola, 1987, pp. 14–15).

The document further defined African non-governmental organizations as organizations: (a) that have risen in response to the need of the African peoples; (b) whose policy-making organs fully consist of Africans; (c) where senior staff whose decisions are likely to influence policy are also African; (d) that have a constituency and a framework for democratic participation and accountability (Wangoola, 1987, p. 7). This suggests that African development was primarily the responsibility of Africans, with an essential role for African non-governmental organizations.

In May 1987, a continent-wide meeting of African non-governmental organizations was held in Dakar. Participants included seventy-one delegates from some twenty-three African countries representing indigenous voluntary organizations from French-, English-, Portuguese- and Arabic-speaking Africa. Also attending were non-governmental organizations from all over the world, as well as African government officials, officials of international non-governmental organizations and of international funding and technical-assistance agencies. The meeting emphasized collaboration among African non-governmental organizations and the establishment of dialogue with African governments 'to secure official recognition for non-governmental organizations and as a means towards non-governmental organization participation and partnership in development' (FAVDO, 1987, p. 5). Additionally, the meeting called for a new understanding and

framework for North–South co-operation. Key outcomes of the Dakar meeting included the following (FAVDO, 1987, p. 40):
- Discussions were held, ideas exchanged and formulated; ideas for further networking, exchange and co-operation were discussed. This eventually will lead to improvement in performance. Since volunteers often work in isolation, coming together to share ideas and experiences can be very helpful.
- The role of FAVDO and African governments was defined: (1) African governments have political responsibility; (2) African governments have prime responsibility for development; (3) indigenous voluntary development organizations have no political ambitions; (4) as far as development is concerned, African indigenous voluntary development organizations have responsibility in consultations with grass roots, whose needs the conference leaders propose to address; Northern non-governmental organizations can only play a supporting role; (5) the African indigenous voluntary development organizations have access to resources which are not normally available to governments; (6) African governments, collectively and individually, must dialogue with Northern governments.

The delineation of the role of indigenous non-governmental organizations is politically expedient. Many African governments have not accepted the non-governmental organization phenomenon as an aspect of development. It is, therefore, necessary for indigenous non-governmental organizations to assure African governments that they need the government's approval, formal recognition and consideration as collaborators in the society's economic well-being.

The theoretical relations between North–South non-governmental organizations

It has been increasingly felt that a partnership between Northern and Southern non-governmental organizations would enhance the significance of transparency, equality and mutual accountability. Funding and technical-assistance agencies such as the United States Agency for International Development (USAID), EDF, the World Bank and UNDP attached some importance to the relationship between national non-governmental organizations and funding and technical-assistance agencies. The latter felt that highlighting institutional development as a specific objective of the partnership would help transmit needed management, monitoring and networking skills. As part of the discourse on foreign aid, the twin concepts of 'partnership' and 'institutional development' were actively advanced towards the end of the 'non-governmental organization decade' (1970–80).

Jones (1993, pp. 7–8) has outlined the following reasons for close working relations between Northern and Southern non-governmental organizations:
1. Traditional Northern-dominated, 'top-down' assistance has failed to provide sustainable improvements in the lives of the poor.
2. The interdependent nature of complex problems demands collaborative problem-solving approaches and can be understood only with the benefit of insight from many vantage points.
3. The South's right and ability to control its own development is forcing Northern non-governmental organizations to change their role. Recognizing the South's growing leadership capacity, the international donor community is beginning to look to Southern non-governmental organizations for programme initiatives.

Thus, it is becoming increasingly beneficial to work with Southern non-governmental organizations. According to Action Aid (1993), there are some worthwhile reasons why a collaborative relation is needed between the two non-governmental organization constituents. One quite practical reason is that

> collaboration is more cost-effective than direct operation; expedites project start-up time, facilitates Northern non-governmental organization work in countries/situations where their direct operations are prohibited; provides access to non-governmental organization skills and resources (such as innovative strategies, sensitivity to local conditions and culture, positive relations with the community, regional contacts with state agencies), allows Northern non-governmental organizations to focus on other key tasks, for example, regional networking, policy influence, documentation and dissemination of innovative strategies, mass public education, etc.; and enhances each organization's legitimacy with key stakeholders (p. 8).

Collaboration can also enhance local control over the direction of sustainable development and help build capacity and confidence. Such an effort can increase sustainability by developing local independent structures and strengthening 'civil society institutions'. It can also lead to cultural understanding and the establishment of development strategies.

The NGLS meeting in Geneva in 1985 was a landmark in the relationship between Northern and Southern non-governmental organizations. At that meeting, role distinctions were outlined with Southern non-governmental organizations claiming to be responsible for development in developing countries, but welcoming Northern non-governmental organization collaboration – not initiative – in the process. It was felt that if Northern non-governmental organizations see their role as messengers, rather than providers, then their message can be viewed from a different perspective. On the one hand, the Southern non-governmental organizations claim that the image of Africans projected by Northern non-governmental organizations – as passive, helpless and pathetic, and needing Northern non-governmental organizations to provide the solutions to all problems – is not generally true. On the contrary, Southern non-governmental organizations hope that their counterparts will project an image of Africans as resilient, capable human beings with endurance and ingenuity (Elliot, 1987). The Northern non-governmental organizations often have a tendency to justify their activities as if they had sole responsibility for African development – a stance which Southern non-governmental organizations resent. The Southern non-governmental organizations see the principal roles for their counterparts in the North as providing support and seeking change in Northern economic and development policies.

It was expected that the coming together of both Northern and Southern non-governmental organizations would bring more satisfying, legitimate and visionary partnerships (Flower, 1988). In a North–South partnership, goals and objectives, it was felt, would be co-determined to the satisfaction of all participants. It was felt that the time was ripe for a catalytic programme to enhance collaborative efforts among partners. This would help in disseminating information about each other's work. Above all, such a relationship could provide seed monies for Southern non-governmental organization initiatives.

The partners were to bring to the table various views and areas of expertise. Southern non-governmental organization staff had at their disposal a set of culturally attuned and place-specified implementation skills (Brinkerhoff and Garcia-Zamon, 1986; Hyden, 1991). The Northern non-governmental organizations were to provide funds, human resource skills and technical know-how. Both nationals and non-nationals were to discuss the importance of mutual trust and respect, transparency, complementary strengths, reciprocal accountability, joint decision-making and a two-way exchange of information.

In the case of African developing countries, the 1987 London symposium of funding and technical-assistance agencies on Development Alternatives: The Challenge for Non-governmental Organizations was a most resonating event for partnership and institutional development. Partially financed by the Overseas Development Institute and the journal *World Development*, the symposium brought together 120 representatives from forty-two countries (twenty-eight so-called developing and fourteen developed countries) to discuss 'a genuine partnership between northern and southern non-governmental organizations to replace previous dependencies, mistrust and paternalism' (Drabek, 1987, p. x). A suggested code of conduct that provides guidelines for North–South relationships received approval. Areas considered included: evaluation effectiveness, research priorities, networking, development education and advocacy, and non-governmental organization relations with governments. It is noteworthy that this was the first time that the relationship between the two was moving in the direction of a more collaborative model and away from the assistantial model. This greater collaboration would, it was hoped, strengthen non-governmental organization development strategies.

The conference provided a cathartic airing of frustrations and anxieties over the continued Northern dominance of non-governmental organization activity in Africa. After the symposium, Southern non-governmental organizations stayed in London to discuss North–South co-operation. It was decided to emphasize the use/exchange of Southern experience and expertise in the fields of community mobilization, credit union management, environmental issues, technology and other pertinent areas, such as the role of women in development. Also discussed was the exchange of information and personnel. The focus of the information was to be on water development, soil conservation, health, women's rights, women's roles in development and traditional medicine. Documentation centres were to be established in Dakar, Manila, New Delhi and Dominica.

Eight years after the London symposium, another major conference, the World Summit for Social Development (Copenhagen, 1995) held under the auspices of the United Nations, brought together more than 160 delegations. The conference document declared:

poverty should be eradicated across the world, as should unemployment and the existing social inequality between the sexes; the debt burden of developing nations (especially Africa) should be reduced through debt relief or outright cancellation; the IMF and the World Bank must, in designing structural adjustment programs for implementation in developing countries, take into account the social factors in those countries so as to avoid or at the very least, minimize disruption; aid to the Third World should be bumped up, with 20 per cent of the total set aside for social development (World Summit for Social Development, 1995, p. 2).

Dilemmas in collaboration

Despite the two conferences, nothing much has changed in the development arena. The partnership envisaged has *not* been realized. The controllers of resources can, in many instances, dictate which projects are to be funded. In some areas, such as transparency and advocacy, little progress has been made.

Part of the frustration of the Southern non-governmental organizations is determining whether a true partnership can be built between the rich North and the impoverished South. As one participant at the London conference declared: 'No amount of well-intentioned dialogue can remove the asymmetry of power in a North–South partnership' (Elliot, 1987, p. 65). One delegate summed the views of most developing countries at the Copenhagen Summit in his assertion that 'the requirement that recipient countries spend 20 per cent of GDP on social needs is an infringement of their sovereignty' (Group of 77 member).

Poverty in the South is an ominous backdrop to the practice of true partnership and institutional development. The difference in environments of both types of non-governmental organizations is a critical factor in translating the theory and practice of North–South non-governmental organization partnership and institutional development. The motivations and expectations of the actors, the content and approach of the collaboration, and the historical and political context in which their work is undertaken are equally important considerations. For example, Southern non-governmental organization movements are placed in the larger, historically evolved state–society nexus. In order to improve national non-governmental organization institutions, one needs, a priori, an appreciation of the determinants that historically have favoured or disfavoured social organization independent of the state.

In most developing countries, the state is all-powerful, and voluntary organizations must operate carefully vis-à-vis the state. It is implicitly known that voluntary organizations cannot, for example, become too powerful. Non-governmental organization workers, therefore, need to understand how the socio-political environment operates.

The colonial superimposition of an inorganic governing model and the removal of decentralized decision-making bodies have had implications for the state–society relationship and for the positions and role of the non-governmental organizations within that relationship. In countries such as Sierra Leone, the state–society nexus is still dynamic and fluid. Full understanding of the historical backdrop to state–society relations could possibly encourage collaborating non-governmental organizations to invest more purposefully in partnerships with other organizations.

Another area of difficulty for national non-governmental organizations relates to the production of quick results desired by foreign non-governmental organizations. Producing quick results is the means whereby national non-governmental organizations prove themselves 'competent' and 'earn' the confidence and reputation deemed essential by funding and technical-assistance agencies. Attaining 'quick results' is sometimes difficult for national non-governmental organizations which may want to invest in long-term activities with less visibility. This is especially true with agriculture, whose gestation period can be longer. As Schultz (1984, p. 141) observed before the United States Congress Sub-committee on Foreign Affairs:

Financial supporters can create a situation where staff of U.S. Private Voluntary Organizations (PVO) does much of the work themselves, rather than support the efforts of the local group to carry out the project. The pressure to produce quantifiable results often constrains PVO effectiveness in building local capacity.

Thus, the acclaimed non-governmental organization partnership and institutional development can be muzzled by competing and often contradictory development priorities.

Northern non-governmental organizations face several problems that have a major impact on national non-governmental organizations. One problem is the growing difficulties that they experience in raising constituents and bilateral support. The constant tragedies in developing countries – famine, outbreak of disease, military coup d'état, dictatorship – have contributed to what has been referred to as 'donor fatigue'. The sensitivity of the rich has become numb to television-portrayed tragedies in the developing countries. The catastrophe of developing countries is no longer striking news in the rich North. This translates into fewer and fewer dollars in aid contributions from those who can afford it. As the Northern non-governmental organization bank accounts dwindle, they have less and less money to pass on to their national counterparts. The insistence on partnership also means that funds available for non-governmental organization initiatives that require collaboration with local partners can become a legitimization strategy, not only in accessing these funds, but also in justifying the presence of a project in the field. Hence, Northern non-governmental organizations can continuously rationalize their existence in the South *ad infinitum*.

A second question relates to timing. At the same time that larger funding and technical-assistance agencies are requiring international non-governmental organizations to play a more prominent role in developing countries, the national non-governmental organizations want their foreign counterparts to maintain a lower profile in the non-governmental organization development community and in communities where projects are being implemented. Dependency and unequal relationships, the antithesis of the objectives of partnership and institutional development, are being enforced when they are least needed.

Although both Northern and Southern non-governmental organizations agree in theory that they must have a mutual relationship, this has not been easy to achieve in practice.

Typology of North–South collaboration

In viewing a typology of North–South non-governmental organization collaboration, it should be noted that these classifications are idealized and that a combination of elements may coexist. Leach (1994) has identified seven types of relationships that could exist between Northern and Southern non-governmental organizations:

Contracting: In which a Northern non-governmental organization pays an independent non-governmental organization to provide a well-defined package of services under conditions established largely by the Northern non-governmental organization. This is an example of 'fee for service' exchange.

Dependent franchise: In which a formally independent non-governmental organization will function as a field office of a Northern non-governmental organization which provides most or all of its direction and funding.

Spin-off non-governmental organization: In which a dependent franchise or Northern non-governmental organization field office is expected over time to become organizationally and financially independent of the Northern non-governmental organization.

Visionary patronage: In which Northern and Southern non-governmental organizations with a shared vision of development jointly agree on goals, outcome measures and reporting requirements for a programme which the Southern non-governmental organization implements and the Northern non-governmental organization supports with funds and other resources.

Collaborative operations: In which both the Northern and Southern non-governmental organizations share decision-making power over planning and implementation of joint programmes implemented by the Southern non-governmental organization with funding and technical support from the Northern non-governmental organization.

Mutual governance: In which the Northern non-governmental organization and the Southern non-governmental organization each have decision-making power, or at least substantial influence, over each other's policies and practices at both the organizational and programme levels.

Sustainable development: In which the Southern non-governmental organizations are fully responsible for all aspects of project development and implementation without Northern non-governmental organization involvement. This is the ideal typical model of most Southern non-governmental organizations.

Ideally, the relationship between the non-governmental organizations should follow the last three mentioned typologies: collaborative operations, mutual governance and sustainable development, which make provisions for joint sharing of vision, decision-making and implementation strategies. The mutual governance typology tries to maximize each organization's effort, especially in cultural and programmatic planning. The other typologies (contracting, dependent franchise, spin-off, visionary patronage) are what African non-governmental organizations do *not* want. However, given the asymmetrical relation between the North and the South, mutual governance can be difficult to realize, as illustrated below.

Influential factors in North–South non-governmental organization collaboration

Using highlights of case studies from education and agriculture in Sierra Leone – i.e. the Bunumbu Teacher Education Project and the Eastern Area Integrated Agricultural Development Project (EIADP) – this section analyses facilitating and constraining factors in the collaboration between the South and the North. The database of this empirical work is limited to 1993 because of the chaos and war situation in Sierra Leone since that time. Sierra Leone is one of the countries categorized as 'least developing' by the World Bank. Both per capita GNP and food production have been falling since the early 1980s. This is a paradoxical situation given the relatively rich resources with which the country is endowed, namely, bauxite, iron ore, diamonds, gold, forest, land and a small population estimated at 4 million. Because of rampant corruption and mismanagement, the country has relied heavily on international funding and technical-assistance agencies, including non-governmental organizations, to meet its food and development needs (Banya, 1994). There are currently more than fifty non-governmental organizations in the country, working in areas ranging from education to water supplies.

Facilitating factors to successful North–South non-governmental organization relationships

Building on the NGLS meeting in Geneva and the London symposium, it seems clear that there is concern by non-governmental organizations, both Northern and Southern, to provide appropriate and meaningful aid to developing nations. This willingness on the part of providers can serve as a facilitating factor in responsible and transparent governance. In addition, there are basic and undeniable considerations that can make non-governmental organization assistance viable.

Non-governmental organizations as partners in Africa: a cultural analysis of North–South relations
Juliet Elu and Kingsley Banya

First and most obvious, the need is present and basic in sub-Saharan Africa. Some 40 per cent of African children under the age of 5 go through a period of malnutrition severe enough to cause mental or physical damage (Lamb, 1987). Lands that could produce enough agricultural products to sustain a nation are marginally farmed and many African nations rely on imported food. Not only is the need evident, but the needs are basic, not highly technological. Agriculture, education, health, water, electricity and a transportation system form the foundation for this basic need. Non-governmental organizations, both Northern and mature Southern, have the expertise and wherewithal to provide needed aid.

Second, the population welcomes meaningful aid. As demonstrated in both the Bunumbu Teacher Education Project and EAIAP, residents are ready to provide 'in kind' labour and work diligently to facilitate the completion of the projects. In the latter project, swamps were cleared, loans taken and plans to plant swamp rice carried on by the people of the eastern area. The population has demonstrated time and again a willingness to participate in meaningful ways in developmental projects. Assistance clearly transcends any Western notion of a 'hand-out'.

Third, geographic areas are small and workable for the provision of aid. While the scope of needed aid may seem daunting, the actual areas within which non-governmental organizations assist are relatively small. Bunumbu, for example, has a population of 1,000, many of whom contributed much needed and important work on the project. While the vision and goals are large, the actual areas of contract are small and manageable. In addition, the population tends to be stable, so that purposeful aid provided will be useful for a considerable length of time. The each-one-teach-one concept of assistance can be beneficial and long-lasting.

Finally, cultural mores work for aid projects. The significance of tribalism cannot be denied. Families are closely knit and supportive. Tribes provide self-help to members. Children and the aged are cared for. Co-operation is practised as a beneficial tradition and mutual help expected in village life. Village-level governance is interactive and consensual rather than entrepreneurial. Life in a subsistence economy tends to inculcate into members of the society a work ethic focused on mutual assistance, survival and the betterment of the village itself. The cultural standards, therefore, bode well for appropriate non-governmental organization intervention.

At the macro-planning level the sheer size of the continent and nations, as well as the immensity of the need, could lead one to believe that the problems associated with aid and Northern and Southern non-governmental organization co-operation are insurmountable. When considered in the light of the facilitating factors briefly discussed above, the necessity for more collaborative efforts with non-governmental organizations – as has been voiced in Geneva, London and elsewhere – becomes essential.

Constraining factors

It is clear from both the Geneva and the London meetings that mutual transparency and joint decision-making are important factors in any North–South collaboration. There are, however, constraints in achieving the stated goals, among which are the following.

Needs assessment. In both the Bunumbu project and EIADP, the time spent on needs assessment was inadequate. Northern non-governmental organizations tend to rely on the few meetings they have with chiefs and elders to determine the need for a particular project. Anyone who is familiar with African chieftaincy will know that the chiefs are not necessarily the best barometers by which to gauge local needs.[1] The British system of indirect rule ensured that the chief could seldom speak for the interests of their people and there is no evidence that the independent government has changed the mode of operation. Indeed, all indicators show that successive independent governments have used the chieftaincy system to buttress their hold on power, hence further alienating the chiefs from the people. Thus, project goals and objectives are not mutually co-determined.

Personnel. Another area of concern is the number of expatriate personnel employed in almost all projects initiated from the North. In the case of the teacher-education project at Bunumbu, more than sixteen UNESCO experts were employed from agricultural science to woodwork and crafts, despite the availability of internal experts. Problems of post classifications,

1. Interview with Paramount Chief Mustrapha, 5 June 1984. Paramount chiefs are traditional rulers supposed to represent the interests of their people to the government and through whom government policy is made known to the people. There are currently 147 chiefdoms in Sierra Leone, of which the chiefs are elected indirectly by 'Chiefdom Councillors', each of whom is supposed to represent nineteen taxpayers. Candidates must belong to a ruling family.

the time for processing applications and, in many cases, the lack of experience of rural living all exacerbated the personal problems.

Equipment. The improvement of teaching or farming presupposes the use of technology that is appropriate or relevant to the local situation and of resources available at low cost locally. Unfortunately, this has not been the case in most projects in Sierra Leone. Both the Bunumbu project and EIADP came with equipment that was inappropriate for its context and relied heavily on outside experts and inputs to function properly. The Instructional Resource Center at Bunumbu was equipped with a highly sophisticated video system that was hardly used because of inadequate spare parts, irregular power supply and lack of proper maintenance. Tractors brought from Europe to work on Valley Swamp rice were not suitable for the soil in Sierra Leone, hence the blades had to be constantly replaced. Also, the availability of diesel oil to run the tractors was a constant problem, as the government did not have enough foreign exchange to import oil regularly. Cheaper, less complex and more cost-effective equipment could be utilized. For example, at Bunumbu, audiovisual aids for teaching, slides, charts, films, audiotapes and cassettes can perform similar functions to closed circuit television. For printing purposes cyclostyling (mimeograph) machines are appropriate for the college and pilot schools. It appears that three decades or more of proselytizing by advocates of 'appropriate technology' made no impact on the Northern non-governmental organization agencies designing and implementing the projects. Local expertise could have been utilized in producing many of the materials as well as working on the project.

Recipient countries are not spared the vicissitudes of budgeting in international organizations. The whims and caprices of the power that finances such organizations affect projects in developing countries. For example, in the 1970s, UNDP faced liquidity problems caused largely by the refusal of Western powers to put more money into the organization. The Bunumbu Project had to stop much of its activity, which was not revived when the crisis ended. Smaller projects managed within the budget of the host country could eliminate such problems.

Training. Providing adequate and timely training for indigenous personnel is a critically important aspect of all development projects. The two projects discussed here are no exception. From the very beginning, provision was made to further train the tutors at Bunumbu. As counterparts to expatriate personnel, they went abroad for study for a year or two. Ideally, the counterparts were supposed to work with the expatriate advisers for a year or two before going for further training. On their return, the counterparts were to work with the advisers for a year or so before the advisers finally left. In practice this never happened. The counterparts generally left for study abroad as soon as the expatriate adviser arrived – usually just when a new department was being set up – and returned on the eve of the expatriate's departure. The lack of proper co-ordination was mainly responsible for the mismatch.

Bureaucracy. Both Northern and Southern non-governmental organizations face major hurdles when it comes to working together on a project. Some of the hurdles are bureaucratic in nature, which directly affects the relationship between both organizations. For example, in the case of EIADP, layer upon layer of bureaucracy was built: five top managerial positions plus a Project Management Unit, which was transformed into a Project Executive Committee (PEC) reporting to the Permanent Secretary of the Ministry of Agriculture and National Resources; a Project Advisory Committee consisting of representatives from the Ministries of Finance and Agriculture, the Bank of Sierra Leone and the Sierra Leone Marketing Board which became the overall policy-making body. In addition, two Southern non-governmental organizations were created – the Project Farmers Advisory Committee and the Project Farmers Working Committee – in an attempt to involve farmers' representatives from all the project chiefdoms. This had a serious impact on both planning and implementation of the project.

In the case of Bunumbu, it took four months to select a candidate for a post. UNESCO first selected four candidates, who were then submitted to UNDP, which in turn referred to the Ministry of Development and Economic Planning. That ministry sent the curricula vitae of the candidates to the Ministry of Education, which sent the documents to the principal of the college, who is the National Director of the project. The National Director deliberated about the candidates and made a selection. The finally selected candidates were rank-ordered and sent to the Ministry of Education, which approved or disapproved their ranking. The list was then sent through the same channels to UNESCO which made the final offer.

In consequence, there were many instances, especially in cases of high-level posts, when candidates had accepted positions with other agencies before the UNESCO offer came through. This meant that the process was repeated again and again. There were also times when jobs were offered to candidates who turned out to be medically unfit. This caused additional delay, as the next best candidate might already have been employed elsewhere.

Conclusion

In an effort to alleviate poverty and human deprivation, establish civil society and increase the GDP of developing communities, non-governmental organizations have become an integral part of the development effort. The concept of development is increasingly being questioned and expanded to include issues such as the environment, politics and the war on narcotics. At the same time that the recipients of 'development aid' have increased, there has been a significant decline in aid provided globally.

The importance of the Northern non-governmental organizations through which much aid is channelled is becoming increasingly critical. Their role has been questioned and challenged by both governments and voluntary organizations of the South. To promote collaboration between the Northern and Southern non-governmental organizations, a code of conduct has been established from both the Geneva conference (1985) and the London symposium (1987). In reality, as shown in this chapter, it takes considerable time before equity can exist between Northern and Southern non-governmental organizations in terms of collaborative operations and mutual governance.

Both types of non-governmental organizations need each other to provide assistance for sustainability and capacity-building in developing countries, and future relationships between the two kinds of non-governmental organizations may become collaborative out of necessity. The North cannot and should not develop the South without the input and active participation of Southern non-governmental organizations. On the other hand, the South needs Northern resources, both technical and financial, in the development of the South. A symbiotic relationship may be what is needed, with a healthy dose of respect for each other's ideas and feelings. As development takes time, so does the building of mutual respect, trust, transparency and collaboration between the two kinds of non-governmental organizations. Clearly, a new typology of relationships needs to be developed.

References

ACTION AID. 1993. *Task Force Report on Working with Local Institutions*. Bangalore, New India Press.

BANYA, K. 1994. The Role of Teacher Education in Education Reforms: A Case Study. In: C. Sunal. (ed.), *Teacher Education in the Caribbean and Africa*, pp. 1–8. (Points of Contract, Vol. 2.)

BRATTON, M. 1988. *Poverty, Organization and Policy: Towards a Voice for Africa's Rural Poor*. (Paper prepared for a colloquium on The Changing Nature of Third World Poverty: A Policy Perspective, Michigan State University, Michigan.)

BRINKERHOFF, D.; GARCIA-ZAMON, J. 1986. *Politics, Projects and People: Institutional Development in Haiti*. New York, Praeger Publishers.

COMMONWEALTH FOUNDATION. 1991. *Report of the First Commonwealth Nongovernmental Organization Forum*. London.

——. 1995. *Non-Governmental Organization: Guidelines for Good Policy and Practice*. London.

CRUSH, J. (ed.). 1994. *Development Discourse*. London, Routledge.

DRABEK, A. 1987. Development Alternatives: The Challenges of Non-governmental Organizations – An Overview of the Issues. In: A. Drabek (ed.), *World Development Alternatives: The Challenge for Non-governmental Organizations*, Vol. 15 (Supplement), pp. ix–xv. Washington, D.C., Bank Press.

DUBOIS, M. 1991. The Governance of the Third World: A Foucauldian Perspective on Power Relations in Development. *Alternatives*, Vol. 16, No. 1, pp. 1–30.

EDWARDS, M. 1989. The Irrelevance of Development Studies. *Third World Quarterly*, Vol. 11, No. 1, pp. 116–35.

ELLIOT, R. 1987. *Final Report Non-governmental Organizations and Africa: A Strategy Workshop*. Geneva, United Nations.

ESCOBAR, A. 1992. Imagining a Post-Development Era? Critical Thought, Development and Social Movements. *Social Text*, No. 31/32, pp. 20–56.

FAVDO (FORUM OF AFRICAN VOLUNTARY DEVELOPMENT ORGANIZATIONS). 1987. *Dakar Conference Proceedings*. Dakar, OAU.

FERGUSON, J. 1990. Feminism, Postmodernism, and the Critique of Modernity. *Cultural Critique*, Fall, pp. 33–56.

FLOWER, A. 1988. *Non-governmental Organization in Africa: Achieving Comparative Advantage in Micro-development*. Brighton Institute of Development Studies, University of Sussex. (Discussion paper 249.)

GOETZ, J. 1991. *Gender and International Relations*. Bloomington, Ind., Indiana University Press.
GRISCHOW, J. 1993. *Creating Underdevelopment in the Northern Territories of the Gold Coast: The Damonon-governmental Organization Groundnut Scheme (1947–1957)*. (Paper presented at the Canadian Association of African Studies Conference, Toronto, May.)
HYDEN, G. 1991. Creating an Enabling Environment: A Long-term Perspective Study on Sub-Saharan Africa. *Institutional and Socio-political Issues*, Vol. 3, pp. 75–80. (World Bank Background Papers.)
JAYCOX, E. 1993. *Capacity Building: The Missing Link in African Development*. (Address to the African-American Institution Conference on African Capacity Building: Effective and Enduring Partnerships, Reston, Virginia, 20 May; mimeo.)
JOHNSON, D. 1990. Constructing the Periphery in Modern Global Politics. In: C. Murphy and R. Tooze (eds.), *The New International Political Economy*. Boulder, Colo., Lynne Rienner.
JOHNSTON, B. 1991. The World Food Equation: Interrelations among Development, Employment and Food. *Journal of Economic Literature*, Vol. 22, pp. 531–74.
JONES, R. 1993. *Choosing Partnership: 'The Evolution of the Katalysis Model'*. Stockton, Calif., Katalysis North/South Development Partnerships.
LAMB, D. 1987. *The Africans*. New York, Random House.
LEACH, M. 1994. *Models of Inter-organizational Collaboration in Development*. Boston, Institute for Development Research.
MANZO, K. 1991. Modernist Discourse and the Crisis of Development Theory. *Studies in Comparative International Development*, Vol. 26, No. 2, pp. 3–36.
MATHUR, G. 1989. The Current Impasse in Development Thinking: The Metaphysics of Power. *Alternatives*, Vol. 14, pp. 463–79.
NINDI, B. 1990. Experts, Donors, Ruling Elites and the African Poor: Expert Planning, Policy Formulation and Implementation – A Critique. *Journal of Eastern African Research and Development*, Vol. 20, pp. 41–67.
OECD. 1986. *Development Co-operation*. Paris, OECD.
PARPART, J.; MARCHAND, M. 1995. Exploding the Canon: An Introduction/Conclusion. In: M. Marchand and J. Parpart (eds.), *Feminism/Postmodernism/Development*. London, Routledge.
PIETERSE, J. N. 1992. Emancipations Modern and Post Modern. *Development and Change*, Vol. 23, No. 3, pp. 5–41.
ROE, E. 1991. Development Narratives, Or Making the Best of Blueprint Development. *World Development*, Vol. 19, No. 4, pp. 287–300.

SHULTZ, G. 1984. Foreign Aid and U.S. National Interests. In: *Realism, Strength, Negotiation: Key Foreign Policy Statements of the Reagan Administration.* Washington, D.C., Department of State, Bureau of Public Affairs.

TANDON, R. 1989. *Non-governmental Organization – Government Relations: Westview A Source of Life or a Kiss of Death?* New Delhi, Society for Participatory Research in Asia (PRIA).

UNDP. 1993. *Human Development Report.* New York, Oxford University Press.

WANGOOLA, P. (ed.). 1987. *Consultation Workshops on AALAE Networks as an Instrument to Strengthen the Adult Education Movement: Theory, Process, and Programme.* Nairobi, AALAE.

WORLD BANK. 1988a. *Operational Manual Statement: Collaboration with Non-governmental Organizations.* Washington, D.C., World Bank (No. 5.30).

——. 1988b. *World Development Report.* Washington, D.C., World Bank.

——. 1989. *Sub-Saharan Africa: From Crisis to Sustainable Growth.* Washington, D.C., World Bank.

——. 1996. *Human Development Atlas.* Washington, D.C., World Bank.

WORLD SUMMIT FOR SOCIAL DEVELOPMENT (Copenhagen, 6–12 March 1995). 1995. *The Copenhagen Declaration and Programme of Action.* New York, United Nations.

Part Three.
New directions for aid practice: constraints and opportunities

Aid co-ordination through the other end of the telescope
Henry Kaluba and Peter Williams

This chapter considers whether, in the education sector, developing countries collectively have been, are, or might be the co-ordinators of education assistance flows and policies. In spite of an increased interest in aid co-ordination generally, rather little seems to have been written about this particular aspect. The chapter is basically exploratory in intent, designed to raise questions and provoke a wider discussion.

Aid co-ordination is a goal ostensibly commanding wide support in international development circles, implicitly representing an orderly and planned approach to the supply and use of external resources for development, and minimization of wasteful duplication, competition and conflict. A more effective application of domestic and foreign resources to development purposes should result. In conditions of international resource shortage, aid co-ordination is seen as one avenue to greater aid-effectiveness and improved resource use.

In practice, of course, aid co-ordination frequently proves not to fulfil the hopes placed in it. Conflicts and resistances are inevitably experienced in attempts to bring it about. The role of 'co-ordinator' is surely more attractive than that of 'the co-ordinated', with all the inferences of discipline and self-restraint that are implied by adherence to agreed sets of rules and consultative procedures. It may thus be more realistic to look on co-ordination as a guiding star than to regard it as a destination likely to be attained, and to recognize the many pressures that tempt individual donors and recipient-government agencies to step outside agreed guidelines. It is well to acknowledge, too, that developing countries will always be wary of international funding and technical-assistance agencies 'ganging up' and – seeking safety in numbers – making pronouncements in their collective name that would be construed as blatant and unacceptable interference if uttered by just one of them. Moreover, co-ordination imposes burdens on both donor and recipient. It can be laborious and time-consuming to gather and disseminate information, to consult and seek consensus, to organize meetings and distribute agendas and records.

Co-ordination of external assistance to the education sector raises many of the same issues as co-ordination in general. However, education is in some respects a rather special case, as Williams (1995, pp. 12–13) has pointed out in relation to Namibia. For several reasons, the education sector is prone to attract a large number of international funding and technical-assistance agencies. One of these is the 'cultural diplomacy' dimension in much educational co-operation, where a donor's desire to promote the study in recipient-country schools of the donor-country's language or culture, or the politically motivated offer of a scholarship as a tangible outcome of a head of state's visit abroad, become incorporated into a bilateral programme of educational assistance. Another factor is that education provides, for example at individual school level, scope for mini-projects that even the smallest agency can afford to sponsor. The plethora of non-governmental organizations with interests in education and training constitutes a third factor leading to a proliferation of donors.

Educational co-operation is technical-assistance-intensive. This compounds the problem of multiple donors, by spawning a wide variety of remuneration packages and different terms of service for personnel, and an array of scholarship offers to which different conditions are attached. The involvement in the education sector of major semi-autonomous institutions (universities, colleges), each operating its own bilateral links and exchange programmes with partner institutions and agencies abroad, can create special difficulties. It greatly complicates the task of those charged with compiling inventories of assistance, and also poses problems for the higher-education authorities responsible for funding higher-education institutions, given that even the most attractive exchange agreement is likely to require counterpart local cost contributions from the developing-country partner.

The education sector is also particularly subject to boundary disputes. The most notable of these is the demarcation line between education and training, and whether vocational training in formal education institutions is the responsibility of, and accounted for under, Education or the sector for which the training is provided, e.g. Agriculture or Health. The boundary between education assistance and cultural co-operation, alluded to above, is another grey area. Overlapping spheres of interest are also carried over into the field of multilateral co-operation where UNESCO, UNICEF and the International Labour Organization (ILO) are often in danger of stepping on each other's toes: and in bilateral co-operation where some kind of understanding is needed between the aid agency and the cultural relations body; in the British case, as an example, between DFID and the British Council.

Co-ordination mechanisms

At one level aid co-ordination can be viewed as a global enterprise among funding and technical-assistance agencies, of the kind attempted by DAC or in the shape of world campaigns providing a framework within which many major bilateral and multilateral agencies agree to apply their efforts. Aid co-ordination through OECD has taken various forms. The DAC annual review of development-assistance programmes and policies generates information which makes possible monitoring of the scale of the international effort, and highlights comparisons and contrasts between different agencies' programmes. OECD's consultative mechanisms tend to promote closer alignment of agency policies and procedures, and their commitment to certain priorities, including in recent years the adoption of development targets, such as the achievement of universal primary education by 2015. OECD also generates self-regulation agreements on subjects such as the tying of aid or the mixing of aid and trade.

The best example in education of a co-ordinated world campaign involving the participation of many agencies is perhaps the Education for All initiative, launched at Jomtien in 1990.

Second, at subglobal level there are regional co-ordination mechanisms for agency co-ordination. A prime example is the European Union, which has an interest in alignment of the assistance policies of its member states. The European Union's policy paper on education assistance (Commission of the European Communities, 1994) forms part of a broader European Union thrust, Horizon 2000, to co-ordinate development co-operation policies in Europe.

Third, aid co-ordination may also have a national focus or intent. Support may be mobilized for a national development programme or plan, or sometimes even for a single, particularly large, project. Co-ordinated efforts may involve the pledging of financial support through consortia and consultative groups established for the purpose, often with World Bank leadership, or through the round tables convened by UNDP (Barry, 1988). Normally, such exercises have been multisectoral, but there have been consultative meetings convened specifically in support of the education sector: for example the Donors' Consultative Meeting held to consider Mauritius' Master Plan for Education in November 1991 (Mauritius, 1991, 1992) or the high-level meeting convened at UNESCO in July under the United Nations Special Initiative on Africa to consider the Education Sector Strategy of Mozambique (United Nations Special Initiative on Africa, 1997). Sometimes an individual institution, such as a university, has drawn up its own development plan and invited a group of potential donors to examine it at a specially convened meeting. Examples include the 1987 donors' conference at Makerere University, Uganda, to mobilize support for the rehabilitation of the university or the November 1994 consultative conference at the University of Namibia which preceded the publication of the university's first five-year development plan (University of Namibia, 1995).

However, a large part of national-level co-ordination activity involves no separate pledging event, but is rather an ongoing consultative mechanism and process in the capital city of the recipient, providing a framework for information exchange, consultation and dialogue on needs, resources and plans with a view to shaping the flow of external assistance and its utilization. There are three distinct but related functions of such co-ordination:

- To secure the articulation of aid resources with the development plans and priorities of the recipient country, and to integrate the application of domestic and external resources in national priority programmes. Here the co-ordination is essentially of external assistance with domestic effort, in support of the recipient country's own goals and strategies.
- To standardize technical specifications (e.g. of vehicles and equipment), documentation and procedures arising from the existence of a multiplicity of donors, so as to economize on the efforts needed to supply, receive and apply external assistance.
- To secure a rational division of labour among agencies so as to avoid duplication and overlap; and as far as possible to ensure that each agency specializes in areas where it has comparative advantage.

Mechanisms which primarily serve and are serviced by donor agencies should be distinguished from those that involve and serve recipients. In some countries the co-ordination machinery was initially set up as a kind of donors' club whose meetings the recipient country could only attend by invitation. But now one is seeing a shift towards fuller recipient-government participation in the co-ordination process. In an increasing number of instances, the national government either convenes the assistance forum itself, or establishes a structure, parallel to the donors' club, that meets under its own chairmanship. There is widespread agreement that the lead in aid co-ordination properly belongs to the recipient government.

As a back-up and base for this, a number of countries are also elaborating their own machinery within government for handling external assistance and for integrating it more effectively into the development process. This, it should be noted, poses challenges of internal co-ordination – both intra-ministry and interministerial – to tax the ingenuity of even the ablest specialist in organization and management of government machinery.

There is growing experience of and interest in aid co-ordination at the national level. Several African countries have been actively grappling with the issue and have recently been the focus of analysis and commentary, most of it by outsiders. The Association for the Development of Education in Africa (ADEA) has published studies of Namibia (Williams, 1995) and Ghana (Sawyerr, 1997). The International Working Group on Education (IWGE), in which most of the principal official aid agencies and several foundations participate, has considered aid co-ordination on a number of occasions in the past (see for example Sack, 1995) and more recently commissioned a study on the United Republic of Tanzania (Buchert, 1997). The present volume contains important companion pieces on the United Republic of Tanzania (Buchert), Botswana and Namibia (Kann) and South Africa (King).

Co-ordination between developing countries

The discussion so far in this chapter, and in much international discourse, has focused mainly on co-ordination among donors, and on co-ordination of bilateral and multilateral assistance by individual recipient governments.

But there may also be potential for co-ordination and collaboration among the users of assistance. Is there scope for developing countries to get a better deal out of the donors and to use aid more effectively by working together?

A number of avenues for developing-country co-operation suggest themselves: see for example the United Nations review of the state of South–South co-operation with its index of co-operation organizations (United Nations, 1995). One possibility is the orchestration of effort through a mechanism like the Group of 77 (which now has over 130 members), established in 1964 and relating chiefly to UNCTAD. It aims to provide the means for the developing world to articulate and enhance its joint negotiating capacity on major economic issues in the United Nations system and to promote economic and technical co-operation among developing countries. Of possible relevance, too, is the South Centre, established in 1990 to follow up the work of the South Commission and under whose auspices the Group of Fifteen heads of state meets each year. At its first summit in June 1990 the heads of state agreed to explore the setting up of an advisory group to assist developing countries in their dealings with multilateral financial institutions and to give advice on the possible impact of conditionalities imposed by such institutions. The focus of both these organizations is the broad area of trade and economic relations, rather than narrower specialized sectoral concerns.

A second phenomenon is collective developing-country organization and response in relation to particular programmes or agencies. A major example is the African, Caribbean, Pacific (ACP) group of countries in relation to the Lomé Convention and the associated EDF of the European Union. Here, through the existence of formal machinery for consultation, review and negotiation, the ACP states have succeeded on occasion, as in the renegotiation of the Financial Protocol at Cannes in June 1995, in securing a larger commitment of funds than the industrialized countries originally intended. However, they appear to have made less progress in the simplification and streamlining of EDF procedures, or in improving the rather abysmal disbursement rate of committed EDF funds. In this case the partnership has appeared to be unequal and the negotiating position of developing countries to have been relatively weak. Possible explanations include a lack of collective identity of interest between the many individual developing countries, and weaknesses in the ACP Secretariat in Brussels.

It may be doubted whether developing countries have been much more successful in affecting the policies or sector analyses of major agencies such as the World Bank. While World Bank policies are continually shifting in response to changing circumstances and to the realities encountered in programme and project implementation, these shifts have not obviously owed much to formal collective consultation processes with representatives of developing countries. Girdwood (1995), in her review of the processes leading to the production of the World Bank's higher education paper (eventually issued under the rubric of a 'best practice' review rather than the 'policy paper' that had been heralded), raises doubts about the efficacy in that instance of the regional consultation seminars to canvass opinion. In her words (p. 55):

The real test of a consultation exercise is the manner in which discussions are recorded and then incorporated into subsequent versions of the text. Despite the assertion in the higher education paper's introduction that the consultative process had 'proved a valuable channel for sharing information and receiving constructive feedback to guide the study', little record is available of the extent to which this feedback was indeed utilized.

One factor impeding the ability of developing countries to get their act together and to strengthen their own negotiating position is the difficulty of gaining access to the experience of other countries. The texts of assistance agreements, with the terms and conditions they contain and the background documentation underpinning them, are not generally public documents. The content of agreements with donors may even be concealed from affected nationals of the recipient country. To cite an example, one of the present authors learned at first hand in a West African country of a case where the university authorities were party to a secret agreement with the World Bank about implementation of target staffing ratios that had not been disclosed to faculty and department heads of the institution. The call for transparency and accountability in public affairs, for which so many of the more affluent countries are nowadays wont to press, does not generally appear to extend to a demand that developing-country governments publish the full details of the terms and conditions of assistance agreements into which they have entered!

In the context of this chapter, the confidential status of so many reports, documents and agreements in the co-operation field does not only have an adverse impact on internal democratic debate and accountability. It may also weaken the bargaining position of recipients of assistance in their dealings with donors and may limit the transfer of experience more generally. First, without an accessible body of 'case law', country A is impeded from calling in evidence the concessions that have been made to country B as a precedent for a more favourable deal in its own negotiations with the same agency. Second, opportunities for learning 'best practice' lessons and for adapting others' experience to one's own parallel situation are diminished.

The hand of developing countries in negotiations could be strengthened if two conditions were met. First, developing countries could benefit from having a forum for the exchange of views and comparison of experiences of aid negotiation both in general and with particular agencies. Perhaps international agencies and regional bodies could usefully orchestrate such exchanges of experience and build up a bank of 'case law' on which developing member countries could draw to support their negotiating position. This activity could usefully be supplemented by training programmes for education ministry staff in aid-negotiation procedures. The authors are aware of one such initiative jointly undertaken by the Commonwealth Secretariat and Caribbean countries, which has included two workshops, with the intention that the associated materials may be issued as a resource book.

Second, documentation must be made more accessible. This requires an energetic approach by the international community to the lifting of confidentiality restrictions on documentation emanating from assistance agencies. This should cover the content of aid agreements including the conditions agreed, as well as background information and appraisals supporting the agreement. Progress does of course presuppose greater openness on the part of developing-country governments as well as of assistance agencies: it should not be assumed that donor attitudes and requirements are the only, or invariably the principal, obstacle to transparency.

Experience drawn from Commonwealth education co-operation also suggests that developing countries would put themselves at greater advantage if they consulted together and orchestrated their efforts more effectively in advance of international conferences and negotiations. In the Commonwealth, this is partly a matter of making early contacts and doing the necessary prior 'homework' on agenda topics for forthcoming Commonwealth meetings. Unfortunately there are obstacles in the shape of communications problems, given that – unlike the position at UNESCO – Commonwealth countries do not maintain permanent delegations at the Commonwealth Secretariat headquarters in London. Their ministries of education also suffer a shortage of staff with specialist knowledge of Commonwealth programmes of education co-operation, and a lack of time and capacity to organize the necessary actions. Their wealthier Commonwealth partners, on the other hand, have usually prepared detailed national briefs and have frequently agreed common positions among themselves before proposals are discussed in Commonwealth forums, especially for those initiatives which involve expenditure of more funds. Such consultation is understandable in a situation where present funding formulae result in Australia, Canada and the United Kingdom carrying the lion's share of the cost of Commonwealth collective programmes and enterprises.

This in turn suggests that exerting leverage on developed-country funds is more than a matter of better consultative procedures. Developing countries must also be prepared to commit resources of their own to international programmes and common endeavours, if they want a stronger voice in shaping them. That is something they have been slow to do in the case of important Commonwealth institutions for education co-operation, such as the Commonwealth Scholarship and Fellowship Plan and the Commonwealth of Learning.

Association for the Development of Education in Africa: a new model

ADEA is an informal consortium of international, national and private donor agencies launched in 1988, originally as the Donors to African Education (DAE). It aims to provide a forum for policy dialogue, consultation and joint planning between ministries of education and training in sub-Saharan Africa and agencies, as well as among international funding and technical-assistance agencies themselves (Woodhall et al., 1994). The evolution of ADEA has been rapid, dynamic and sensitive to the principles and objectives for which it was established. It has created a framework within which collaboration among agencies has increased, and more development partners have come forward to join ADEA in recent years. This reflects increasing confidence in ADEA's neutrality and focus.

Although there was initially some criticism of ADEA as being primarily a 'Donors' Club' (Woodhall et al., 1994), the organization can claim to be fulfilling its original purpose by providing opportunities for high-level dialogue and consultation between African ministers and agencies on current programme activities, resource allocation and emerging issues in development aid to education. The forum has given ADEA members greater insight into problems facing donors and recipients. The ADEA biennial conferences are forums in which the parties exchange views openly; they serve as valuable information-sharing platforms.

In addition, ADEA has helped to forge links between African ministers themselves and to raise their awareness of issues and problems of education development in neighbouring countries, and of the initiatives being undertaken to address them. The Bureau of African Ministers of Education, for example, has emerged as a useful consultative structure within ADEA.

The substantive work of ADEA is conducted mainly through its eleven working groups which focus on specific areas of education development. Where the working groups are regularly convened and properly managed, they can assist member countries to focus more sharply on issues and to channel development aid to areas of priority need. The ADEA Working Group on the Teaching Profession (WGTP), the one with which the authors are personally most familiar, has established annual meetings of Principal Secretaries of Education in eight Southern African Development Community (SADC) countries to act as a consultative and decision-making body on regional teacher-management and support issues and action plans. The structure has potential to tackle broader issues such as aid co-ordination, thus helping to avoid wasteful use of aid resources on uncoordinated project activities.

The ADEA system enables agencies to participate in the programme while maintaining their own separate bilateral aid arrangements uninterrupted, which makes it an attractive and non-threatening co-ordination framework from the agency point of view. Lessons learned through their participation in ADEA activities may well have inspired some donors to provide additional resources to particular causes in education. But any initial hopes that substantially greater resources overall might be mobilized for African education have not so far been realized.

From a recipient standpoint, the same benefits of wider insights and understanding have been gained, but it is not clear that ADEA's creation has either brought African countries greater control over aid procurement and deployment or has enabled them to engage much more effectively in collective bargaining about amounts and conditions of education aid. The jury is still out on whether or not ADEA's existence will lead to any marked improvement in the mechanisms for seeking, recording and accounting for aid to education, and whether more fundamentally it can redress some of the inequalities in donor–recipient relationships.

Certainly one might hope that ADEA will be able to spread good practice among developing countries themselves. Responsibility for articulating aid resources with national development priorities and for securing a more rational division of labour among agencies at country level are matters within the responsibility of developing-country governments. They would surely benefit from the good offices of a catalyst and intermediary body in helping them to capitalize on the extensive, but largely uncharted, experience they have had in such areas.

Conclusion

This chapter has reviewed a number of developments in the co-ordination of aid to education. It is a subject that is attracting greater interest as part of a more general recognition of the need to make more effective use of scarce resources for education development. The community of professionals engaged in improving the processes of education co-operation has certainly developed its understanding of co-ordination potential and constraints, and there have been useful institutional developments, like the creation of ADEA, which could hopefully give developing countries a greater say in managing aid flows to the education sector. The principle that recipients must take the lead, and must develop and strengthen their capacity to manage the process of requesting, negotiating and applying external resources, commands wide assent.

Yet the overall impression one is left with is that co-ordination efforts have so far not served to increase developing-country influence on the process at all significantly, and that agency policies and practices have not been greatly affected by dialogue with developing countries. For many agencies it is the dialogue within DAC, at the World Bank or in the councils of the European Union that exerts the major co-ordinating impact on their aid behaviour.

The tensions and constraints inherent in any attempt at co-ordinating education assistance are deep-seated and one cannot be complacent about the likelihood of finding ideal solutions. The developing countries least able to co-ordinate external assistance are often the most needy ones and, as King has shown in this book, even a country such as South Africa which started out with a considerable capacity for policy formulation and a determination to call the tune in directing aid to its own purposes in a closely regulated way has found itself yielding a significant part of the initiative to agencies.

Some suggestions have been put forward for strengthening the hand of receiving countries in collective efforts to negotiate for, and direct, assistance to the education sector. But experience confirms that there are no short cuts in this area. For a long time to come, the world may have to be satisfied with travelling hopefully towards best practice in this area, rather than with arriving.

References

BARRY, A. J. 1988. *Aid Co-ordination and Aid Effectiveness: A Review of Country and Regional Experience.* Paris, OECD Development Centre.

BUCHERT, L. 1997. *Education Policy Formulation in Tanzania: Co-ordination between the Government and International Aid Agencies. A Report from the IWGE.* Paris, UNESCO/International Institute for Educational Planning.

COMMISSION OF THE EUROPEAN COMMUNITIES. 1994. *Co-ordination between the Community and the Member States on Education and Training Schemes in Developing Countries.* Brussels, CEC. (Doc. COM(94) 399 final.)

GIRDWOOD, A. 1995. Shaping the World Bank's Higher Education Paper: Dialogue, Consultation and Conditionality. In: L. Buchert and K. King (eds.), *Learning from Experience: Policy and Practice in Aid to Higher Education*, pp. 41–74. The Hague, Centre for the Study of Education in Developing Countries (CESO). (CESO Paperback, 24.)

MAURITIUS. Ministry of Education, Arts and Culture. 1991. *Education Master Plan for the Year 2000.* Mauritius, Ministry of Education Arts and Culture.

——. Ministry of Education and Science/UNDP/UNESCO. 1992. *Donors' Consultative Meeting on the Master Plan for Education 1991–2000, Mauritius, Paris, 5–6 November 1991. Report.*

SACK, R. 1995. *Donor Co-ordination at the Country Level: Experience from an 'Upstream' Education Policy Analysis Project and Conceptual Explorations.* Paris, UNESCO. (BER-95/WS/3.)

SAWYERR, H. 1997. *Country-led Aid Co-ordination in Ghana.* Paris, ADEA.

UNITED NATIONS. 1995. *State of South–South Co-operation: Statistical Pocket Book and Index of Co-operation Organizations.* New York/Geneva, United Nations.

UNITED NATIONS SPECIAL INITIATIVE ON AFRICA. 1997. *High-level Meeting on the Education Sector Strategy, Mozambique, 7–8 July 1997: Executive Summary.* (Mimeo.)

UNIVERSITY OF NAMIBIA. 1995. *University of Namibia: First Five-year Development Plan, 1995-1999.* Windhoek, University of Namibia.

WILLIAMS, P. 1995. *Government's Co-ordination of Aid to Education: The Case of Namibia.* Paris, ADEA.

WOODHALL, M.; KWAPONG, A.; TROWBRIDGE, I. 1994. *Evaluation of Donors to African Education.* Paris, DAE.

Co-ordination of aid to education at the country level: some experiences and lessons from the United Republic of Tanzania in the 1990s
Lene Buchert[1]

Context

One of the central issues in the discussion of international development co-operation and aid to education in the 1990s is how to co-ordinate the efforts of all actors. The concept of co-ordination is far from clearly defined and the nature of co-ordination may differ at different times and in different contexts. It may include all or part of: consultation and exchange of information; common understanding of policy and programme objectives and priorities; policy and sector analysis at the country level; co-operation in project and programme design and execution; and co-operation in policy formulation (for a useful conceptual exploration, see Sack, 1995, pp. 15–21). Co-ordination may be undertaken in several major ways: by all or some of the international funding and technical-assistance agencies in a given country; by all or some of the international funding and technical-assistance agencies led by the government of the country in question; or by all or some of the international funding and technical-assistance agencies in co-operation with the government but predominantly directed by the agencies.

---

1. This chapter has been written in a personal capacity and does not necessarily express the views of UNESCO.

Co-ordination of aid to education at the country level: some experiences and lessons from the United Republic of Tanzania in the 1990s
Lene Buchert

Nature and implications of co-ordination

The very nature of co-ordination is highly political. One of the necessary preconditions for the occurrence of the 'ideal' form of co-ordination as understood in the 1990s, namely government-led co-ordination of international funding and technical-assistance agencies within the framework of nationally determined policies, would be overcoming the well-known political and economic self-interests of the aid providers in the North, which have led to a net flow of resources from rather than into the developing world (see, for example, Riddell, 1987). Establishing partnerships and consistency in educational development in order to increase the efficiency and effectiveness of international aid to education would also be important. As stated in both the World Declaration on Education for All and the Framework for Action to Meet Basic Learning Needs, partnership in education must include all actors, such as the national governments in the South, international funding and technical-assistance agencies, administrators and other education personnel, non-government organizations, religious and other civil society organizations, the business community and other private communities, and parents, students, teachers and their corresponding associations (World Conference on Education for All, 1990). Some technical-assistance agencies, for example the Norwegian Agency for Development Co-operation (NORAD) and the Swedish International Development Co-operation Agency (Sida), now emphasize transparent contractual arrangements between two equal government partners as a way to improve the mutual responsibility and accountability for development co-operation and to decrease the level of dependency even in an unequal global context (DAE, 1996, p. 1; Karlsson, 1997; see also Wolgemuth's contribution in this book).

Such anticipated equal partnership demands co-ordination in terms of articulation of aid flows with a country's development programme. As pointed out by Williams (1995, p. iv), 'In one sense, coordination focuses on the goal of articulating aid with the development plans and priorities of recipient countries, in such a way that it enhances the capacity of the receivers to pursue successfully their own freely chosen goals.' At least three implications, which will be discussed in this chapter, follow from this: first, that aid providers are willing to articulate their aid efforts with the development plans and priorities of recipient countries; second, that development plans have been formulated and priorities set by the recipient country; and third, that recipients have the capacity to manage aid flows, co-ordinate their providers and deliberately pursue their own goals.

Underlying the listed implications are, therefore, a range of issues which partly concern the control of aid, partly the coherence in thinking on development issues and priorities among recipients and providers, and partly the existence of capacity, procedures and mechanisms that would allow for aid co-ordination to take place to the satisfaction of both recipients and providers. As the underlying objectives of aid provision are multiple, often determined by the different kinds of organizations involved, including international funding organizations, international and national technical-assistance agencies, profit and non-profit non-governmental organizations, and humanitarian and church organizations, the aid scenario and the options for co-ordination differ from one country to the next. The prospects for successful co-ordination must, therefore, be seen in relation to multiple, not always overt, factors and actors in a given country context.

Focus of analysis

Aid co-ordination has been analysed at different levels: some analyses have been concerned with specific projects (for example, Magnen, 1994; Sack, 1995), others with governments in specific countries (for example, Williams, 1995; Sawyerr, 1997) and yet others with comparative country experiences (for example, Panday and Williams, 1990). The issue has also been analysed as part of formulating education policies (for example, DAE, 1996). This chapter supplements the already existing perspectives by focusing on what has been seen by some authors as a deficiency in our knowledge (see, for example, King, 1992), namely the extent to which policy reform in the South has been 'donor-induced'. This issue is analysed in the following in the context of recent formulation of education policies and actual practice in the Tanzanian education sector.

The chapter is based on a wider study undertaken for the IWGE during 1996 (Buchert, 1997), which concentrated on the following major areas: (1) whether and how an interaction between the Tanzanian Government and the international agencies took place in the recent formulation of selected Tanzanian education policy papers; (2) whether and how the Tanzanian Government and international agencies, on the one hand, and the international agencies, on the other, co-operated in educational prac-

Co-ordination of aid to education at the country level: some experiences and lessons from the United Republic of Tanzania in the 1990s
Lene Buchert

tice; and (3) implications for future co-ordination of work in the education sector in the United Republic of Tanzania. The study was based on extensive document analysis, interviews with key government and agency officials at headquarters and field levels, and observations from international meetings of government and agency officials. The data collection was completed in August 1996.

The chapter addresses the three study areas mentioned above and is concerned with the mentioned implications concerning articulation of aid flows with a country's development programme. It is, in particular, concerned with three matters: the relative coherence in thinking concerning broader development and education issues and concerning education priorities among the government and the international agencies in the United Republic of Tanzania; agency willingness to be co-ordinated; and government capacity to co-ordinate. While the outcomes of the study reflect the Tanzanian reality in mid-1996 and while the situation in the country has already altered, there seem to be generalized lessons to consider in other country contexts.

Government and agency interaction

As is well known, numerous international government and also non-government agencies of various kinds have both supported and directed national development efforts in the United Republic of Tanzania at different times. More recently, as in other countries in Africa, the international financial agencies have – since the government agreement with IMF in 1986 – continued to play an important role in the formulation of the macro-economic policies. An increasing number of agencies have also made their impact on the education sector in the wake of seriously deteriorating conditions in the 1980s.

In the 1990s, the most influential international funding and technical-assistance agencies measured in terms of monetary inputs to the Tanzanian education sector are Danish International Development Assistance (Danida), the European Union, NORAD and the World Bank (each contributing in the range of an estimated US$50–70 million). They are followed by DFID, the General Directorate for International Co-operation of the Netherlands (DGIS), the German Organization for Technical Co-operation (GTZ), Irish Aid and Sida (estimated at US$15–20 million) (for full details, see Buchert, 1997).

The relative impact of the international agencies seems not to be dominant in the government education budget. Government recurrent expenditures on education are still by far higher than the inflows from international aid agencies which have mostly financed (the larger proportion of) the development budget – although the latter seems to have increased somewhat proportionately during the mid-1980s to 1990s (Mukyanuzi, 1996; Samoff and Sumra, 1994). A comparative analysis of government and agency investment in the education subsectors seems to indicate that the government has persistently emphasized the primary education subsector, whereas the larger part of project support by external agencies has been channelled into the higher and tertiary education and technical and vocational education subsectors. There are indications, however, that a larger part of planned project funding will be allocated to the primary education subsector during the 1990s, although a full picture could not be established at the time of this research (Buchert, 1997).

Co-ordination within the education sector

In the United Republic of Tanzania, co-ordination of educational efforts has, so far, been relatively weak in terms of both systematic agency–government interaction and interagency interaction. The issues of control of aid inflows and co-ordination of the many external actors in the development process are, however, of central concern to the government which was installed after the election in October 1995. They have also been pushed along by some of the agencies working in the education sector in the United Republic of Tanzania. There are, therefore, signs of change in terms of increased interaction between government and agencies. Increased government interest in co-ordinating the inputs of the international funding and technical-assistance agencies is slowly appearing in new agency practices, including the development of education sector programmes, whereas agency pressure was more apparent in the recent policy formulation processes which will be analysed below.

Until very recently, the nature of co-ordination of education sector work in the United Republic of Tanzania was largely limited to interagency information sharing and dialogue at regular (every two months) meetings, held since 1992. Government representatives have been invited to these meetings when considered relevant for the discussions. Little co-

Co-ordination of aid to education at the country level: some experiences and lessons from the United Republic of Tanzania in the 1990s
Lene Buchert

ordination has taken place of the numerous education projects in terms of both co-financing and/or implementation of the full project cycle. There has, however, been some co-operation concerning one or more elements of the project cycle among a number of agencies, especially in projects initiated by Irish Aid. Signs of more substantial co-ordination of subsector work between the government and some of the agencies appeared in late 1996 when Danida and DGIS began to co-ordinate their work in primary education in close interaction with the Ministry of Education and Culture (MOEC). This work is expected to be supported by other agencies, in particular Irish Aid, UNICEF and the Ministry for Foreign Affairs of Finland.

As a likely result of the lack (until quite recently) of overall co-ordination of education sector work by the Tanzanian Government and of fluidity in the responsibility of different ministries for different subsectors of education, agencies have negotiated projects through a range of different ministerial entry points and have been able to set their own agenda in terms of both project content and location. A typical example is that multinational funding organizations, such as the World Bank and the European Union, have negotiated chiefly with the Ministry of Finance and Ministry of Planning while having the substance matter of the individual project approved by the 'line' (functional) ministry, i.e. MOEC or Ministry of Science, Technology and Higher Education. The national technical assistance-agencies have, on the other hand, negotiated directly with MOEC (for example, Irish Aid) or, depending on the project, with a number of ministries, such as MOEC, the Prime Minister's Office and the Ministry of Local Government (for example, Sida). Some of the agencies have deliberately bypassed MOEC because of perceived higher efficiency in other ministries.

A more long-term solution to the issue of interministerial responsibility for education is to result from the work on the Civil Service Reform. Meanwhile, an education sector committee was set up within MOEC in autumn 1996 with six months' support from the European Union. Based on the work areas defined in its original Terms of Reference, the committee was primarily a 'think tank' on education policies and strategies liaising with other ministries and institutions on education matters. With redefined Terms, this committee could become the central entry point for all education sector work.

Co-ordination of policy development

During the 1990s, in addition to information-sharing and project work, some agencies have actively supported education and wider social sector policy formulation, in particular Danida and the World Bank. Others have had a direct impact on specific education policy areas and subsector policies, for example the formulation of a textbook policy (Sida) and a strategy for vocational education and training (Danida and Sida). A number of agencies have also played a critical role in somewhat controversial discussions between the World Bank and national technical-assistance agencies concerning the content and direction for education policy development and implementation.

Tanzanian Government officials considered it to be appropriate to include agency officials in policy development because of, as one official put it, 'their rich knowledge of the education situation in the United Republic of Tanzania and elsewhere'. The officials were, however, as appears below, highly concerned about losing power over the agenda. Agency officials, on the other hand, saw a need for active agency involvement in policy development because of what they considered to be a wide vacuum in local policy development both for education specifically and for the wider development process, and because of considerable scepticism concerning local capacity in policy development. The established co-ordination of policy thinking, and policies will be discussed in the following with particular reference to three selected policy documents: *Education and Training Policy* (United Republic of Tanzania, 1995); *Primary Education. Master Plan. 'A Framework'* (Government of Tanzania, 1995); and *Social Sector Strategy* (United Republic of Tanzania, n.d.).

While it is always difficult, in particular retrospectively, to isolate the relative impact of one actor over another, it is possible to identify trends in the thinking of individual actors and to see whether priorities, key themes and underlying understandings are congruent. In the case of concomitant change of thinking of the government and one or more of the agencies, in particular when the agency(ies) in question has(have) been directly involved in government policy development, it can be asked whether the policy documents express new nationally owned policies which can serve as frameworks for future work because of widespread support, whether they express the priorities and agenda of the agency(ies) involved in policy formulation or whether they are nationally owned policies which overlap in priorities and agenda with the agencies involved in the formulation process.

Recent policy development: considerations of ownership and process

Tanzanian Government thinking on education has been expressed in a number of documents since *Education for Self-Reliance* (1967), many of which have been issued after the onset of the economic crisis in the late 1970s. Present official government policy appears in *Education and Training Policy*. Of the documents produced in the 1990s, Danida funded the production of *The Tanzania Education System for the 21st Century* (United Republic of Tanzania, 1993), *Education and Training Policy* and *Primary Education. Master Plan. 'A Framework'*. The new education policy document was produced simultaneously with the production of the *Social Sector Strategy*. The latter was closely related to the *Tanzanian Social Sector Review* produced by the World Bank and funded by JICA (World Bank, 1995).

With respect to the agencies involved in education sector work in the United Republic of Tanzania, most, if not all, have recently formulated aid policy statements and many also have formulated policies on education (Buchert, 1995a). There is a high degree of convergence in the thinking across the agencies, including concerns for poverty alleviation, social sector development and support for basic education. Of the critical differences that remain, it was the relative emphasis on supply- or demand-driven approaches to education as well as the relative understanding, interpretation and emphasis on capacity-building, partnership and ownership which, as will appear below, determined the space for co-operation and co-ordination among the agencies in the United Republic of Tanzania (see also Buchert, 1995b).

Agency rather than government steering and closed rather than open processes

There were critical differences in the perception of the 1995 documents, i.e. *Education and Training Policy, Primary Education. Master Plan. 'A Framework'* and *Social Sector Strategy*. *Education and Training Policy* was understood to be a Tanzanian Government product by both government and agency officials. *Primary Education. Master Plan. 'A Framework'* was seen as a Danida document by most, if not all, government and agency officials. *Social Sector Strategy* was considered to be a World Bank document by government and agency officials, except for those (few) government officials who had been directly involved in its production.

Work on *Education and Training Policy* started in February 1993. It was initiated both because of an internally felt need for an official policy that reflected the state of the art of education in the 1990s and because of agency pressure for a policy framework to guide education assistance. The point of departure for the policy paper was the Task Force report, *The Tanzania Education System for the 21st Century*, work sponsored by Danida but never acknowledged as official Tanzanian Government policy.

Education and Training Policy was formulated by Tanzanian officials in an interministerial committee headed by a professor of the University of Dar es Salaam and supported by three specialist subcommittees, additional resource persons and an editorial committee. The formulation process can be characterized as 'open', but not inclusive of all stakeholders in the education sector. A first draft was discussed at an internal seminar with the directors of education and with representatives of different ministries, education parastatals, agency officials and a university representative. A summary paper of this draft was discussed at the University of Dar es Salaam. A reworked draft was shared widely at meetings with headmasters, principals and regional and district education officers. By contrast, representatives of teachers, students, pupils, parents, community, non-government and other civil society organizations were not invited to comment and there was no widespread debate in the media or in Parliament. Inclusion of the wider educational constituencies in the debate was partly prevented by the fact that there was no condensed version available to the public in Kiswahili.

The primary purpose of the public meetings was information sharing. A number of critical issues were, however, discussed at the meeting at the University of Dar es Salaam and considered in the ensuing policy discussions within the ministry and in Parliament, including: whether to keep or abolish the quota system guiding access to secondary education; the nature of decentralization from ministerial to lower administrative levels; whether vocational and technical schools should form part of the formal education system; and the use of English versus Kiswahili as the language of instruction in the education system. It appeared from the interviews that final decisions on the individual issues were made by the policy-makers. Agency officials also discussed the draft in the interagency meetings and had direct contact with the ministry throughout the process. Government and agency officials agreed that this interaction has been reflected in the final version of the policy paper in stronger emphasis on some of the themes and issues, for example gender and local autonomy.

Primary Education. Master Plan. 'A Framework' was, on the other hand, initially pushed along by Danida which required a Master Plan in order to implement a planned twelve-year Primary Education Programme (PEP). The Plan, which was to be a tool with priorities and strategies for the subsector, was completed in March 1995 (Ministry of Education and Culture, n.d.). The document was not, however, recognized as a ministry document, and in February 1996 the new Principal Secretary for Education restarted the process, the underlying issue being lack of ownership of the produced Plan rather than disagreements concerning its substance. This process resulted in 1997 in the production of a number of master plans for different areas of basic education that do not form part of the analysis in this chapter.

Compared to the process of the *Education and Training Policy*, that of the Danida-initiated Master Plan was virtually closed and highly exclusive. This was reflected in the fact that most of the government and agency respondents were uncertain about the purpose and status of the Plan. Initially in 1994, the Plan was to be produced by a small group (three internal people from MOEC and the Prime Minister's office) supported by consultants recruited through four agencies: Danida, Sida, UNESCO and UNICEF. The Danida Chief Technical Adviser played a key facilitating role. Initial work was disrupted in early 1995 owing to disagreements among the team members and another exclusive committee was set up – consisting of two government officials, one academic from the University of Dar es Salaam and the Danida Chief Technical Adviser – which produced the draft Master Plan.

When restarting the process in February 1996, a new ministry team was appointed. It was supported in its work by local, not external, experts and funded by two external agencies. The Technical Secretariat, consisting of nine internal officials and originally set up in 1994, was set up again in April 1996. A team of educationists was appointed to review the existing Master Plan and to produce a synopsis of issues, programmes and projects to be included in the new Plan. The synopsis was essentially a shopping list for specific projects and was, by some of the respondents, identified as the product of the Technical Secretariat set up in 1994. It had no correspondence with the draft Master Plan, but differed, *inter alia*, by not being concerned with broader educational issues or by considerations regarding the function of the Master Plan in wider policy formulation and development in the United Republic of Tanzania. This work has since been followed up with the production of the 1997 Basic Education Master Plan.

The same exclusive process was adopted in the production of the *Social Sector Strategy*. The need for the strategy was first voiced at the Paris consultative group meeting in November 1993 and can be seen in the context of the move from project to programme and sector approaches that has taken place among most international funding and technical-assistance agencies. Its production should also be seen in the context of a felt need among Tanzanian Government officials for a coherent approach to social services delivery.

A steering committee for the strategy work was set up in July 1994, led by the deputy Principal Secretary for Planning and involving top officials from the concerned ministries, including MOEC. Work on the strategy was discussed with top officials both in Washington and the United Republic of Tanzania and was completed in February 1995. The underlying data came from the *Tanzania Social Sector Review* conducted in 1994 by a World Bank team constituted of Washington officials and Tanzanian consultants, and co-ordinated by the Planning Commission. The work on the strategy was never broadly shared and caused concern within the education agency community owing to uncertainties concerning its linkage with the *Education and Training Policy* and the possible distraction of the production of the latter.

Underlying substantive issues: privatization and liberalization

Both the Tanzanian Government and the most influential education agencies in the country – in particular the World Bank, Danida, Sida and DGIS – are concerned with the need to develop a market economy and to blend private and public initiatives. Concepts of cost-sharing, partnership and devolution of authority to lower levels are central policy themes for all of them. However, their interpretation of the core themes and the translation into practice are not uniform and not uniformly delineated in different documents by the Tanzanian Government or by individual agencies. In the case of the agencies, this can be explained by the continued evolution of thinking within the organization or because different individuals have different perspectives. In the case of the Tanzanian Government, the issue is also whether differences in thinking reflect an impact by different agencies.

One of the critical differences between the *Education and Training Policy* and the *Social Sector Strategy* is that the education policy introduces privatization and liberalization in broad terms but does not define specific roles for the government, the private sector and the international community. The focus in the *Social Sector Strategy* is, on the other hand, on the needed participation levels and interactions among the government, international aid agencies and households in the financing of the social sector for which specific strategies are drawn up. In the *Social Sector Strategy*, the government is said to have 'a special role to play in complementing, not substituting for investments in human capital that are made by the household'. Another difference is that financing is but one aspect of the *Education and Training Policy*, which is overall concerned with improving quality and learning in the education sector. By contrast, there is no learning perspective in the *Social Sector Strategy*. Neither of the two documents is concerned with their possible interlinkages or with their linkage to the primary education Master Plan.

The nature of privatization and liberalization has also been the critical substantive issue that has continued to create differences within the agency community, rather than between the government and the agency community. One of the six strategies in the *Social Sector Strategy* aims at moving resources closer to the household and promoting household investment in human capital. This has been tested by the World Bank in a Community Education Fund project within the overall Human Resources Development Project. The implementation of the project was at the core of the controversy between the World Bank, on the one hand, and a number of the national technical-assistance agencies, on the other, and led to some change in traditional standpoints and working relationships among some of the national agencies. The Tanzanian Government has negotiated funding for further implementation with the World Bank.

The controversy between the World Bank and the national technical-assistance agencies revolved around a number of issues, including: the relative balance between government and private responsibility for and investment in the education sector; the anticipated role of local government in the project; the focus on demand- versus supply-side approaches; the relative involvement of other actors, including other international agencies, in the project; the linkage to the *Education and Training Policy*; and the underlying assumption that parents had a choice of school.

In 1996, after completion of the test phase and after continuous discussions between the World Bank and the national agencies, differences had mellowed in some areas but still remained in others. Thus, as summarized in the internal correspondence of one of the agencies, most agencies could agree on 'the decline in access and quality of primary education; the need to strengthen the financial base of schools; the need for school planning; the need for improved parents' participation and accountability towards parents with regard to their financial contributions; and increased decision-making of parents in issues of use of school funds and improving quality of teaching and learning'.

They continued to differ, however, with respect to: 'the relative emphasis on demand-side versus balanced demand-side plus supply-side approaches; the relative importance of working through the existing structures, having capacity-building as an integral component, and seeking to achieve local ownership; the relative focus on output versus process; conditions of funding, time perspective and geographical scope; and relative attention to equality, sustainability and general contextual experiences'. These differences determined the nature of interaction not only between the World Bank and the national agencies but also among the national agencies, some being closer to World Bank views than others.

Co-ordination of aid in the United Republic of Tanzania: some perspectives

The case of the United Republic of Tanzania has shown that despite, or perhaps because of, the long presence of numerous international agencies of different kinds, co-operation and co-ordination of external aid are recent on the agenda of both government and agencies. It demonstrates the distance between the ideal of government-led co-ordination within a framework of nationally designed policies and programmes, and the reality in which policies have been recently formulated to fit agency as much as government needs. Finally, it shows the differences in interpretation among the agencies and within the Tanzanian Government of the approaches to liberalization and privatization which have been identified, and accepted by the government and most agencies, as critical means of improving the economic and educational situation in the United Republic of Tanzania.

Both government and agencies have accepted the need for co-ordination of external assistance with national endeavours. The government has committed itself to government-led co-ordination, has set up, with outside assistance, the foundation for a co-ordinating mechanism for education, namely the Education Sector Co-ordinating Committee, and has started to work with two agencies in the implementation of a common programme for primary education. The initiative seems, however, to be with the agencies rather than the government. In the same way, agencies have committed themselves to government-led co-ordination, accepted the *Education and Training Policy* as a guiding policy framework and acknowledged the stipulated government priorities for the education sector, namely primary education, quality, teaching materials and management. This expressed commitment coexists with underlying scepticism concerning government capacity in policy formulation and co-ordination, and agency flexibility in this respect.

Despite the softening of differences between the Tanzanian Government and the international funding agencies, on the one hand, and between the international funding agencies, in particular the World Bank, and some of the national technical-assistance agencies, on the other, policy differences continue to exist. The analysed controversy among the agencies highlights the difficulties in establishing aid co-ordination among agencies as long as basic socio-economic philosophy and ways of operation differ. Agency differences appear in ongoing practices, lack of consistency in certain cases between formulated and implemented policies, and insufficient knowledge of other agency policies and practices. Agency flexibility is hampered at the field level by the procedures which have to be followed vis-à-vis headquarters. Specific procedures differ from agency to agency and often determine the nature and level of co-operation that can be established with other agencies and with the government. Furthermore, staff turnover and interpersonal issues are often strongly inhibiting wider co-operation.

Thus, while there is a favourable climate in terms of government commitment to co-ordinate education sector work in the United Republic of Tanzania and, in general, agency willingness to be co-ordinated, there remain inhibiting factors on both sides. Co-ordination led by the government might facilitate common views if it were undertaken within strict frameworks of government thinking and, therefore, accepted the participation of specific external agencies only if there were consistency in underlying aims and understandings between the government and the participating agency. In a situation of unequal partners and continuous dependency on external aid, government-led co-ordination may, however, in reality represent only an approximation to the ideal situation and governments may achieve more by establishing individual relationships with agencies rather than interacting with them as a group. The difficult choice for many governments would be to refuse non-conforming aid in a situation of fiscal constraint. Such a case might be educationally sound but probably would be considered economically questionable and politically unwise by most government officials.

In order to proceed, therefore, it seems to be of particular immediate importance to strengthen the national leadership in order to pursue nationally defined policies and to allow the kind of mutual relationships to occur that are presently sought by some of the national technical-assistance agencies. Furthermore, the wider national constituencies must play a more prominent role in order to ensure widespread support for the government agenda. On their side, agencies have to evaluate and critically analyse the policies and practices of their aid operations. If government-determined aid co-ordination is to take place as it is presently discussed, current agency procedures are likely to be as inhibiting as the lack of government capacity that is often identified as the primary obstacle to improvement.

References

BUCHERT, L. 1995a. The Concept of Education for All: What has Happened after Jomtien? *International Review of Education*, Vol. 41, No. 4, pp. 537–49.

—— 1995b. *Recent Trends in Education Aid: Towards a Classification of Policies.* Paris, UNESCO/IIEP.

——. 1997. *Education Policy Formulation in Tanzania: Co-ordination between the Government and International Aid Agencies. A Report from the IWGE*. Paris, UNESCO/ IIEP.

DAE. 1996. *Formulating Education Policy: Lessons and Experiences from Sub-Saharan Africa. Six Case Studies and Reflections from the DAE Biennial Meetings (October 1995, Tours, France)*. Paris, Association for the Development of African Education.

GOVERNMENT OF TANZANIA. 1995. *Primary Education. Master Plan. 'A Framework'*. Dar es Salaam, Ministry of Education and Culture, Prime Minister's Office. (Draft 1.)

KARLSSON, M. 1997. *Biennial Meeting of the Association for the Development of Education in Africa (ADEA), Dakar, Senegal, 14–18 October: Introductory Statement*. (Mimeo.)

KING, K. 1992. The External Agenda of Aid in Internal Educational Reform. *International Journal of Educational Development*, Vol. 12, No. 4, pp. 257–63.

MAGNEN, A. 1994. *Donor Co-ordination in Education. A Case Study on Bangladesh*. Paris, UNESCO-IIEP/UNICEF.

MINISTRY OF EDUCATION AND CULTURE. N.d. *Primary Education Master Plan. A Synopsis of Issues, Programmes and Projects*. Dar es Salaam, Ministry of Education and Culture.

MUKYANUZI, F. 1996. *Financing of Education in Tanzania*. (National Conference on Education and Training Policy, Arusha, 10–13 September.)

PANDAY, D. R.; WILLIAMS, M. 1990. *Aid Co-ordination and Effectiveness: Least Developed Countries 1981-1989*. New York, United Nations. (Second United Nations Conference on the Least Developed Countries.)

RIDDELL, R. C. 1987. *Foreign Aid Reconsidered*. London, James Currey/Overseas Development Institute.

SACK, R. 1995. *Donor Coordination at the Country Level: Experience from an 'Upstream' Education Policy Analysis Project and Conceptual Explorations*. Paris, UNESCO. (BER-95/WS/3.)

SAMOFF, J.; SUMRA, S. 1994. From Planning to Marketing. Making Education and Training Policy in Tanzania. In: J. Samoff (ed.), *Coping with Crisis. Austerity, Adjustment and Human Resources*, pp. 134–72. London/Paris, Cassell/UNESCO.

SAWYERR, H. 1997. *Country-led Aid Coordination in Ghana*. Paris, Association for the Development of Education in Africa.

UNITED REPUBLIC OF TANZANIA. 1995. *Education and Training Policy*. Dar es Salaam, Ministry of Education and Culture.

UNITED REPUBLIC OF TANZANIA. MINISTRY OF EDUCATION AND CULTURE AND MINISTRY OF SCIENCE, TECHNOLOGY AND HIGHER EDUCATION. 1993. *The Tanzania Education System for the 21st Century. Report of the Task Force.* Leeds.

——. n.d. *Social Sector Strategy.* (Prepared for the Consultative Group Meeting.)

WILLIAMS, P. 1995. *Government's Coordination of Aid to Education: The Case of Namibia.* Paris, ADEA/UNESCO/IIEP.

WORLD BANK. 1995. *Tanzania Social Sector Review.* Washington, D.C., World Bank.

WORLD CONFERENCE ON EDUCATION FOR ALL (Jomtien, Thailand, 5–9 March 1990). 1990. *World Declaration on Education for All and Framework for Action to Meet Basic Learning Needs.* New York, Inter-Agency Commission for WCEFA. (3rd impression, Paris, UNESCO, 1994.)

Aid co-ordination in theory and practice: a case study of Botswana and Namibia
Ulla Kann

This chapter examines aid co-ordination in two southern African countries, Namibia and Botswana, and provides a number of important lessons derived from the author's and others' experiences. The two countries are neighbours and have many similarities, for example, a huge surface area with small populations. But there are also differences, for example, in the way they handle the co-ordination of foreign aid to their countries and to the education sector.

A number of international funding and technical-assistance agencies, including development banks, are active in both countries. They all have their own policies regarding support to less developed countries. Donor relationships form part of foreign affairs and diplomatic activities, and the agencies, therefore, do not necessarily operate in the same way in the two countries. The recipient country may, similarly, act differently in relation to different agencies.

Even though both government and agencies have overall policies and guidelines regarding objectives, areas of support and overall administration and management of aid, individual programmes and projects often turn out differently. Furthermore, many individuals are involved on both sides during the negotiations, and the implementation and monitoring of the programmes and projects – individuals with different personalities and views.

Almost all funding and technical-assistance agencies have in their policies a statement concerning the importance of listening to the recipient country, providing aid on the conditions of the recipient and so on. This is the theory. The practical implementation of this policy often differs from the theory.

What is aid co-ordination?

From most writings on the subject, it appears that aid co-ordination is a good thing, something to strive for (Cliff, 1988; Hallak, 1995; Jallade, 1993; Lister, 1991; Magnen, 1994; Macfarlane, 1996; OECD, 1992; Sack, 1995; Samoff, 1992; Wolfson, 1972; World Bank, 1995). Logically, aid co-ordination is the responsibility of the recipient government. It concerns co-ordination of the support provided by various international funding and technical-assistance agencies, including development banks, in order to ensure, *inter alia*, that overlaps between different agencies are avoided, that support is in line with national policies and priorities, and that aid will not be too costly in the long run, i.e. that projects or programmes are sustainable.

In practice, however, aid co-ordination is rarely the responsibility of the recipient country, but rather of the agencies. In fact, aid co-ordination appears to mean co-ordination among agencies. Left to the recipient government is aid management or rather aid administration and reporting.

Several papers (Jallade, 1993; Saasa and Carlsson, 1996; World Bank, 1995) differentiate between three different kinds of aid co-ordination:

- Co-ordination within the recipient government system.
- Co-ordination between government and agencies.
- Co-ordination among agencies.

All three are necessary for the successful implementation of aid. The most important, however, is co-ordination within the recipient government system.

This classification forms the basis for a comparison of aid co-ordination in Botswana and Namibia in the following.

Co-ordination within the government system

There are two dominant systems in developing countries as far as co-ordination of foreign aid is concerned. Some countries, as is the case in Botswana, have a joint Ministry of Finance and Development Planning. Others, like Namibia, have a Ministry or a Commission for National Development Planning and Aid Co-ordination separate from a Ministry of Finance.

The level of centralization or decentralization to local authorities in connection with co-ordination of aid also varies. Both in Botswana and Namibia all agreements with foreign governments are signed at the central level. However, foreign non-governmental organizations sometimes sign agreements with local non-governmental organizations without government approval or involvement. The negotiation and signing of development loans are the responsibility of the ministries of finance in both case study countries. At the implementation stage some aid organizations deal directly with the district or regional offices of the central government, often to the frustration of the civil servants at headquarters who tend to be left out of the process.

Botswana

Botswana gained independence in 1966 following many years as a Protectorate under the British Crown. At the time of independence, it was one of the twenty-five least developed and poorest countries in the world. It was totally surrounded by the apartheid regimes in South Africa and the then Rhodesia. Its poverty, geopolitical situation and the fact that Botswana was one of very few democracies in Africa attracted substantial foreign support. During the first years of independence, Botswana was totally dependent on its former colonial master, the British Government, for most of its recurrent budget. Botswana was also dependent on foreign personnel to fill many of the positions in the civil service. The discovery of diamonds soon after independence changed this situation. The financial success story of Botswana is now well known.

Not as well known is Botswana's aid co-ordination and aid management system, which is also a success story. As far as aid co-ordination is concerned, Botswana has an integrated system through its Ministry of Finance and Development Planning. Since independence Botswana has had national development plans co-ordinated by this ministry. The annual budget process is closely linked to development plans. Development projects are included in the long-term plan that guides the agency and the recipient country in their co-operation. Projects are included in the capital and development part of the budget, which provides more flexibility than the recurrent budget, because the development budget allows for financial commitment beyond one financial year. This provides clarity and openness. It also 'reduces the extra work involved in managing aid, and gives less scope for aid agencies to impose their own priorities on the government' (Lister, 1991, p. 19).

All development planners are part of a cadre of economists in the Ministry of Finance and Development Planning, seconded to line ministries and transferable between ministries. There are no subject specialists, only economists. This system has its great advantages. Every Monday morning, all planners from all ministries meet for one hour in the Ministry of Finance and Development Planning – among the planners this meeting is referred to as 'the weekly prayer meeting'. It is an excellent way of sharing information on policy development, financial issues and planned visits by international funding and technical-assistance agencies. Within the education sector, some changes have taken place during recent years as the Ministry of Education has employed an educational planner from within its own cadres. In addition, some of the directorates within the Ministry of Education have increasingly taken over the responsibility for project preparation and monitoring.

Namibia

Namibia gained independence in 1990 following some thirty years of military struggle against the South African apartheid regime and some seventy-five years of colonial rule. The pre-independence government had little experience with foreign aid, although the South West Africa People's Organization (SWAPO), while in exile, had substantial contacts with and support from international agencies. Thus, at independence, after SWAPO won the elections in 1989, a number of civil servants were rather confused regarding the role of the foreigners who flooded their country to help. Many of the technical-assistance staff had in various ways been working with SWAPO in exile. However, not all had the necessary understanding of the situation or the necessary knowledge of the pre-independence history of Namibia. The political opposition took the presence of a substantial number of foreign technical-assistance staff as an indication that the new government could not run the country on its own.

Namibia had been considered by South Africa as its fifth province. A substantial part of the administration, not least the financial part, had been co-ordinated from Pretoria in South Africa. There was insufficient knowledge among the Namibians regarding budgeting and financial planning at the time of independence. During the apartheid regime, Pretoria had not properly differentiated between the financing of the operations of the South African Defence Force in Namibia and normal state activities. Top-level government civil servants were South Africans, many of whom returned to their home country at Namibia's independence. To build a new administrative system – a system based on democratic principles and less hierarchical than the pre-independence administration – takes time. During the negotiations for independence, SWAPO agreed not to dismiss any existing personnel from the civil service. In order to obtain a balance between the old and the new, the civil service was therefore inflated. Many new civil servants were employed at independence, sometimes with little or no experience in government administration. On the other hand, many of the civil servants had worked under the previous administration and were neither interested in nor capable of changing their approaches to work. In fact, they have sometimes been obstructing the implementation of the new policies.

Compared to Botswana, Namibia had at independence a well-educated civil service, many of whom had obtained their training and academic qualifications in exile. Some also had work experience from a programme of work attachment for students from the United Nations Institute for Namibia (UNIN) in other friendly African countries, for example, Botswana. Others had obtained work experience while being employed as civil servants in other countries while in exile. In addition, quite a few of the Namibians who had not been in exile had obtained qualifications at South African universities and technikons.

As regards aid co-ordination, Namibia established the National Planning Commission (NPC) with a Secretariat. In addition to co-ordination of aid, NPC is also responsible for overall development planning, compilation of national development plans and the capital budget.

Only a few months after independence, the Namibia Economic Policy Research Unit (NEPRU) convened a workshop entitled Aid, Donors and Development Management (Lister, 1991) with substantial participation from the Botswana Ministry of Finance and Development Planning. Study visits to Botswana were also made by NPC staff. However, Namibia remains weaker than Botswana in its approach to international funding and technical-assistance agencies mainly owing to lack of networking between NPC, the Ministry of Finance and the different line ministries. In theory, NPC is the co-ordinating body. In practice, however, a substantial part of the aid co-ordination regarding education is carried out by a section within the Ministry of Basic Education and Culture.

Williams (1995, p. 44) gives the following description of the relationship between the Ministry of Education and Culture (MEC) and NPC:

> In a very small country like Namibia this [aid co-ordination] would seem at first to be a straightforward task. . . . In practice things are more complicated, and while NPC and the Ministry generally work harmoniously, there is room for misunderstanding. Namibia does not, unlike some countries, have a system of cross-posting of planners from a central pool to sectoral ministries so there is not at present a built-in arrangement for ensuring that MEC and NPC are each fully attuned to the culture of the other. . . . In NPC there is a feeling that education often goes its own way in discussions with external aid donors without keeping NPC fully informed at the appropriate time, and that it too readily resorts to technical assistance from abroad. In MEC *per contra* one hears the criticism that NPC has a tendency too readily to equate development expenditure with physical capital, despite the fact that in education much of the investment is in the form of curriculum development, staff training and setting up of management information systems.

The document provides a comprehensive picture of aid co-ordination in the field of education in Namibia.

Co-ordination between governments and funding and technical-assistance agencies

Co-ordination between governments and agencies is a complicated issue. One way of co-ordination is to set up so-called 'round tables'. Inviting to and arranging a round table is the prerogative of UNDP. A UNDP round table is a meeting of bilateral and multilateral agencies with representatives of a particular recipient country, its government and sometimes representatives of the private sector. Similar meetings and consultative groups are arranged by the World Bank. Multilateral agencies generally do not allow a recipient government to take the initiative of inviting bilateral agencies to a meeting without first consulting them.

With respect to Botswana and Namibia, there are some similarities concerning the kind of agreements between the funding agencies and the recipient. In most cases, an overall country agreement guides the aid.

There are also specific sector agreements, for example in education and training. While the contents of the sector agreements are usually worked out between a line ministry (e.g. education) and the division in the agency in question responsible for the sector concerned, these bodies have to follow the overall country agreement. Line ministries are usually not permitted to sign a sector agreement on their own. It is, furthermore, common that project agreements fall within the sector agreements. In some cases, project agreements can be signed by the minister of the line ministry, provided that the body responsible for aid has agreed. Many meetings have been held and substantial correspondence exchanged between the agency and the recipient before signature can take place. Each party seeks to ensure its own interests. The period of negotiation is facilitated if both parties are knowledgeable of each other's policies, plans and procedures.

A major issue during the negotiation process is the time frame. This is usually a rather lengthy procedure. It is not unusual that project preparation, with its various phases, takes two years or more. Meanwhile, the recipient country has two options: to await the agency decision regarding funding of the project, or to obtain government or other funding for the project in question. The agency usually requires that the project be afforded high priority by the recipient government. But high-priority projects and programmes should not be delayed while negotiations and pre-feasibility studies take place. Thus, if possible, the recipient government should take responsibility for high-priority projects. Projects funded by international agencies are uncertain until they have been signed and sometimes even after that. Countries undergoing structural adjustment programmes have less negotiating power, but both Namibia and Botswana are in a position to negotiate.

In order to overcome this problem, agencies, mainly under the guidance, co-ordination and leadership of the World Bank, have begun a more powerful initiative in the form of joint sector analyses (Working Group on Education Sector Analysis, 1997; Kemmerer, 1994). The intention is for individual agencies to 'buy into' a subsector or a project. While the negotiations and preparations for a final agreement tend to take quite a long time, there is almost always a great rush to complete the sector analysis. The recipient is rarely asked to participate in the exercise and usually does not have the capacity to release people to participate in or carry out the sector analysis. A substantial number of technical-assistance staff and short-term consultants are, therefore, recruited in order to assist in undertaking the analysis. This is an improvement from the previous situation when each agency carried out its own separate sector analysis. The concern, first, is that the recipient country does not have the capacity to participate in the process and, second, that the recipient country's own sector analyses as presented in development plans and country reports presented at international conferences are never taken as the starting point for the sector analysis. The approach is top-down. It is the agency approach to sector analysis that guides the process while the recipient – too busy managing crisis situations in the existing system – rarely has a chance to catch up with the agencies' analyses and plans.

Interest in the policies of the international funding and technical-assistance agencies has recently increased (Buchert, 1995, 1996) and agencies have begun to understand that their varying and ever changing policies and procedures are difficult to handle for the recipient. One small example is the almost mandatory inclusion of the so-called logical framework in all project documents, which is to assist in the development and monitoring of a project. In the case of Namibia, NPC has issued a *Manual for Planners* which includes a Namibian version of a logical framework. This is, however, not used by the planners. Instead they use a Swedish version for Swedish-funded projects, a German version for German-funded projects, a European Union version, a Luxembourg version, and so on. Several agencies have arranged training sessions on their special logical framework version. Why not agree on using the Namibian version for projects undertaken in Namibia?

There are substantial differences, but also similarities, between Botswana and Namibia. Already in early 1973, the Ministry of Finance and Development Planning in Botswana had a well-developed system for accounting and dealing with foreign support. In fact, many agencies accepted the Botswana Accountant-General's certification as evidence that funds had been properly used. There is a clear understanding of the roles of government and agency funding in development activities. Namibia is still working towards achieving a similar situation.

It is the well-functioning, internal administrative set-up in Botswana regarding aid co-ordination which makes the difference and which has made Botswana a success story in this regard. Other factors of importance are political stability and a long period of co-operation with international funding and technical-assistance agencies, including development banks.

Of importance both in Botswana and Namibia are comparatively strong economies. Both countries can set their own conditions. Many years ago, Botswana requested the return of a new mission from one of the major development banks, because the government did not agree with the conclusions of the first mission. The bank in question had never before experienced such an incidence.

Only a few years after independence Namibia declined to sign an extension of education support from one of its major funding agencies because the conditionalities linked to the support were unacceptable to the Namibian Government. A new programme of support was later developed.

Only politically stable and economically strong countries can afford to decline support.

Co-ordination among agencies

The main responsibility for aid co-ordination, in theory, lies with the recipient governments. However, international agencies have certain advantages. They know the jargon and the acronyms. They have the latest information. They have access to the top level in recipient governments, to ministers, permanent secretaries and sometimes even to the president. In addition, they organize their internal meetings both at country sector level and internationally, for example, IWGE meetings. They are much better informed about the aid situation and about general recipient-country affairs than the civil servants in the ministries in the country concerned.

Among the many papers, journal articles and books available on the theme of aid co-ordination (Buchert and King, 1995; Griffin, 1991; Hawes and Coombe, 1986; Hewitt, 1991; King, 1992; London, 1993; OECD, 1991; Riddell, 1988; Saasa and Carlsson, 1996; Saravanamuttoo and Shaw, 1995; Verspoor, 1993; World Bank, 1995), few are written by a national of a recipient country. However, almost all papers on aid co-ordination highlight the importance of recipient-country ownership of projects and programmes. Can this situation be improved? One of the best pieces of advice available to recipient countries can be found in Hallak (1995). In a checklist for negotiations, Hallak provides sixteen pieces of advice divided into four: prior to negotiation; what to negotiate; how; and when. During the last couple of years an increasing awareness regarding the importance of leaving more space for the recipient countries to take the lead in the co-operation process has developed among funding and technical-assistance agencies, including development banks. The recent initiative 'Partnership Africa' by the Swedish Government is one example of this. Another initiative taken recently by the European Union at the Horizon 2000 meeting of education experts is to develop a code of conduct for education sector funding agencies.

The issue of varying and changing policies both at macro and sector level by individual aid agencies is a problem for recipient governments. Steps have been taken by agencies to harmonize their policies, for example currently within the European Union. Will this facilitate the situation for the recipient countries or will it only make the giant even more powerful? One of the problems with a harmonized policy has already become evident following the Jomtien conference. It is no longer easy to obtain funding for non-basic education projects, since basic education is now the worldwide, global, overall goal. Most countries aim at a balanced education system. Recipient countries now and then use the possibility of playing agencies against one another in order to obtain their own goals. If agencies harmonize their policies, this approach is less likely to succeed.

Exchange of experiences between recipient countries

From the above, it is evident that international funding and technical-assistance agencies, including development banks, have an advantage in the aid co-operation process. They have human resources, funds and know-how in connection with planning both projects and the whole education system. They have extensive networks at local and international levels. Countries in the South need similar networks in order to learn from one another.

Recipient countries only rarely meet to discuss the policies of international funding and technical-assistance agencies including the development banks. However, since the establishment of ADEA, there have been better opportunities for ministers of education in Africa to learn from one another through South–South co-operation. This has been the most significant development in creating a forum for African exchange of experiences regarding support from the North. The development of common guidelines for development co-operation, however, still remains to be agreed upon by African states.

Lessons learnt

In conclusion, there are a number of different factors that affect the success of aid co-ordination. In comparing Namibia and Botswana it is evident that the internal networking between various government institutions is a critical ingredient towards effective aid co-ordination. In addition, as mentioned above, the current globalization trend has led to closer co-operation between funding and technical-assistance agencies and development banks. This has the advantage that agencies and banks now speak, if not with one voice, then at least with similar voices. They are easier to understand for the recipient country. However, it also has the disadvantage of making this voice very powerful. There is less room for bargaining by the recipient country in that situation. What is the solution? There is, of course, no one single answer as to how to improve aid co-ordination. Only joint attempts by agencies and recipient governments will improve the current situation.

The final section of this chapter is an inventory of learning experiences. Some of them emanate from the author's own experiences. Others are from other writers who have added to the debate on aid co-ordination. Unlike most other documents on aid co-ordination, the majority of the lessons represent a recipient-country perspective and are directed to other recipient countries.

1. 'We should keep in mind that *the costs of mistakes to donors . . . are normally small*, if not negligible, whereas the costs to governments could prove to be catastrophic no matter how small the share of aid in the education budget' (Hallak, 1995, p. 7).

2. *Relations with aid agencies.* Tumelo (1991) elaborates on the importance of knowing the agencies well and of cultivating good relations with them. Knowing them well includes knowing their policies, as they change. But even more important is probably the building of a good reputation and trust with the agencies. This involves using funds as agreed upon, preparation and presentation of sound projects (otherwise the agencies will prepare them for you), timely implementation of projects, and good financial control and reporting. The agency desk officers are your allies. They

are the ones arguing your case at headquarters. You should give them as much ammunition as possible (Tumelo, 1991, p. 163).

3. *Do not forget the word NO.* It is admittedly difficult during negotiations to decline an aid offer. It is more difficult for a very poor country than for a less poor country. Whatever the case, it is the recipient country that has to live with the decision made. A NO indicates that the recipient country is serious and may open up for a better discussion. It is the business of agencies to disburse aid.

Aid should not be part of an agency's experiments. We often hear the expression 'It would be nice to know if . . .'. Beware. Find out if it is absolutely necessary to know this for the successful implementation of the project.

4. A substantial part of external support to education and training takes the form of *projects*. Projects are not usually administered or implemented by aid agencies, nor by recipient governments, but by universities and other specialized institutions or companies in the North that enter into international competitive bidding, having often been shortlisted by the funding agency, e.g. the European Union, USAID or the World Bank. Too little attention is paid to the integration of the project into the main activities of the Ministry of Education. According to Macfarlane (1996, p. 5), the potential rewards from securing international funding are very large and well worth pursuing, but they cannot normally be achieved in an optimal way without the receiving side devoting a tremendous amount of both time and effort to all stages of the process. This is not always recognized by the recipient partner.

In some cases a non-project support approach has been used, i.e. direct budget support usually with accompanying conditionalities. The choice between a project approach, direct budget support or sector support is difficult. However, it is an issue to which planners in recipient countries need to pay attention during negotiations. There is a danger both with sector and direct budget support because the financing agency tends to feel responsible for the development of the whole education system. They become more powerful that way. Subsector support with one lead agency is worth considering.

5. *Aid and plans.* Aid should supplement a country's own efforts and resources. Aid co-ordination and educational development planning should not be separate. Government officers responsible for aid co-

ordination should also be involved in development planning. The issues of sector analysis and master plans are receiving increased attention. According to Kemmerer (1994, p. 13), 'Sector analyses are being initiated with increasing frequency by donors as a preliminary step to project definition and design in developing countries.' Recent developments indicate a change in focus towards a more African-based approach to sector analysis (Working Group on Education Sector Analysis, 1997; Sack, 1995). The national development of educational master plans presented to agencies for information as well as funding is also a positive development. However, it requires correct timing between the national development planning institution and the agencies. Different planning cycles make this approach difficult in practice.

6. The importance of *networking and information sharing* cannot be overemphasized. It is not only a question of providing the co-operating partners, the agencies, with information, although this is crucial. It is also a question of sharing information internally in the Ministry of Education, between this ministry and the Ministry of Finance and Development Planning or the National Planning Commission, and sharing information with non-governmental organizations, the private sector and civil society at large. Almost everyone is a stakeholder in education. Aid is usually mistakenly thought as 'foreign'. Government officers tend to forget the support to education from internal sources, not least from parents.

7. *Expatriate personnel – technical assistance.* Technical-assistance staff, consultants and advisers are usually, though not always, expatriates or foreigners. They come in different shapes and forms, with different types of contracts and for different lengths of time. The short-term consultants especially eat time and reports. They want copies of, or at least access to, all previous reports and often start off with a summary of these reports. Unfortunately, most countries rarely have the opportunity to recruit their own technical-assistance staff or to choose between candidates. It is a positive step forward that some countries now insist on doing so.

Several international agencies have repeatedly outlined what the procedures ought to be. According to OECD (1992, p. 53):

Recipient countries must be involved throughout the Technical Co-operation [TC] process. They must determine their needs and articulate their requests, rather than simply respond to offers from donors, even though they might wish to seek outside help in formulating their needs. The full active involvement in TC projects by recipient countries and beneficiary groups and institutions is basic to promoting sustainability and self-reliance and should be encouraged by donors.

As mentioned above, it has become almost standard to invite universities and other institutions or private companies to bid for projects even in the field of education. These projects often include technical-assistance staff who are difficult to negotiate. The group of staff comes as a package. The recipient country can accept or reject the whole package, but not replace anyone of the proposed staff members. Often the key persons who have won the project are unavailable in the end, or resign when the project is to be implemented. The system has many problems, even if it is more impartial than previous practice.

Samoff (1992) has noted that consultants use a standard approach, a standard view of education and standard concepts. Globalization in the field of education seems not to have improved the situation. The impact of Jomtien is that concepts such as Education for All and Basic Education are used in every report. Even the University Library project in Namibia was initially referred to as a Basic Education project because the financial institution involved only funded basic education.

A major concern is the 'fly-in, fly-out' consultants. They have little time and/or little interest in developing local capacity in research and general analysis. Their Terms of Reference rarely include capacity-building. This ensures that they will continue to have contracts to do these kinds of jobs, paid for by international funding and technical-assistance agencies.

A new kind of ethics, morals and standards must be adhered to by agencies and external consultants. All Terms of Reference should include local capacity-building and must be taken seriously by all parties. Recipient country staff must understand that capacity-building consists not only of seminars, lectures, long-term academic degree courses, but also tapping on the experiences of the advisers, consultants and technical-assistance staff. Those who belong to the latter must be much more inventive and serious in their attempts to work themselves out of their jobs. Only then can they be seriously trusted by the recipient countries.

References

BUCHERT, L. 1995. *Recent Trends in Education Aid towards a Classification of Policies*. Paris, UNESCO/IIEP.

———. 1996. *Education Policy Formulation in Tanzania: Coordination between the Government and International Aid Agencies. A Study Commissioned for the IWGE*. Paris, UNESCO/IIEP.

BUCHERT, L.; KING, K. (eds.). 1995. *Learning from Experience: Policy and Practice in Aid to Higher Education*. The Hague, CESO/NORRAG. (CESO paperback, 24.)

CLIFF, C. 1988. Aid Co-ordination: Are There Any Lessons to be Learnt from Kenya? *Development Policy Review*, Vol. 6, pp. 115–37.

GRIFFIN K. 1991. Foreign Aid after the Cold War. *Development and Change*, Vol. 22, pp. 645–85.

HALLAK, J. 1995. *Negotiation with Aid Agencies: A Dwarf Against a Giant*. Paris, UNESCO/IIEP. (IIEP Contributions, 19.)

HAWES, H.; COOMBE, T. (eds.). 1986. *Education Priorities and Aid Responses in Sub-Saharan Africa*. London, ODA/University of London/Institute of Education/HMSO.

HEWITT, A. 1991. Aid without Power. *Development Policy Review*, Vol. 9, pp. 217–26.

JALLADE, L. 1993. *How to Improve Donor Coordination: Options and Issues Drawn from Field Experience*. (Paper presented at the Meeting of the International Working Group on Education, Nice, 14–16 April 1993.)

KEMMERER, F. 1994. *Utilizing Education and Human Resource Sector Analyses*. Paris, UNESCO/IIEP. (Fundamentals of Educational Planning, 47.)

KING, K. 1992. The External Agenda of Aid in Internal Educational Reform. *International Journal of Educational Development*, Vol. 12, No. 4, pp. 257–63.

LISTER, S. (ed.). 1991. *Aid, Donors and Development Management*. Windhoek. (NEPRU Publications, 2.)

LONDON, N. A. 1993. Why Education Projects in Developing Countries Fail: A Case Study. *International Journal of Educational Development*, Vol. 13, No. 3, pp. 265–75.

MACFARLANE, I. 1996. *The Handling of Donor-funded Projects within NIED*. Namibia. (Internal discussion document, INSTANT project.)

MAGNEN, A. 1994. *Donor Co-ordination in Education. A Case Study on Bangladesh*. Paris, UNESCO/IIEP/UNICEF.

OECD. 1991. *Development Co-operation. 1991 Report*. Paris, OECD.

———. 1992. *Development Assistance Manual. DAC Principles for Effective Aid*. Paris, OECD.

RIDDELL, R. C. 1988. *Foreign Aid Reconsidered.* London, ODI/James Currey.

SAASA, O.; CARLSSON, J. 1996. *The Aid Relationship in Zambia. A Conflict Scenario.* Lusaka/Uppsala, Institute for African Studies/Nordic Institute.

SACK, R. 1995. *Donor Coordination at the Country Level: Experience from an 'Upstream' Education Policy Analysis Project and Conceptual Explorations.* Paris, UNESCO. (UNESCO doc. BER–95/WS/3.)

SAMOFF, J. 1992. *Advisers and Their Advice: A Review of Recent Major Studies of Education in Namibia.* Windhoek. (Paper prepared for Sida and the Namibia Ministry of Education and Culture.)

SARAVANAMUTTOO, N.; SHAW, C. 1995. *Making Debt Work for Education – How Debt Swaps Can Contribute to African Education.* Paris, ADEA.

TUMELO, S. 1991. Botswana's Aid Management in Practice. In: S. Lister (ed.), *Aid, Donors and Development Management,* pp. 154–61. Windhoek. (NEPRU Publications, 2.)

VERSPOOR A. 1993. More than Business-as-usual: Reflections on the New Modalities of Education Aid. *International Journal of Educational Development,* Vol. 13, No. 2, pp. 103–12.

WILLIAMS, P. 1995. *Government's Coordination of Aid to Education: The Case of Namibia.* Paris, ADEA/UNESCO/IIEP.

WOLFSON, M. 1972. *Aid Management in Developing Countries. A Case Study: The Implementation of Three Aid Projects in Tunisia.* Paris, OECD Development Centre.

WORKING GROUP ON EDUCATION SECTOR ANALYSIS. 1997. *Summary Report of the Working Group on Education Sector Analysis (WGESA) Meeting of the Steering Committee, April 28–29.*

WORLD BANK. 1995. *Strengthening the Effectiveness of Aid. Lessons for Donors.* Washington, D.C., World Bank.

Part Four.
National responses to changes in international development co-operation

Aid to South African education: a case of the reluctant recipient?

Kenneth King[1]

Historical background: aid via non-governmental organizations not via the state

In April 1995, just a year after the then Government of National Unity had come to office, the range and diversity of connections between education in South Africa and the outside world had become so evident that the Department of Education felt it necessary to establish a Directorate of International Relations. It had also set up a Directorate for Project Funding. While the latter was primarily concerned with national project initiatives, externally funded projects also fell within its remit. The sheer variety of this outside interest in South African education (and training) was partly historical and partly the result of the department's success in articulating highly challenging reform initiatives in the education and training sector within an extraordinarily short space of time. Many of these created considerable interest within both the external academic and the development assistance constituencies.

As far as the historical dimension was concerned, an enormous number of external bodies had been very closely connected to South Africa's education and training needs even when direct relations with the South African state were regarded as illegitimate. In the case of some organizations, external financing of the educational requirements of disadvantaged non-white populations goes back twenty-five to thirty years. Such external financing covered not only the routine provision of overseas scholarships

---

1. An early version of this chapter was presented to the Department of Education, South Africa (see King, 1996). Work on that report was supported by the Overseas Development Administration, now DFID.

but also the indirect – and often covert – support to educational initiatives within South Africa. A whole range of 'popular' movements concerned broadly with education, adult learning and community development were the recipients of this aid. The spectrum covered everything from trade-union education to adult literacy, from innovative science education within formal schools to popular alternatives to the content-based curriculum of formal education, from innovatory higher education to freedom schools situated outside South Africa's borders. The vehicles for these myriad transactions during the era of apartheid education were sometimes bilateral and multilateral agencies (from both East and West), prevented by the illegitimacy of the South African state from employing their usual government-to-government modalities, finding themselves developing special programmes of assistance to South Africa. And sometimes, it was the 'Northern' non-governmental organizations with resources from many different government and non-government bodies in OECD countries as well as from Africa and other parts of the so-called developing world that had organized and delivered very wide-ranging measures of support to their counterpart organizations within South Africa. Such was the international concern at the implications of Bantu education for human development that it was particularly in respect of the education sector that such non-governmental organizations found themselves supporting the creation of appropriate programmes and projects to assist in reducing the fall-out from apartheid measures. Understandably, large numbers of committed individuals both within and outside South Africa became used to dealing with these many alternative channels of aid to education and training.

In due course, with the release of Nelson Mandela and the prospect of a transition to democratic rule within a number of years, a period of further very intensive interaction between the multiple actors in the democratic movement and external sources of finance can be noted. The objective now was much more focused on capacity-building for the coming transition. Within the education sector, as in a number of other areas, this meant support to policy development, so that when there was change in the government, it would not be necessary to start from scratch in the reconstruction and development of policy.

There have been few historical parallels to these two to three decades of interaction between the progressive forces within South Africa and their multiple supporters outside. Namibia offers a parallel on a

Aid to South African education: a case of the reluctant recipient?
Kenneth King

much smaller scale, as does Zimbabwe. For most of the rest of Africa, the transition from colonialism to independence was much earlier, and in many cases even preceded the establishment of the bilateral development-assistance agencies. The closest parallel is perhaps Chile, which endured exceedingly oppressive authoritarian rule for almost twenty years (from the early 1970s to the very late 1980s). During that period, a whole range of 'popular education' and development alternatives to the illegitimate state received external funding from a huge array of external non-governmental organizations, church organizations and foundations. This external support was also directed to the development of research and policy capacity for a democratic Chile. This latter proved so effective that, with the transition to democracy, many of the key personnel in the Chilean non-governmental organizations and private (non-profit) research and development centres found themselves in positions of very substantial authority in the new ministries.

It should be noted that the non-governmental organization sector that expanded so rapidly in South Africa to complement and compensate for the huge gaps in state provision was also the recipient of significant funding from within South Africa, from the private sector, from charitable foundations and, perhaps paradoxically, in some cases from the state itself. This latter point is important for our subsequent discussion for it would appear that, faced with the increasing illegitimacy of the Department of Education and Training (responsible for African education) in the latter years of white rule, the state itself channelled large public funds via non-governmental organizations, such as the Independent Development Trust, to support initiatives in such crucial areas as school-building.

The other reason for the proliferation of interest by the international development assistance community in South Africa in the last two to three years is that there has been an extraordinary level of policy reform activity within South Africa's education and training programmes. Much of this was able to build on the earlier investment in policy analysis already referred to, but in South Africa, as in Chile, when the many individuals who had been involved with policy development outside the state transferred into line departments, including Education, they were rapidly in a position to articulate new policies that were genuinely creative. These education reforms included, most notably, massive plans for the integration of education and training in the new South Africa, plans also for early childhood intervention and development, and high levels of commitment to the massive populations of adults and inadequately schooled young people whose education had been neglected by the apartheid regime.

Assisted by this headstart on policy analysis and by the continuity in personnel, the new Department of Education had, within its first two years of existence (1994–96), not only organized and begun to digest some of the enormous challenge of restructuring the diverse apartheid arrangements into a single national department and nine provincial departments, but was also identified with two white papers, as well as major work on a School Finance Policy, a South African Schools Bill, and the completion of a National Higher Education Commission. The department had also found time to participate substantially in the International Donor Conference on Human Resource Development, the International Colloquium on Education in the New South Africa (London), the Commonwealth Ministers of Education Conference and the UNESCO General Conference, and in the regional preparation for the mid-term review of Education for All in early 1996. All of these events, and many, many more require major investments in time as well as in the dissemination of new information on policy.

The same pace of policy development was evident in other sectors, such as Health, Small Business and Labour. In terms therefore of what may be called the new aid paradigm's preoccupation with policy (King, 1992), South Africa had a very impressive array of policy work completed in its first two years of majority rule, and by April 1997 there were further substantial papers on the new education curriculum (South Africa. Department of Education, 1997) and on training policy (South Africa. Department of Labour, 1997). As a result of this historical legacy of multiple connections with the external world and its reinforcement by the quality and innovation of the many new policy initiatives, the Department of Education (and indeed the Department of Labour) found itself increasingly being approached by external interests of every kind. These included offers of bursary and scholarship both in South Africa and overseas. They covered requests for protocols, partnerships, twinnings and linkages at every level of education. They also covered the many new obligations derived from rejoining both the Commonwealth and UNESCO (and the United Nations family more generally). In these first two hectic years, requests for educational collaboration were arriving virtually on a daily basis from prospective partners as large as the Russian Federation and as small as Croatia.

In the development assistance arena, every donor nation and multilateral organization as well as all major and minor non-governmental organizations wished to be identified with the newness of the new South Africa. Even though South Africa as a whole had taken some important foreign policy decisions about aid and had set up mechanisms to channel it into high priority programmes, there was every reason for the Department of Education to want to think through its own policies for dealing with the urgency and insistence of its many international contacts, old and new, who wished to collaborate. After setting up its Directorate of International Relations, it therefore turned to the development of a framework paper for guiding its policy on development co-operation (see South Africa. Department of Education, 1995; Kann, 1996; Coombe, 1996; King, 1996).

South Africa's two worlds and the aid relationship

A very substantial number of non-state South African groups, organizations and individuals had been in touch with multiple external sources of moral and financial support for a long time. By contrast, the formal state apparatus with its regular departments such as Finance, Education and Labour had absolutely no tradition of receiving earmarked external funds during the apartheid era. The complex universe of development co-operation was an unknown quantity. And at the time of the democratic transition, it was certainly thought by some who had been closely associated with the previous government that, as South Africa was a relatively rich and industrialized country, it was not a sphere they particularly wanted to enter. To consider becoming an aid recipient in many sectors – from Water, to Land, to Education, Health and Constitutional Affairs – was probably not for some a welcome prospect.

First, there was no experience of aid and, second, there was fiscally no mechanism to treat aid as special. In combination, we shall see that these two factors produced some very major barriers to South Africa becoming rapidly an aid-friendly environment. As far as the first of these two factors is concerned, there was an additional obstacle which was itself the result of the way the aid paradigm had changed over the previous three decades. In earlier years, it was commonplace for both bilateral and multilateral funding and technical-assistance agencies to provide straightforward infrastructural projects. By the early 1990s, it was much more common for funding and technical-assistance agencies to be actively concerned about the larger policy environment in which their aid would be located and, therefore, for their aid to be in part conditioned by the desire to change policy.

This policy-oriented aid had been very obvious to many of the groups that had been receiving aid in the period prior to the democratic transition. Some external aid, in the period before majority rule, had very specifically targeted the policy development process of the democratic movement and, within the sphere of education particularly, aid had been intimately associated with the Education Policy Units and the Centre for Education Policy Development (King, 1993). This policy focus was regarded very positively by those most closely associated with it, since aid was providing the space to develop what would become South Africa's new education policies. Several of these same individuals were, however, well aware that elsewhere in Africa and the developing world, the policy conditionality of aid had proved extremely controversial. It had meant the imposition on financially weak countries of policies approved by particular funding and technical-assistance agencies. In other words, many of those who had moved into key departmental positions in the New South Africa had not only been assisted by aid to develop their own alternative policies, but they would also be very anxious to ensure that the policy development process remained firmly in South African hands.

Paradoxically, this characteristic caution about the role of aid amongst the new adherents to the Departments of State in the new South Africa corresponded with a rather different kind of caution amongst those who had for years been responsible for seeking to maintain the traditions of South African financial probity and parliamentary accountability. These latter, typically located in positions concerned with financial administration in the line departments or in the Department of Finance itself, had firm views about the role of this new money that was quite suddenly on offer to the South African state from many different quarters. First and most crucial to this particular view of aid from the perspective of fiscal discipline was that aid should not be special. The Exchequer Act cannot allow targeted funds to be accepted into the Treasury. There could, therefore, be

Aid to South African education: a case of the reluctant recipient?
Kenneth King

no special deal for aid so that it was an 'additionality' to what had already been voted. Rather it should be firmly located within the budget, and only thus would it be reported on to parliament. Few other countries have argued as strongly as South Africa that aid should not be organized through the back door of the different line departments. It should enter openly by the front door, become part of the regular eighteen-month budget cycle, and thus be susceptible, like any of the other departmental projects, to being audited and reported upon in due course as part of the budget to parliament.

Before dismissing this view as hopelessly unrealistic, it is worth examining it a little more closely. First, the new aid paradigm which we referred to above as being concerned with policy can also be characterized as being a front-door-of-the-department business. New thinking about aid strongly suggests that aid should not be a series of enclave projects, separated from line departments, with their own project implementation units, their own procedures for staffing, procurement, salaries and accounting. If aid is to be influential, arguably it has to be integral to the programme and to the policy of the department or ministry being aided. In one sense, therefore, aid should not be an add-on to the programme of a particular department. If it is really going to make an important contribution, it should be thought through as early as any of the other major initiatives of the particular department. In other words, it should fit into the eighteen-month cycle of regular departmental projects. That way it can be thoroughly discussed with the province (if it is for example to be located in the school sector over which provinces have operational responsibility) and with the national Department of Education; it can be appraised carefully by the agency in question, and it can be situated firmly within the department's regular programme of estimated expenditure for the national and provincial levels in a particular financial year. That way, the agency money is in the budget and 'on the books', and there is no question of it not being accounted for fully.

The objection to large and important agency projects being treated as 'on the books' and part of the budget is hard to sustain. If such projects really are important, why should they be identified, developed and implemented according to a fundamentally different time-frame than the department being aided? Why, for instance, should an agency project expect to be developed, signed and sealed within a few months, and the money begin to be drawn down at a much greater speed than the regular budgetary allocations?

By early 1997, there would appear to have been some change in this original position. One bilateral agency that had been negotiating a project was sent information by the Department of Finance that suggested, in March 1997, that grant aid could be off the books:

Grant aid to the Government should not form part of the budget process. Grant aid to departments and provinces, should, therefore, be over and above their budget allocations. A copy of the relevant memorandum is available on request (South Africa. Department of Finance, 1997).

However, later discussion on this very issue in the Department of Finance suggested that disagreement remained about what can be allowed. This was confirmed by Sida, in South Africa, which has been financing a consultant to the Department of Finance to examine what legislation needs to be changed in this whole area of external funding.

How this debate may work out is not clear, but originally the more substantial agency objection has been to the South African notion that the aid money should not be additional to the state budget. Instead, the aid money should formally enter the budget and save money to the state expenditure. At first sight this apparent absence of additionality in aid money may seem very problematic both to the potential funding or technical-assistance agency and to the line department. But again it may be worth examining this in a little more depth as this may clarify what precisely is the role of international aid in what is by comparative standards a relatively wealthy country – one that, for example, does not even qualify on per capita GNP grounds for the concessional International Development Association (IDA) funds from the World Bank. Presumably, the international aid community is interested in assisting South Africa because there are particular areas, such as the low quality of education in what are locally termed 'historically black' schools or colleges, or the absence of effective literacy skills in much of the adult black population where they feel that external resources – both financial and human – could make a difference.

Agencies are not on the whole saying that more money should be allocated to the education sector of the national budget which represented 7 per cent of GNP in 1995–96. Nor are funding and technical-assistance agencies saying that the current intersectoral allocation between primary, secondary and higher education is necessarily inappropriate. Their main concern is of course with the wide (if decreasing) disparities between the formerly African, coloured, Indian and white sectors of education. There has also been some concern at the relative neglect of early childhood education, adult basic education and training, especially for the majority African population. But the agency agenda is principally about redistribution and redress — about targeted support to constituencies that have historically been massively neglected.

The South African response to this emphasis, including views from within the Department of Finance, is broadly in agreement. But a very powerful thread in the response has been concerned with getting the balance right between redress and sustainability. It might be argued that agency offers of educational aid (which everyone assumes are essentially short term, and may not actually even be available to South Africa in five years' time) could have the result of establishing new institutional capacity and high cost inputs in many of the areas of current deprivation. However, if this were to lead, at the end of the funding, to significant and unsustainably higher recurrent expenditure in education overall, this might not be regarded as an appropriate use of international funding. It should be noted that there has, in fact, been a much greater concern in South Africa about the sustainability of agency inputs than has been the case in many other African countries.

In summary it could, therefore, be said that much of the discourse on aid was essentially concerned with refocusing and redistributing education budgets, and with re-emphasizing equity and quality issues in their application.

Aid in the context of the Reconstruction and Development Programme

Effectively, what agencies wanted to do was paralleled much more dramatically by the new role assigned to the Reconstruction and Development Programme (RDP). This was meant to act as a lever for change and for new priorities in all government departments. The concept was very openly projected during the International Donor Conference on Human Resource Development in the Reconstruction and Development Programme in Cape Town (October 1994). But it is worth noting that

RDP underlined for its own operations some of the very same things that had been urged upon agency offers of support. There was the same concern that RDP programmes be new but not additional.

Equally, there was an assumption that RDP should be a lever for redistribution and redirection, and certainly not just a source of new staff for new and separate 'development' activities. To re-emphasize this concern with financial sustainability, the government wanted to underline the fact that RDP was not a slush fund that would allow business-as-usual in the line departments while offering additional money and staffing for visible one-off projects. All RDP projects had the challenge of combining being new and yet being integrated into the various departments. They had to be path-breaking and yet fiscally very disciplined, empowering and affirmative and yet sustainable and viable (Naidoo, 1994).

RDP was to be the vehicle for the twenty-two Presidential Lead Projects that were to be at the heart of this attempt to reform the way that the government worked and assigned itself priorities. Several notable projects in the education sector, such as the Culture of Learning, school nutrition and adult literacy, were identified amongst these twenty-two. But the RDP fund to support such programmes was not, strictly speaking, new money; it was the result of top-slicing the annual budget, to create a sufficiently large amount – no less than R7.5 billion in 1996–97 – that could be bid for and redistributed for programme implementation at provincial and local levels. In accounting terms, therefore, RDP money could be seen as being within the budget and, from 1996–97, any such money allocated to national projects was explicitly 'on the books' and could be reported on to parliament as a line item, whether in national or provincial budgets.

In a sense, RDP's central concern about programme reorientation, the reform of both the spirit and the practice of line departments, and the identification of high visibility areas of national need that were fiscally sustainable, was not fundamentally dissimilar to the discourse of the agency community just discussed. That too was substantially concerned with redistribution and redress in favour of large disadvantaged communities. It should not therefore have been surprising that RDP expected the development-assistance constituency to be closely associated with this programme of major reform. This way, agency activity would not be a scattershot of myriad large and small initiatives driven by hundreds of different negotiations between agencies and different actors in South Africa, but would be

Aid to South African education: a case of the reluctant recipient?
Kenneth King

within the agreed programmes of the government. Accordingly an interdepartmental committee had been set up in 1994 whose central purpose had been to bring aid money on line, within this framework of major priority projects, with the spirit and purpose with which few agencies could disagree.

Here, then, was the vision of an aid partnership that would substantially reinforce the agreed transformation programmes of government. It would surely commend itself to the development-assistance community, since the RDP emphasis on changing the whole policy environment rather than running add-on projects in agency or RDP enclaves was so akin to the thrust of the new aid paradigm. But it did mean that a funding and technical-assistance agency had to accept the basic assumption that government-to-government aid was not special but was to be integrated into both the budget and the medium-term investment profiles. In the words of Alec Erwin, former Deputy Minister of Finance:

The assistance is not additional resources to a department but will lower the cost of borrowing as a whole, therefore, indirectly releasing resources that can be used for reprioritizing. Clearly the use of foreign currency development assistance will be of benefit to the balance of payment position (Erwin, 1994, p. 10).

Almost exactly a year and a half after these bold aspirations for a creative government–aid partnership were publicly expressed on 27 October 1994, the RDP office was closed as an independent entity and incorporated into the Department of Finance, and its minister without portfolio was transferred and not replaced. It was possible to conclude that this particular strategy for agency co-ordination had simply not worked out. Indeed, very little external assistance appears to have been channelled through RDP in the interim.

It is not the purpose of this case study to examine the achievements of RDP or the new modalities for its continuation. Rather, it is to understand, from the perspective of the education sector, something of the way in which educational aid has in practice sought to attach itself to South Africa. By contrast, with the expectation that aid would be solidly situated within this government framework and would thus be on the budget, any observers could be forgiven for concluding that almost the opposite has transpired over the past year and a half (up to the changes on

28 March 1996) and in the year following that. A good deal of aid is, strictly speaking, 'off the books' and not embedded in the regular budgets of the line departments and the provinces. It does not appear to be concentrated on a small number of really major projects and programmes in the manner proposed by RDP. Nor have the shape and quality of external aid been at all easy to judge by the key South African determinants of its sustainability and accountability. In terms of our discussion earlier in this chapter, the existence of a strong national policy line had not made the negotiations with agencies any easier. Nor had it apparently aided the development of greater co-ordination amongst them.

The shape of the aided component of the education sector in South Africa

Given the very considerable historical exposure of several South African education policy-makers to the aid constituency and given also the attractiveness to international funding and technical-assistance agencies of supporting South Africa's innovative educational reform plans, what can actually be said of the character of this educational aid some two to three years after the democratic transition? Here we shall limit ourselves to a number of comments noted in just two short periods in South Africa.

Apparently relatively small amounts of educational aid actually received

Compared to the overall budget for education in the financial year 1996–97 of some R34 billion, it would be difficult to argue that the extent of educational aid money received by the government through their preferred route had been significant. Some, for example from the Netherlands Government, had been granted in a manner close to what might be called the RDP mode just described. As part of budgetary support to RDP of some 40 million florins agreed by the Netherlands Minister of Development Co-operation for certain of the broad RDP programmes, a substantial amount could be released for education themes. It would appear that the money was held in the Netherlands and was to be transferred for particular activities on the basis of agreed business plans. Several years later, less than half of the amount available had been drawn upon by the South Africans.

There had also been agreement in principle with USAID on a basic education programme of some $15 million, but the modalities for dispersal to the three agreed provinces do not appear to have been completely settled. And there had also been a single project agreed by the European Union (library books and training for historically disadvantaged institutions) which was for 11 million ecus. Other agencies, such as the United Kingdom's DFID, had been active in project development. However, up to April 1996, no significant money had actually been granted by DFID to the South African Government for education sector projects. Germany was another country that had had government-to-government talks at the highest level in June 1995. From the total German allocation of DM7.5 million for 1995, there had been agreement in principle about the importance of German co-operation in support of technical and vocational education and training (to the Department of Labour for DM4.5 million).

But this was not necessarily quite the same as supporting the RDP lead projects in the way outlined by RDP. Even if there were an audit of all other agencies' education aid programmes in these first two to three years, it is doubtful if there would be much that could be counted as falling within RDP's approved budget and programme support modality. It is also doubtful if there would be many others that came as close to the preferred budgetary support of RDP as did the Netherlands. And if those amounts were then to be set against the sheer size of the education budget for this period, they would probably appear to be minuscule in comparison.

From the illegitimacy to the complexity of the state: the non-governmental organization option for external support to education

One of the paradoxes of development co-operation in South Africa has been the continuity in the use of non-governmental organizations as an alternative to direct support to the state. For the period prior to April 1994, we have already referred to the widespread use of South African non-governmental organizations by multilateral and bilateral agencies as well as by Northern non-governmental organizations as the main channel for getting funds into the country for the support of education and training initiatives for Africans. But even after the state had become legitimate, several agencies continued to make use of non-governmental fundholders because of the alleged difficulty in rapidly developing education projects through the approved channels. Agencies such as Sida, which would have preferred regular government-to-government collaboration, found themselves being advised to resort to various arrangements with non-state recipients in order to deliver educational support to the new South African state.

These developments are widely known about and discussed in the government and agency worlds, and they are by no means restricted to the Department of Education. But they do not appear to have been thoroughly analysed or written about. It is difficult, accordingly, to be clear what has been the influence of several different factors in producing this rather contradictory and unsatisfactory situation. It is, on the one hand, alleged that the rules and regulations of the tender board (in South Africa as in Namibia) place major obstacles in the way of external agencies or government departments wishing to get work done speedily by identified groups. Equally, it is suggested that procedures for commenting upon or ratifying proposals for external funding have been exceedingly slow. Again, the challenge of following the agreed route for project development and approval suggests that in some quarters it is not even clear to funding and technical-assistance agencies what is the status of the different guidelines on development co-operation. In addition, there is in some quarters a genuine degree of hesitation about the values and assumptions embedded in aid. It is difficult also to generalize about this because it does not appear to have been written up as an input into the process of formulating a position paper on aid to education.

The result is that in some situations where agencies would have preferred to have used bilateral government-to-government agreements but where the legal capacity to accept these is not yet in place, it would seem that non-governmental organizations are used as fundholders to implement particular projects in schools or in adult education. If there were a listing of all such non-governmental organization projects in the education sector, it might be quite large. But as we shall see, even that is difficult to be sure of.

What is so complex about the current status of non-governmental organization and public sector aid projects in South Africa is that many agencies had every intention of continuing to support non-governmental organizations as key actors in civil society after the democratic transition, in addition to developing new programme relations with the government departments. What would be unfortunate would be a situation in which

Aid to South African education: a case of the reluctant recipient?
Kenneth King

external bodies continue increasingly to avoid the important controls associated with tendering, auditing and monitoring because of the comparative ease of making their aid arrangements with the non-governmental organization sector.

Tracking and inventorying direct and indirect aid flows to education

One of the results of some aid having initially gone via the older RDP route in favour of education, and other aid being destined for public-sector education but being routed via the non-governmental organizations, and other aid, again, being provided for education but being allocated entirely for foreign or local technical assistance (and therefore not transferred to government at all), is that it is extremely difficult to know precisely what is the tally of external support to education. There had been initiated a series of annual consultations between the International Development Co-operation Committee (IDCC) and individual agencies which have resulted in agreed minutes of what the particular agency was already supporting and committed to support in the near future in all sectors including education. These could in principle be drawn together, and at the end of a particular year a listing of projects could then be deduced for the education sector.

In many countries, this tracking of external development co-operation on a yearly basis has been carried out both by a national planning unit and by the local UNDP office (Williams, 1995). In the case of South Africa, it was decided early on by the new government that this was a function that could be handled nationally by RDP and need not involve UNDP. Quite how the closure of the RDP office has affected this responsibility is not yet clear, though individual discussions with funding and technical-assistance agencies continue, even though IDCC has been disbanded. But even before the changes, it was already difficult, in spite of the existence of a Directorate of International Relations, for a single department such as Education to track the status of particular aid programmes or to get an overall picture of aid commitments and disbursements to the sector.

The view within the Department of Finance at this period was that the only aid that should formally be reported on to DAC was aid that followed the official route and had involved IDCC and RDP. The obvious difficulty with this position is that other aid that has utilized the non-governmental organization route to avoid the alleged complexities and delays of the official pathway is effectively invisible as official aid flows. It has proved problematic to calculate the proportions of aid going through these different routes. But it is certainly the case that more aid destined ideally for the government-to-government path is actually made invisible as an official aid flow by being located with non-governmental organizations rather than directly with the particular line departments.

This is clearly an anomalous situation in terms of aid reporting. But it is even more serious from the perspective of formal accountability. When external moneys which the Department of Finance would have wished to see built into budgets and therefore on the books for accounting to parliament are actually being channelled via a non-governmental fundholder, it would seem to be unfortunate. At the moment, there are only a few such projects in education where the bilateral route has been dropped in favour of the non-governmental route. But, again, it could become very difficult to be sure what should be classified as a non-governmental organization in its own right and what should be classified as a non-governmental organization in the sense of fundholder for government. If it becomes commonplace to regard the government route as problematic, projects could begin to be negotiated *ab initio* directly with non-governmental organizations that might in other circumstances have been located with government. If this same principle also became commonplace at the provincial level, it could become extremely difficult to monitor the extent and pattern of external aid to education in South Africa.

The changing dimensions of 'additionality' in educational aid

We noted earlier that the government's intention had originally been that external aid not become a series of add-ons to government's plans and projects, but that it be fully integrated or added in to the budgets of line departments through formal agreements with RDP and IDCC. Within a relatively short time of the then Government of National Unity being in office, it had become clear that not a great deal of aid was following this add-in route. The precise reasons probably differ from agency to agency. Some felt that they could not become involved in what looked like budgetary support to RDP for reasons of their own agency's accounting proce-

Aid to South African education: a case of the reluctant recipient?
Kenneth King

dures. Others felt that their own principal, potential contribution was in the transfer of know-how through technical assistance at the national, provincial and local levels. They would not need to have head office staff in South Africa at all, they might argue, if the agencies were merely content to put their money into RDP agreed projects as a form of budgetary support.

In a way, the add-in add-on debate surrounding aid funds goes to the heart of the debate about development assistance in South Africa. Add-in suggests that the government has done its homework, developed its own set of policies and is asking for external aid to reinforce these in ways that avoid a whole separate set of regimes for aid money. Add-on points to the special role of agency money, and the need for funding and technical-assistance agencies to feel that they are bringing something new and extra to the ordinary budget of the state. Add-on also speaks of the importance of agencies being able to identify, track and make accountable their own particular contributions. Add-in, by contrast, may be relatively invisible, and while it may be nationally accountable within the regular state budget, it may be much harder for the agencies to earmark and make specially accountable through their own channels and procedures.

In reality, this either-or approach to aid may be misleading. There are certain projects where the external agency might make a relatively invisible (add-in) contribution to a national priority such as a lead project but where the technical assistance (know-how or add-on) element could be completely off the books of the national government; it would, however, be known about by both governments but only be on the books of the funding and technical-assistance agency. This 'mixed economy' of development co-operation could mean that budgetary support to a key project, such as the Culture of Learning in the education sector, could be combined with a potentially influential role for technical assistance. But there seems to be no good reason why the latter should be off the books of official aid flows.

As a result of the rethinking of RDP and development co-operation in late March 1996, it would seem that there has been a recognition of the importance of allowing smaller projects (say, of less than R5 million) to be agreed directly with line departments without going up through what was once the whole IDCC–RDP route. These would tend to be add-on, predominantly technical-assistance projects, that would seek to address particularly short-term know-how needs. They would still need to be carefully checked for their implications for recurrent costs and financial sustainability. Larger projects certainly do need in some sense to become part of the particular line department's own planning frame and financial cycle if they are to avoid being seen as special deals with their own rules and regulations. Such projects will tend to have both a technical-assistance component and some direct financial contribution. Precisely how the cash element gets treated so that it is a regular part of the department's and parliament's control and accounting concerns may need further to be discussed in the aftermath of RDP changes and of externally funded projects that have led to very public accountability disputes.

The centre–province dimension of the external assistance debate

One of the still unresolved dimensions of international assistance concerns the question of how external funds can relate to the many very pressing demands from the provinces for both technical assistance and institutional and infrastructural support. It should not be surprising, given many agencies' concerns with basic education, that it should be in particular provinces, with their constitutional responsibility for school education, rather than in the centre that agencies are looking to make a contribution. Some of the same discussion about agency money being within the budget or off the books has surfaced in this sphere, along with the issue of agencies being encouraged to use non-governmental-organization fundholders. Obviously an additional dimension of agency negotiations with the provinces is clarity about the control function of the substantive line department and the Department of Finance as well as of the procedures that follow the changes in RDP.

The centre–province debate is of course much larger than the issues concerning education, but it is clear that agencies are not aware of the precise degrees of freedom to be allowed to the provinces. This is entirely understandable as the division of powers and responsibilities has not been completely sorted out. In the interim, it would seem to be important that a whole series of relatively invisible projects do not get agreed with different agencies through the non-governmental-organization fundholder route. The present situation has been described as a 'free for all' or 'a Wild West', with agencies individually approaching different provinces. None of this can be very helpful if the aim is to develop a coherent management of aid within the fiscal disciplines of the national state.

Again, there seems to be an absence in the sphere of education of a comprehensive tally of which agency is doing what in which province through which funding modality. And although there are occasional department–agency informal meetings on education, these have thus far excluded the possibility of provincial policy initiatives being represented in their own right. Once the centre and the provinces have worked out a division of responsibility, it would presumably be timely to have provinces set out their policies for integrating external support into their own frameworks.

Agency desire for projects versus departmental concern for policy coherence

A number of agencies have been disappointed at how little they have managed to get agreed in the first two or three years since April 1994. In many cases, special money was allocated for potential support to South Africa and, it is alleged, fundable projects have just not been forthcoming. It must be remembered that, during this same time, line departments have had a huge number of very major internal changes to digest and, particularly in education, have been seeking to put in place really major legislative initiatives. Responding to the agency desire for projects has had to take second place. And it has probably been quite important that the department did get its own policies established before feeling obliged to accommodate grant assistance, let alone loans for education.

Nevertheless, there is clearly very major underutilization of the grant aid that has been made available, not just in education but more generally. In April 1996, there was a meeting of the South African International Development Forum at which it was claimed that procedures for aid negotiations would henceforth be simplified through what was termed 'a one-stop shop'. But there had not been much noticeable difference. For instance, of the R500 million per year from the European Union, only 10 per cent had been used, according to senior agency sources. Other bilaterals, notably the Japanese, who have been less certain about using the non-governmental-organization route, possibly through lack of non-governmental organizations known to themselves, have felt it problematic to have to continue to explain to the Department of Finance in

Japan that education projects may eventually be coming. Even the Canadians, who have been one of the most active donors in the education sector, continue to find that there is a problem getting aid to government. It would be possible to illustrate a degree of frustration amongst several other agencies.

However, on the government side there continues to be a strong feeling that getting the right policies in place must take precedence over accommodating the many and various requests of agencies. There has been one major exception to this hesitation, and that would encompass what has been termed the President's Educational Initiative (PEI). It had its origins in the crisis of teacher redundancy in Western Cape and it took the form of direct requests from the President to his counterparts in several donor countries; but it has since developed into a major initiative on teacher-training strategies. In a sense, it could be described as another Presidential Lead Project, but, unlike the earlier series, this was one that many agencies were, at the highest political level, encouraged directly to support.

Now that the first set of national education policies is almost in place and that there clearly have been important changes in the IDCC–RDP route for project identification, it could well be that the South African education authorities and international funding and technical-assistance agencies need a restatement of how external funds can be most appropriately added in and added on to the many very urgent developments, especially at the provincial level.

Implications for aid to South Africa in the context of the new aid paradigm

It is appropriate before ending this account to see what light the South African experience sheds on what was called the new paradigm in the Introduction to this volume. First, in respect of the new emphasis on policy-based aid, South Africa was a country which had no shortage of thoroughly developed policies. Several international funding and technical-assistance agencies had played key roles in creating the space for policy development through generous support to Education Policy Units (EPUs) (Samoff, 1995) and the Centre for Education Policy Development (UNESCO, 1994, pp. 13–19). Much of this support had been available in the period prior to majority rule. Second, the style of trustfulness and respect in the patterns of early support during the anti-apartheid era right up to the time of majority rule could in many ways be characterized as having that 'mutuality' and partnership feeling that Sweden in particular has been exploring more generally for Africa in the very recent period (Sweden. Ministry for Foreign Affairs, 1997). The paradox is that the special quality of that aid relationship with those bodies battling against the illegitimate apartheid state has not yet been found with the now legitimate state.

Third, there is no denying that there has been little attention paid to the role of agency co-ordination in the period after majority rule. UNDP was actively discouraged from what has been its usual role in aid reporting. The meetings of education agencies that had once been convened by Sida soon stopped altogether once the agencies had abandoned their lead role and ceded that, appropriately, to the Department of Education. But then this is not the whole truth. The government had actually set out to co-ordinate the agencies in the ultimate sense of asking them simply to contribute to the lead projects through RDP. The agencies had mostly refused to do this, with one or two exceptions. So what was called in the Introduction 'policy-based educational aid' had not appealed, presumably because either the policies or the process or both were not attractive.

Fourth, what is more surprising, given the surety of purpose in proposing agency support to RDP, which we could call a straightforward add-in to the budget of the state, is that government should then apparently turn round and allow a number of agencies to do their own thing. Several were able to choose their own recipients, including at the provincial level, with the result that what looked like being a very carefully modulated aid framework became a 'free for all'. One explanation of this rather dramatic shift is that there was a shift within South Africa in the short space of a few years from the highly centralized model of development associated with RDP to a much more pragmatic and increasingly decentralized model. It could well be in this new situation that external aid could flow into what Hyden has termed autonomous development funds instead of into non-governmental organizations as fundholders (Hyden, 1997).

Fifth, there is, nevertheless, in South Africa still a legacy of concern about the invasiveness of aid. So, like Namibia, there is still not a World

Bank project in the education sector, although individual World Bank staff may from time to time play key advisory roles, most recently in the *Higher Education White Paper*. And there is still some radical questioning in the International Relations Directorate of the appropriateness of aid for particular purposes. But at the same time, many funding and technical-assistance agencies, from the British to the Canadians, Irish, Australians, Americans and the European Union, are developing relatively large technical-assistance projects, including with the provinces. In this situation, there are a lot of questions to be asked about the role and character of aid to South African education. The national policies in most cases are in place. The real challenge now will be to implement them. And here, aid which has had experience of putting in place whole systems of local level training, administration, inspection, and teacher in-servicing may well have something to offer, as an add-on or add-in to the huge amount that South Africans have already achieved.

In approaching this, South Africa could well be a test case of the 'genuine partnerships' or 'the more equal and respectful relationships' that the United Kingdom and Sweden respectively have emphasized in their recent policy papers on aid (DFID, 1997; Sweden. Ministry for Foreign Affairs, 1997).

References

COOMBE, C. 1996. *International Relations Policy and Practice: A Draft Discussion Paper*. Pretoria, Department of Education.

ERWIN, A. 1994. *Financing Mechanisms*. (Paper to the International Donor Conference on Human Resource Development in the Reconstruction and Development Programme (RDP), Cape Town, 26–28 October.)

HYDEN, G. 1997. The Battles for New Formulas: Foreign Aid in Longer Term Perspective. In: Sida, *Project 2015: Development Cooperation in the 21st Century*. Stockholm.

KANN, U. 1996. *Report from a Consultancy on International Relations and Aid Co-ordination within the Department of Education, South Africa*. (Mimeo.)

KING, K. 1992. The Role of the External Agencies in Local Education Reform. *International Journal of Educational Development*, Vol. 12, No. 4, pp. 257–63.

——. 1993. *Aid and Education in Africa: A Review of Recent Developments with Particular Relevance to South Africa*. Cape Town, University of Western Cape, Education Policy Unit. (Occasional Paper, 21.)

——. 1996. *Aid Co-ordination in South Africa: Continuity, Accountability and Transformation in the Education and Training Sectors. Report to the Department of Education*, Pretoria, South Africa.

NAIDOO, J. 1994. *Overview and Priorities of the RDP*. (Paper to the International Donor Conference on Human Resource Development in the Reconstruction and Development Programme (RDP), Cape Town, 26–28 October.)

SAMOFF, J. 1995. *Agitators, Incubators, Advisers – What Roles for the EPUs? An Evaluation of South African Education Policy Units Supported by Sweden*. Stanford, Samoff Services.

SOUTH AFRICA. DEPARTMENT OF EDUCATION. 1995. *First Draft Framework Document for Policy Formulation on International Relations*. Pretoria.

——. 1997. *Curriculum 2005: Lifelong Learning for the 21st Century*. Pretoria.

——. DEPARTMENT OF FINANCE. 1997. *Memorandum concerning External Assistance Sent to a Bilateral Donor*. Pretoria.

——. DEPARTMENT OF LABOUR. 1997. *Green Paper: Skills Development Strategy for Economic and Employment Growth in South Africa*. Pretoria.

SWEDEN. MINISTRY FOR FOREIGN AFFAIRS. 1997. *Partnership with Africa. Proposals for a New Swedish Policy towards Sub-Saharan Africa*. Stockholm.

UNESCO. 1994. *Donor Co-operation and Co-ordination in Education in South Africa*. Paris, Division for Policy Analysis and Sector Analysis.

UNITED KINGDOM. DEPARTMENT FOR INTERNATIONAL DEVELOPMENT. 1997. *Eliminating World Poverty: A Challenge for the 21st Century*. London, HMSO. (CMMD 3789.)

WILLIAMS, P. 1995. *Government's Co-ordination of Aid to Education: The Case of Namibia*. Paris, ADEA/UNESCO-IIEP.

Educational policies, change programmes and international co-operation: the case of Chile

Cristián Cox and Beatrice Avalos

Introduction

In the education sector in Chile, transition towards democracy began in 1990 with a government programme designed to improve the quality of the poorest primary schools in the country. A grant-in-aid from the Swedish Government, supplemented a year later by the Danish Government, contributed substantially to what became known as the 900 Schools Programme. Two years later, and assisted by a World Bank loan, a major reform effort began in order to improve quality and equity in pre-school and primary-school education; in 1995, a similar programme for secondary-school education was started.[1] To date, despite a change of government and five ministers of education, results of these programmes are noticeable both as regards the innovative character of the change efforts involved and their stability over time.

In this chapter, the development of these reform efforts and the mode in which international co-operation was at work in their design and implementation have been sketched. In the first part, the educational policy context surrounding educational changes and the key features of selected reform efforts are described. In the second part we look particularly at the case of programme development assisted by multilateral agencies as represented by the World Bank.

---

1. For a recent analysis of the secondary-school reform programme, see Lemaitre (1998).

The educational policy context of the 1990s

Over the last thirty years there have been three major interventions in the Chilean education system. In the 1960s, a highly centralized state system in a democratic context accomplished a reform focused on *expanding access* to schooling. In the dictatorship context of the 1980s, a radical neo-liberal reform affecting the school system's administration and finance focused on *efficiency, decentralization* and *privatization* of educational services. In the regained democracy of the 1990s, educational reform in Chile is grounded on the principles of *quality* and *equity* in educational provision, combining state control and market orientation in the implementation of change.

The overriding principle of the educational reform which began in 1990 has been to provide equal opportunities for all children and young people to develop the capacities required by the complex world in which they have to live: the ability to think systematically and critically, to communicate with others and work as a team, to learn how to learn, to make appropriate moral judgements and participate intelligently in a democracy. In practice, this has meant instituting reforms that affect the organization, processes, curriculum and supporting structures of the education system. The new policy framework for educational reform, building on the competitive finance mechanisms introduced in the early 1980s by the military regime, strengthens the state's leadership through installing institutional capacity to design and conduct comprehensive social and educational programmes aimed at enhancing the quality and equity of education, providing information tools for public evaluation of programmes and institutions and opening of schools to external 'support networks', especially universities and business enterprises.

The key orientations of this approach, resulting from the findings of over a decade of research conducted by independent centres[2] opposed to the military government, also coincided with principles set in the early 1990s by the World Conference on Education for All (1990) and by

2. The ideas and experiences resulting from work in these independent centres, funded throughout the 1980s by non-government aid agencies such as the International Development Research Centre (IDRC, Canada), the Swedish Agency for Research Co-operation (SAREC) and the Ford Foundation, amongst others, are described by García-Huidobro (1989) and PIIE (1989).

ECLAC-UNESCO (1992). Between 1990 and 1992, Chilean educational policy gradually came to incorporate the following set of guiding principles:
- Shift from concern about educational inputs to concern about learning processes and outcomes.
- Sensitivity to differences and discrimination in favour of those most at risk.
- Regulatory norms governed more by provision of incentives, information and evaluation results than by bureaucratic and administrative concerns.
- Opening of educational institutions to societal demands and connections amongst themselves and with other institutions.
- Shift from top-down directed change and linear planning to incremental change harnessing the innovative capacity of schools.
- National strategic policies based on consensus among key stakeholders.

Key reform interventions

While there were four main areas targeted for action by government policies (finance, the teaching profession, the context and processes of education, and building political consensus regarding educational change), this chapter deals with programmes designed specifically to improve the quality of schooling and its social distribution.

Improvement of school quality in poor districts: the 900 Schools Programme

The 900 Schools Programme began in 1990, assisted by a Swedish grant, with the purpose of serving the 10 per cent of schools (around 900) with the lowest level of attainment as measured by national examinations. The programme, which is ongoing and now fully part of the Ministry of Education's structure, aims at improving the physical environment and educational processes in these schools, provides textbooks, teaching materials and classroom libraries and offers professional support to teachers. It also supports a monitorial scheme to assist pupils with learning difficulties during the first four years. The scheme is aimed not only at improving these children's reading, writing and maths skills, but also at enhancing their self-esteem and communication capabilities.

Over time, the target schools have changed. Those that clearly improve their results, as measured by national examinations, are deemed ready to 'graduate' and become part of the mainstream reform efforts for primary schools. Other schools are then brought into the programme and the same sort of assistance is provided for them. Evidence of success of the programme lies in the pace of learning of children in these schools compared to pupils in their mainstream counterparts, the municipal schools. In fact between 1990 and 1996, the 2,099 schools that were part of the programme increased by almost 13 percentage points their attainment in maths and mother tongue as opposed to 9 percentage points in municipal schools, suggesting a narrowing of the quality gap between the lowest-ranking schools and the rest of the system.[3]

Improvement of quality and equity for the pre- and primary-school levels (Primary MECE or MECE Básica)

Launched in 1992, the Primary MECE Programme is a systematic effort to improve the quality of educational processes in all state-subsidized pre-primary and primary schools (around 90 per cent of the school population). The programme was implemented on a six-year basis by means of a financial loan and technical support from the World Bank. The loan period has been completed and the Primary MECE Programme is now part of the Ministry of Education's structure and fully funded by the national education budget.

The Primary MECE Programme has supplied textbooks to the entire student body of subsidized schools (some 6 million textbooks per year for the 1992–97 period);[4] it has equipped libraries in all classrooms between Grades 1 and 6 and provided teaching materials to all classrooms between pre-kindergarten and Grade 4. Additional investments in infrastructure

3. See Chile. Ministry of Education (1997).
4. Access to textbooks is regarded as one of the important factors for achieving improved learning outcomes. Between 1988 and 1990, the state invested an average of $1.6 million per year in basic textbooks. Between 1991 and 1996, the average of annual spending on textbooks (three books per student from years 1 to 4 and five books per student from Grades 5 to 8) was $4.7 million (in December 1995 US dollars) (Cox, 1997).

repairs and a programme of health care are intended to ensure better learning conditions.[5]

In its effort to enrich the school work, three major innovations were introduced: the Rural Schools MECE, the Educational Improvement Projects designed to stimulate innovative capabilities at school level and Enlaces, a computer-linked educational information network.

1. The Rural MECE covers over 3,000 rural primary incomplete schools with one to three teachers, supplying them with textbooks, libraries and teaching materials. It assists teachers in developing multigrade teaching skills and communicating with each other through periodical meetings at a nearby centre. At these 'rural micro-centres' teachers learn from each other as well as from outside facilitators.

    This programme attempts to reverse the influence of a traditional urban centralist culture by recognizing that the language and cultural codes of the rural communities are a valid and necessary point of departure for school work. The programme, however, does not seek to 'ruralize' education by limiting its learning to local cultural horizons. On the contrary, while strengthening the sense of place and empowerment of the local culture and environment, it seeks to offer children access to the knowledge and language of the world at large: *aprender de lo cercano para llegar a lo lejano* (learn about what is near to you in order to reach out to what is far).

2. The Educational Improvement Projects are intended to stimulate the school and teachers' ability to respond as a team to the challenge of improving instruction. Public resources are provided for a series of school-initiated projects that compete each year. The themes of these projects broadly coincide with curriculum areas. Schools selected under the schools' project programme receive a grant based on enrolment (averaging $6,000 per school, which may be drawn over a period of up to three years) and a teaching support package (which includes, for example, a television set, videotape recorders, microscopes).

---

5. Between 1992 and 1996, buildings of 2,232 schools were repaired (89 per cent of the original target). The entire student body from Grades 1 to 4 (322,241) was submitted to health examinations by specialists (ophthalmologists, ear, nose and throat specialists and traumatologists) and 233,739 pupils were treated (optical glasses, drugs, kinesitherapy, hearing aids, examinations). This exceeded the original goals of the programme (Cox, 1997).

Even though their goal is to raise school attainment, each school has complete autonomy when it comes to deciding what is to be prioritized in a project. Thus the strategy combines the provision of guidelines and central funding with grass-roots initiatives in the form of locally defined projects.

Evidence produced on the basis of monitoring and managing the Primary MECE Programme has shown that successful implementation of the school-initiated project strategy has involved some or all of the following processes: (i) horizontal communication among teachers in different subjects or grades; (ii) team or joint diagnosis of problems, design of solutions and evaluation of completed tasks; (iii) setting of priorities associated with school routines and proper costing of activities (this allows teacher management of the project rather than bureaucratic following of orders); (iv) parental or community involvement (it expands the volume of available resources and opens the school and its teachers to their external environment); (v) identification of professional development needs on the part of teachers and of how to meet them; and (vi) innovative practices related to curriculum, instruction and the production of teaching materials.

3. The Enlaces network is a computerized interschool communications network project for pupils, students and teachers that was launched at primary level in 1992. Its current funding is $120 million. The original goal of Enlaces – at the time a bold one when networking was in its pioneering stages – was to link up 100 primary schools by 1997 through a user-friendly, multimedia and pedagogically stimulating computer tool that could operate under the technological conditions of the country's then existing telephone system. The programme's initial success and the speed with which its technological base radically improved meant that, by 1994, Enlaces was no longer regarded as a pilot project. New targets for network coverage were set: 50 per cent of publicly supported primary schools by the year 2000 and all secondary schools by 1998. It is expected that by 1999 all 5,000 schools in the country will be reached.

For its operation Enlaces provides between three and twelve latest-generation computers to the participating schools with multimedia and communication capabilities. A programme-developed software known as *La Plaza* (the square) introduces in a user-friendly way teachers and students to the educational uses of the new medium. *La Plaza* integrates tools for e-mail, discussion groups, bulletin boards and access to educational software and productivity tools without requiring the user to master the operating system of the computer on which they are installed.

The development of this computer program drew upon lessons and the experience of the 1980s in North America and Europe, showing that free availability is no guarantee that proper educational use will be made of computers. The process of appropriating new technologies is a gradual one, involving teachers as key actors who require proper introduction to the system. Enlaces relies on universities to assist teachers to learn about the uses of hardware and software in an educational context and to assist them in disseminating electronic culture throughout their schools (use of e-mail and electronic forums to promote collaborative interschool work).[6]

This school—universities network has wide-ranging implications for the quality and equity of schooling in the country. By providing access to networking and information technology, the programme opens up new windows of knowledge and information that should redefine quite drastically the learning possibilities of schools in the future and provide students with the kind of information resources and possibilities that enable cross-cultural fertilization regardless of geographic or social settings.

Improvement of quality and equity for secondary-school education (Secondary MECE Programme, 1995)

Three years of experience with the Primary MECE Programme and five years with the 900 Schools Programme proved the effectiveness of com-

6. Enlaces schools will gain access to the Internet over the next two years; currently, they communicate only through e-mail. Seven Education Information Technology Centres located at universities are responsible for planning and managing the network project within their areas and for delivering training and technical assistance to schools and colleges. Each centre provides training and technical assistance to schools within its area for two years. During those two years, twenty teachers from each school are trained, the schools are linked into the network and efforts are made to bring computer technology into the classroom, the school administration and into extracurricular projects.

prehensive quality improvement programmes. Thus, after two years of work on its technical and policy components and strategies, the Ministry of Education in 1995 began a new programme aimed at secondary-school education. With a budget of $207 million (or more than twice the per capita funding of the primary education programme)[7] and a planning framework of six years, the programme has already covered all publicly subsidized secondary schools (about 1,300). Like the Primary MECE Programme, it has provided funds for improvement of buildings and materials to assist the teaching–learning processes: textbooks, school libraries, teaching resources and the computer equipment needed to join the Enlaces network.

Among the key interventions specific to the secondary-school programme are a new curriculum frame, school-based professional development activities for teachers and a programme for school youth. The development of a new curriculum frame and the specification of minimal required contents have been completed and will mean an important change in the structure of the curriculum areas (both for general and vocational education) as well as updating of its contents. As a means of enabling teacher personal and professional growth, the schools have introduced Teacher Professional Groups.[8] The immediate purpose of these groups is to provide a setting for teacher development as well as a structure for teacher participation in change processes in the school. The ultimate purpose of the groups is to improve the quality of student learning.

In an attempt to provide young people with a different experience of school and a situation where the special features of youth culture may be expressed and recognized as valuable, the secondary-education programme has also institutionalized a highly successful youth activity programme, Actividades Curriculares de Libre Elección (ACLE) that operates outside school hours. Students, mostly from poor neighbourhoods, return to the schools where they find teachers or other facilitators willing to undertake a variety of activities of special interest to them and

7. On average, the MECE-Media programme will invest roughly $34.5 million per year from 1995 to 2000 in publicly supported secondary schools. This annual figure represented 13 per cent of public grants to secondary education in 1996 (Cox, 1997).
8. For a description of these and their effects in the first two years of the secondary-school programme, see Avalos (1998).

which they have chosen to do: for example, expressive arts, drama, crafts and music workshops, sports, journalism and environmental projects.

The positive results of the Schools Improvement Projects at the primary level led to their implementation in the Secondary MECE Programme. In addition, the ministry has established a fund from which schools may draw to buy professional improvement services from universities or other institutions with appropriate expertise. To facilitate selection, the Ministry of Education publishes a directory of relevant institutions and services.

Progress in learning

Changes in the quantitative behaviour of an education system can be a good indicator of the effectiveness of reforms.[9] In the case of Chile's change programmes, which are strongly aimed at improving the quality of learning opportunities especially for the poor, the kinds of results that matter concern the amount and quality of children's learning. While there are a number of studies that have looked into the effectiveness of the various components of the 900 Schools Programme[10] and the Primary MECE Programmes, we note here the available evidence regarding basic skills learning attainment of primary-school children.

SIMCE (Sistema de Medición de la Calidad de la Educación), a national examination which is administered every two years alternately to the fourth and eighth grades, provides data for judging the pace of learning improvement among children who attend MECE primary schools as compared to those in private schools. Table 1 points to differences in Spanish and maths attainment by type of school at fourth-grade level in the period 1990–96 (covering the Primary MECE Programme). Results

9. During 1990–96, illiteracy diminished from 5.3 to 4.8 per cent, and the mean years of schooling increased from 9 to 9.5 years. Primary-school enrolment grew from 95 to 98 per cent and secondary-school enrolment from 80 to 85 per cent. Especially important was the increase in school enrolment of children and young people from the lowest socio-economic groups, making schooling practically universal for the age group 6–13 years. The number of the 14–17 age group has increased from 73.3 to 75.3 per cent. Drop-out rates in primary school decreased from 2.3 to 1.8 per cent and in secondary school from 7.3 to 6.4 per cent. Primary-school retention increased from 68.2 to 81.6 per cent (Cox, 1997).
10. The 900 Schools Programme has been the subject of several assessments (see Undurraga, 1994; Filp, 1994).

TABLE 1. Changes in attainment in Spanish and mathematics
of primary-school children (Grade 4)
by type of school as measured by SIMCE tests (1990–96)

		Type of school		
Year of exam	National average	Municipal	Private subsidized	Private fee-paying
Spanish				
1990	61.2	57.2	64.7	80.0
1992	68.0	64.0	70.8	86.8
1994	67.5	63.5	70.0	83.7
1996	71.9	68.3	74.3	86.2
Increase	10.7	11.1	9.6	6.2
Mathematics				
1990	60.1	56.2	63.1	79.9
1992	67.3	63.7	69.6	85.2
1994	69.3	65.4	71.3	86.4
1996	71.2	67.8	73.1	85.6
Increase	11.1	11.6	10.0	5.7

Source: Chile. Ministry of Education, 1997.

show a slightly higher rate of increase for children in municipal schools (enrolling from the lower socio-economic groups) as compared to the national average; and a definitely higher rate of increase compared to children in private schools (highest socio-economic level). The fact that, over time, it is the poorer children who steadily and more rapidly improve their performance in Spanish and maths as compared to children in the well-to-do fee-paying schools suggests that the goals of greater quality and improved equity in the distribution of schooling benefits are effectively being achieved, without yet reaching satisfactory levels.

International co-operation and agency assistance in the development and implementation of educational programmes

Particularly in the first half of this decade (1990–94), international co-operation played an important role both in the design and implementation of the described reform programmes. The educational budget of the military government (the lowest in a decade) greatly restricted what the new democratic government taking office in 1990 could do. Yet the government was expected to fulfil expectations for short-term visible changes in the health and education sectors affecting the poorer sections of the population. Hence, the decision to seek external aid for programmes in both sectors. In the case of education, the Swedish and Danish governments provided a grant 'aimed at backing the transition to democracy at a very decisive time and with the purpose of assisting the poorer groups of the population' (Gustafsson and Sjöstedt, 1994, p. 10). This funding was crucial for the 900 Schools Programme. At this time, the new educational authorities began to prepare for comprehensive and universal coverage improvement programmes at pre- and primary-school level with technical and financial assistance from the World Bank.

The new government had defined a two-stage strategy for implementing its policies. The first stage was linked to the urgent requirement of responding to the educational needs of the poor if democracy was to show its benefits. The second stage would be a longer-term intervention in the entire education system taking into consideration factors and conditions crucial to the improvement of quality. The unconditional grants of the Nordic countries were perfectly in tune with what the new government wanted to do in its immediate stage,[11] while the preparation of the MECE Primary School Programme was part of the second stage that involved negotiating a loan with the World Bank under its rules and conditions.

While the Swedish donation, with emphasis on moral issues such as poverty alleviation and transition to democracy, may be linked to what King (1998) refers to as the 'new bilateralism' in aid development, the World Bank loan may be referred to as policy-based aid conditioned on the educational policy instruments and macro-economic dimensions of the recipient country. In Chile, both cases of international co-operation have become operational around projects that have been designed and implemented by nationals. A decisive feature of the co-operation process as a whole was the technical strength of the Chilean designs that made it possible to accommodate external aid conditions to the country's own political agenda, even when (as we shall see regarding the World Bank) the external agency did not entirely agree with the national perspective. Furthermore, the capability to design projects as expressed in the 900 Schools

11. The 900 Schools Programme was launched on 13 March 1990 – two days after the inauguration of the new president Patricio Aylwin.

Programme and the MECE Primary Programme was rooted in the research and development experience acquired in non-government agencies financed with international co-operation throughout the dictatorship period.[12]

The rest of this chapter analyses the kind of co-operation that took place between the Chilean Ministry of Education and the World Bank in relation to the Primary and Secondary MECE Programmes. In this context, we shall examine the respective agendas, the conditions of the World Bank, the way of dealing with innovation and the evolution of the relationship between the World Bank and the client country throughout this decade.

Agendas

A key aspect of the Programme for Improving the Quality and Equity of Education (MECE) was its relationship to the transitional government. The political agenda during this period was determined by the coalition government's goal to produce a successful transition to democracy. The MECE programme was guided and structured by that agenda and became a programme strongly defined, led and executed by national capacity. The MECE programme was, however, also designed with technical co-operation from the World Bank. The timing of the World Bank's participation helps one to understand why what we consider to be a positive working relationship could be established with the Chilean Government: two months after the Jomtien conference in 1990 and just before the publication of the Bank's strategy for primary education in the 1990s (Lockheed and Verspoor, 1990).

At the outset of the project, both the Chilean Government and the World Bank had strong initial views on and definitions of priorities and intervention strategies for primary education about which they were essentially in agreement. On the one hand, Chile had defined as the political goal for primary education the improvement of quality and equity, while the Bank had defined its priorities for pre- and primary-school education as improvement of learning.

12. The 900 Schools Programme could be started so soon after President Aylwin's inauguration because, as an innovative project, activities had already been carried out by an independent research centre in the 1980s.

As far as the Bank was concerned, Chile offered a favourable context. On the one hand, education was considered crucial to development and to the transitional process to democracy and, on the other, an 'adjustment' had already taken place during the 1980s under key principles of decentralization, search for efficiency in the use of resources and financial policies that favoured investment in primary (and not university) education.

However, the 1990 political agenda in Chile also included interventions in the secondary-school system and, particularly, a change in its curriculum. Neither of these policies were part of the World Bank's priorities. Thus, no agreement was reached to fund a secondary-level component in the first loan despite the fact that growth in coverage (80 per cent) had not been equalled by growth in the quality of its teaching and learning conditions. Nevertheless, the Bank agreed to fund a series of studies that could provide a sound research base for a later intervention programme in the secondary-school sector. These studies provided diagnosis and change orientation that were later extremely influential for the manner in which the Secondary MECE Programme was designed and is now being implemented with World Bank participation. Thus, even though, on account of its priority definitions, the World Bank was not willing to support secondary education, it did agree to work with the Chilean teams to produce the basis for a later reform. The fact that the Bank did, eventually, support the implementation of a secondary reform project shows how the recipient country was able to contribute to redefining World Bank priorities, probably because of the strong success of the Primary MECE Programme.

Conditionalities

In the course of negotiations for the MECE programme, the Bank set three conditions for its support, all of which were macro in nature: (a) sustainability of MECE actions once the programme was finished; (b) maintenance of the 1980s' balance in the education budget which favoured primary education against the historic support for higher education;[13] and (c) maintenance of policies supporting the role of the private sector in education which had widened and strengthened during the neo-

13. Educational expenditure in 1990 was distributed as follows: 8.2 per cent for pre-school; 52.7 per cent for primary education; 17.6 per cent for secondary-school education; and 18.7 per cent for higher education (Cox, 1997).

liberal reform of the 1980s. Of these three conditions, only the second one was not accepted. A letter from the Minister of Education to the President of the World Bank (Chile. Ministry of Education, 1991) stated that 'factors associated with the policies to be applied, as others of a demographic nature, will . . . affect somehow the way in which expenditure is allocated'.[14] More specific conditions as, for example, cost-recovery for textbooks through charges to parents, though initially accepted by the Ministry of Education with great legal and socio-political difficulties, were eventually discarded by the World Bank once the Primary MECE Programme began to show its fruits.

Locally generated innovations and World Bank frameworks

The approval of the three primary MECE innovations referred to above were considered somewhat differently at the time of their proposal. The World Bank had no objections to the Rural MECE proposal but was concerned about the adequacy and viability of the other two innovations. The Bank Headquarters in Washington (not the team in the field) initially considered that the School Improvement Projects and the Enlaces computer network could be a financial and effectiveness risk because of their highly innovative nature. In relation to the Schools Improvement Projects, they feared that the funds the schools would get might be used by teachers for other purposes. In this respect, however, the Bank was not aware of the traditional probity of Chilean teachers and the very strong control instruments of use of public resources that exist in the country.

In relation to the Enlaces network, the concern was that its institutional and technical sophistication might be beyond the real capabilities of the Chilean education system (still in need of textbooks, teacher training and other items closely related to conventional interventions). In this respect, there were no elements that could enable judgement about Chilean technical capability or whether it could bridge the gap between high technology and educational needs, nor even of the state of development of

---

14. It is a mark of how the Bank has changed its priorities with regard to Chile that a loan proposal to support the improvement of equity and quality in higher education is now under discussion with the Chilean Government.

communication infrastructure. Given this situation, careful persuasion was needed for the World Bank in Washington to review the case and support the programmes. Such a task was mostly carried out by the counterpart World Bank teams in the field which, in turn, were convinced of the technical robustness of the innovation by the Chilean teams.

In stark contrast, the proposed innovations for the Secondary MECE Programme were not questioned by the World Bank. The successful experience of three years of implementation of the Primary MECE Programme, as well as the strong professional links and increased knowledge of the Chilean education system on the part of multilateral agency staff, made it possible for the most innovative interventions of this programme, the Teacher Professional Groups and ACLE described above, to be included in the design and implemented without special probing by the World Bank.

Evolution of a relationship: from funding and technical assistance to technical assistance

From a Chilean perspective, the evolving relationship with the World Bank regarding education-sector policies is reflected in the Bank's mode of participating in the two MECE programmes. For the first programme designed in 1990, the Bank set conditions, assisted technically and also financed 70 per cent of total investments ($170 million of $243 million). For the second programme, designed in 1994 for secondary-school education, the Bank set no conditions, participated with technical assistance and financed only 17 per cent of the total of $207 million. In 1990 the Chilean Government was in need of technical support and finance; in 1994, it only needed technical assistance.

As to political concerns, the experience of four years of joint execution of a successful programme and the development of strong professional links on both parts had dispelled whatever initial apprehension the World Bank might have had in 1990. For the Chilean professional teams responsible for designing and implementing the two MECE programmes, the technical assistance of the World Bank throughout the 1990s has been of a substantive but also procedural nature. As a knowledge-broker about best practices in key domains of policy, the World Bank has played a crucial role as tester and evaluator of the Chilean proposals.

The World Bank has also contributed to know-how about design and execution of projects in the social sector. From this point of view, as the supervisory missions of the multilateral agency, using their monitoring, control and evaluation procedures, repeated once and again their experience in looking at the overall state of implementation of a complex programme, the local teams as participants learned and were able to make use of these procedures for the good of the whole operation. In an invisible manner, the MECE teams benefited from the Bank's forms of keeping tabs on programmes, leaving the Ministry of Education with good expertise in the support and promotion of innovation.

From the political perspective there were two kinds of benefits resulting from co-operation with the World Bank. In the first place, in relation to predictable criticisms from political opponents that government might inject partisan schemes into the reform, the World Bank guaranteed that the projects implemented would reflect international best practice experiences. At another level, the fact of an international agreement backing the projects, signed by the government, specifying programmed activities to be carried out in the following years, served as a symbolic and de facto deterrent of budgetary or other pressures affecting its implementation.

Ideologies

As it began its contribution to education in Chile, the World Bank held to a set of ideas that celebrated without qualification the neo-liberal reform of the 1980s. To the World Bank, Chile meant vouchers and application of a version of the principle of private solutions to public problems. However, the policies of the 1990s in Chile rest on other principles, actors and values. Without attempting to recentralize the system or to act against the private sector in education, the new policies give key importance to the role of the state regarding the quality of education, setting national standards of attainment, equity in the social distribution of results and participation of teachers as a professional body responsible for the sectors' main functions.

After almost a decade of involvement in Chile's educational programmes in the context of a democracy, the World Bank appears to be critical of the laissez-faire reform ideology of the 1980s in the school system of the country and increasingly concerned about the role of the state and the political economy of educational reform with its focus on stakeholders, their interests and meanings (Fiske, 1996).

Conclusion

The case of Chile may not be representative of what could happen in other recipient country situations. Yet, in this chapter, we have noted those main factors that contribute to a constructive provider–recipient country situation: a strong national policy framework, sufficient national capacity to prepare innovative proposals and sustain them both at the discussion stage and in their practical implementation and, finally, a capable and sensitive in-the-field team of professionals representing the bilateral or multilateral funding and technical-assistance agency. Awareness of needs, which is not just of a political nature, but also based on empirical evidence and responsive to pedagogical criteria is a key to imaginative proposals. The contribution of professionals from the agencies as question-posers, information providers and collaborators in the review of programmes is a key factor in the success of programmes such as the 900 Schools Programme and the Primary and Secondary MECE Programmes in Chile.

References

AVALOS, B. 1998. School-based Teacher Development. The Experience of Teacher Professional Groups in Secondary Schools in Chile. *International Journal of Teaching and Teacher Education*, Vol. 14, No. 3, pp. 257–71.

CHILE. MINISTRY OF EDUCATION. 1991. *Documento-letter from Ricardo Lagos, Minister, to the President of the World Bank, Barber B. Conable, on the Background, Objectives and Strategies of the Chilean Government for the Education Sector.*

——. 1997. *Programa P-900 Comparación SIMCE-Escuelas P-900.* Santiago.

COX, C. 1997. *La reforma de la educación chilena: contexto, contenidos, implementación.* Santiago, Ministry of Education.

ECLAC-UNESCO. 1992. *Education and Knowledge. Basic Pillars of Changing Production Patterns with Social Equity.* Santiago, ECLAC-UNESCO.

FILP, J. 1994. Todos los niños aprenden. Evaluaciones del P-900. In: M. Gajardo (ed.), *Cooperación internacional y desarrollo de la educación*, pp. 179–250. Santiago, Agencia de Cooperación Internacional.

FISKE, E. B. 1996. *Decentralization of Education. Politics and Consensus.* Washington, D.C., World Bank.

GARCÍA-HUIDOBRO, J. E. 1989. *Escuela, calidad e igualdad.* Santiago, CIDE.

GUSTAFSSON, I.; SJÖSTEDT, B. 1994. Cooperación internacional y desarrollo de la educación: la perspectiva de ASDI. In: M. Gajardo (ed.), *Cooperación internacional y desarrollo de la educación*, pp. 9–12. Santiago, Agencia de Cooperación Internacional.

KING, K. 1998. The New Aid Paradigm of the 1990s Reviewed. *NORRAG News*, No. 22 (January).

LEMAITRE, M. J. 1998. Turning Improvement into Reform: Secondary-school Education in Chile 1991–2001. In: L. Buchert (ed.), *Education Reform in the South in the 1990s*, pp. 53–73. Paris, UNESCO Publishing.

LOCKHEED, M. E.; VERSPOOR, A. M. 1990. *Improving Primary Education in Developing Countries*. Washington, D.C., IBRD/World Bank.

PIIE (PROGRAMA INTERDISCIPLINARIO DE INVESTIGACIONES EN EDUCACIÓN). 1989. *Educación y transición democrática. Propuesta de políticas educacionales.* Santiago, PIIE.

UNDURRAGA, C. 1994. Pedagogía y gestión. Informe de evaluación del Programa de las 900 Escuelas. In: M. Gajardo (ed.), *Cooperación internacional y desarrollo de la educación*, pp. 99–178. Santiago, Agencia de Cooperación Internacional.

Issues amidst assistance: foreign aid to education in China

Kai-ming Cheng

Introduction

Since its policies of reform in the early 1980s, China has attracted much attention from international funding agencies. In the realm of basic education, the reform is to devolve finance and administration of primary and secondary schools to local governments and local communities. A very large percentage of international aid to education in China is targeted at the poorer provinces so as to reduce the effects of regional disparity in education. The amount that has been spent on China's education, either as grants or loans, is by no means small. It is, however, relatively small when compared with the overall expenditure in the vast system of over 200 million students. Therefore, it is interesting to see what effects such aid has had on the system and what issues have arisen as a result of such investments. This chapter is based mainly on the author's experience in the field; hence it may reflect more the situation at the receiving end rather than that prevailing at the government level.

Insignificant scale of aid

The World Bank, for example, has contributed about $1.4 billion since 1981 to education in China. This huge amount, however, is relatively trivial when compared with the annual national budget, which is around $19 billion per annum, and has been increasing rapidly over the years.[1]

The trivialness can be demonstrated by the following anecdote. During a visit from an international mission, it was discovered that children in underdeveloped villages study in appalling classrooms with no

---

1. Data from discussions with members of the Foreign Affairs Bureau.

heating and a temperature of − 5 °C. Students all shivered in thick clothing, with running noses, in classrooms with only paper as window panes. The mission immediately thought that providing heating for such classrooms should be a matter of priority. A brief calculation revealed that for each classroom, two coal stoves and the necessary chimneys (each made of five linked iron cylinders) would cost around $70. To equip approximately 145,000 classrooms in the province alone would cost $10 million, and that did not include the running cost of coal supply which was extremely rare in the province, and the anticipated replacement in about three years. The idea had to be abandoned because of the huge amount involved.[2]

Investment in physical items is relatively inexpensive. Indeed, much of the first education aims in China related to the provision of libraries and laboratories, and they were relatively affordable by even smaller international agencies. However, it is quite obvious that for education in China, physical facilities are not necessarily what are needed most when the aid is to assist development in underprivileged areas. In most such areas, one would most likely be amazed by the spectacular scale of local contributions which usually go to the construction of school buildings. The problem usually lies with the shortage of funds for teachers' salaries or, more recently, the private costs for schooling which have increased to levels beyond parents' capacities. These refer to recurrent expenditures which are well beyond the capacity of any international organization.

In any case, foreign aid is meant for critical *investments* that could help develop the capacity for further development. It is not meant to be subsidies for shortages in the recipient countries. The Chinese case provides a very good demonstration of this principle. If foreign aid is not playing an investment role, then the huge 'sponge' could easily absorb any enormous amount of resources with little effect.

The pivotal role of aid

The crucial question is, therefore, what role such foreign aid has played in the education development of the nation. A recent example of a UNICEF project serves as an illustration of the issue.

2. The case is reported in Cheng (1997).

In 1995, UNICEF started a project which supported basic education development in disadvantaged counties.[3] There are 102 such counties in the project. In a county that the author visited in March 1998, the amount received was only about RMB 1 million (*renminbi*, the local currency, or around $0.12 million[4]). The actual amount spent on the project was about RMB 6 million. Of this amount, approximately RMB 4 million came from upper levels of government, about half from the prefecture government (the level above counties) and another half from the provincial government.[5] The UNICEF funding has obviously played a pivotal role. It is interesting to understand why governments at each level are willing to spend the money.

The provincial government regards external aid as a useful indication for investment. As was indicated by provincial officials,[6] the provincial government has anyway put aside resources for the development of basic education. There is a national urge for local governments to place priority on basic education and there are stipulations that guarantee it priority funding. For example, there is a requirement that the growth in public educational expenditures should exceed the growth in general revenues and that student unit costs should see positive annual growth. However, an even distribution of the provincial resources to all the counties (often sixty to seventy in number) would have a very thin effect on the actual improvement of basic education. The UNICEF funding, with its rigorous methodology, has helped the provincial authority rationally to identify the areas for heavier investment. In a sense, the external agencies have provided free consultancy for project identification and provincial resources are allocated accordingly.

Politically, the participation of external agencies has also provided legitimacy for the direction of provincial investment. In a system like

3. Counties are the basic comprehensive administrative structure in China. There are around 2,000 counties in all. The average population of a county is around half a million. In terms of education, a county is a unit that comprises schools at all levels before higher education, i.e. primary, junior secondary and senior secondary school.
4. The exchange rate in 1998 was $1 = RMB 8.
5. The common pattern is that there are several prefectures in each province and then fifteen to twenty counties in each prefecture.
6. Discussions on 5 March 1998 with the Deputy Governor, who is in charge of education.

China's where, conventionally, resources are distributed on the basis of either egalitarian principles or competition combined with favouritism, assessment by an external agency provides an impartial element which relieves the provincial government of decisions that would otherwise be politically difficult.

The counties, as the receiving end, welcome external funding for more obvious reasons. In very practical terms, they receive the extra funding from higher levels of government. In this particular case, the county has received almost RMB 4 million, a huge amount for a poor county whose overall revenue is no more than RMB 50 million.

The very fact that the money has come from an international agency has also brought about a sense of prestige to the rather isolated county in the mountains. 'If foreigners are concerned about our children's education, why shouldn't we be?' There is much publicity that the county has been identified as a 'United Nations' target of aid, and this in turn has prompted fundraising in the local communities. Without such an incentive, it would be extremely difficult for the local government to raise the RMB 1 million needed as matching funds.

The professionals in the State Education Commission (i.e. the Ministry of Education) also welcome the participation of foreign agencies. The foreign aid creates the sense of a 'project', i.e. it develops among local officials and educators a sense of 'value for money' and 'investment for success'.[7]

Hence, in this particular case, the UNICEF funding does play a positive pivotal role. It provides a mechanism for the provincial government to direct its resources to crucial investments and it also provides incentives for local governments to mobilize community resources. Other international agencies have played more or less the same role. It has done what cannot be achieved by internal mechanisms. In a way foreign aid has caused some cultural change in resource distribution. Indeed, a number of internal allocation exercises have adopted methodologies similar to those used by external agencies.

7. Interview with some specialists in the State Education Commission, March–April 1998.

Aid vis-à-vis decentralization

The role of foreign aid is particularly significant in the Chinese system, which is undergoing spectacular decentralization. China has launched reforms of substantial decentralization since the early 1980s and education is no exception. Central to decentralization is change in the financial system. In a nutshell, the financing of basic education is now almost completely a local endeavour at the county level.[8] Public teachers' salaries are paid through the general revenue which is based on local tax. Community teachers are paid mostly by a surcharge levied over local taxes. Physical construction is largely built upon local donations and schools generate income for other expenses.[9] The central and provincial governments provide practically no funding, with the exception of minimal sums in special grants for the most deprived regions.

Decentralization has created local ownership and hence new mechanisms of mobilizing local resources, but it has also created a degree of disparity which is unprecedented in the socialist nation. In 1996, for example, the per capita GDP in Shanghai and Guizhou, the richest and the poorest provincial units respectively, differed by a factor of 10.[10] In a recent study, it was also revealed that, in 1996, the per capita GDP of the richest and poorest counties in one province (Jiangsu) differed by a factor of 13.[11] Cheng (1997) observes that even two villages within the same township may have very significant differences in their economic development, because of the difference in natural resources and the conditions of transportation.

While the disparity is recognized as intolerable, there are few identifiable solutions to reduce it. There are intrinsic contradictions which have caused difficulties in solving the problem. The very reason which has caused the disparity has also given local governments and the communities unprecedented autonomy. Estimations have hinted that the central government is only receiving about 20 per cent of the total revenues collect-

8. In more developed and more densely populated areas, financial decentralization goes further down to townships.
9. Detailed descriptions can be found in Cheng (1991).
10. In 1995, the per capita GDP for Shanghai was above RMB 15,204 ($1,900) and that for Guizhou was RMB 1,552 ($194) (*China Statistical Digest*, 1996).
11. Ranges from $220 to $2,800 among the seventy-three county units (Yamaguchi, 1998).

able by the entire nation (Min, 1997). This has rather handicapped the central government in playing an equalization role. However, any change in the balance of central–local distribution would mean a heavier taxation of the local governments by the central government, reducing accordingly the local capacity in the developing economy. Hence, while the local government would like to see more resources handed down from the central government, they would not like to contribute more to the central treasury. In other words, while there is an urgent need to reduce disparity, any governmental movement would disturb the existing pattern of taxation, and the latter is playing a positive role in economic developments.

There are occasional calls for internal aid from the more developed to the less developed provinces. One practice which echoes such calls is to pair rich and poor provinces as 'sister provinces'. Such practices perhaps play little more than a token role, given the keen competition that has prompted provinces to become interest-driven and self-centred.

In this context, the injection of foreign aid provides a welcome solution. Foreign aid has become a means whereby additional and needed resources can be channelled to targeted needy areas, without the degree of decentralization being affected. It is perhaps not an exaggeration to say that the existence of foreign aid helps to stabilize the trend of decentralization. By the same token, the effectiveness of foreign aid is of extreme importance. At times, there has been hesitation (particularly among the less developed provinces) about the trend of decentralization or even calls to reverse the process. Successful use of such funds provides a convincing argument *against* such a reversal.

Aid and improved economy

However, disparity has given birth to another issue in the interaction between China and foreign aid. The decentralization, which has caused the disparity, is also seen as the major cause of economic improvement in the whole nation. In the past two decades, China has seen remarkable economic growth, often at two digits annually. Such economic growth has led to some hesitation among international organizations in providing aid to China.

China's per capita GDP, for example, has exceeded the cut-off point which justifies the country receiving 'soft' loans. This causes a dilemma which is of a fundamental nature. On the one hand, the demonstrated economic strength should disqualify China from receiving aid, which is meant for much more deprived nations. On the other hand, the difficulties in the less developed regions are not easily eradicated by the national government under the existing decentralized arrangements (which all parties seem to favour).

One of the compromises, which is practised by some of the international agencies, is to target the provinces as units of aid. Such a practice may realistically distinguish the poor regions from the national average, but may bring with it problems of repayment. Under the present decentralized system, it is quite unrealistic to expect the central government to undertake the repayment if the loan goes to the province. In any case, the central government may not have the capacity to do so. In an area such as education, where returns to investment are not visible within education per se, provinces may find it difficult, even if it is a 'soft' loan. In reality pure 'soft' loans have, anyway, become very unlikely.

The overall economic performance of China may, therefore, remove it from the entire game of international aid, but then the deprived regions in China would become even more deprived. There does not seem to be an easy solution to this dilemma.

Internal debates

Ever since the starting years of the reform, there have been controversies about the location of priorities. At one point, the basic debate was whether foreign aid should be channelled to the more or less developed areas.

The argument for the more developed areas was very much along Deng Xiaoping's motto of 'let part of the population prosper first'. It saw the more developed regions as more capable of making efficient use of foreign aid, and hence they would bring better returns on the investment. Such views were held more often by decision-makers in the planning and financial sectors.

The counter-argument was that foreign aid should be strategically used to help develop the less developed regions. The underlying philosophy was that education should be seen as a long-term investment and the major means towards sustainable development. Such views were more often held by decision-makers in the education sector.

More recently, with the further development of decentralization and the further weakening of the sense of planning, debates are prompted by more practical causes. For example, in higher education, there is often a controversy about whether foreign aid should be channelled to institutions that operate under the central ministries or those that work under provincial authorities. The debate on the surface is about efficiency and repayment, but suspicions are that it is also underpinned by the responsibilities of repayment. Quite unlike the previous debates, where different sectors (or government divisions) compete for control of foreign funds, the recent debate seems to hint that different sectors are avoiding foreign aid because of implied repayment responsibilities.

Such very realistic considerations perhaps signify an improvement in the nation's handling of foreign aid, but they could well be viewed negatively as a retreat from the proactive role of attracting foreign assistance.

Aid and departmentalization

China is often regarded as a solid decision-maker and decisions were made with rational consideration of the holistic national picture. Recent developments have substantially changed the scene.

International agencies in China are now associated with different sectors of the Chinese Government. The World Bank and the Asian Development Bank are associated with the Finance Department of the State Education Commission (which is due to become the Ministry of Education as a result of government restructuring), UNDP is associated with the Ministry of Foreign Trade and Economic Co-operation and UNICEF with the Department of Foreign Affairs of the State Education Commission.

Such associations are seen as an improvement as they lead to more participation from different parts of the government. Such arrangements, however, sometimes may lead to less favourable situations where each of the hosting departments may not be able to grasp the entire national picture and make decisions accordingly. Although there is little self-interest in such decisions, most of such government departments do not have the information or the expertise to maximize the utilization of foreign aid.

Concluding remarks

China has been undergoing a spectacular economic and societal transition in the past two decades. Foreign aid has brought international elements to this transition. Education is one of the focal points. The studies and interactions have allowed people outside China to understand more about the country instead of relying solely on images presented by the media. By way of foreign aid, China also benefits from international experience. In the realm of education, this is particularly true in terms of problem identification, problem-solving and resource-allocation methodologies. This is quite apart from the pivotal role played by the funds per se.

However, with further development in China, when the entire nation has become a stable decentralized system and when the nation's *average* wealth may challenge its candidature as a recipient of aid, the relationship between China and the international aid agencies may need to be reviewed.

References

CHENG, K. M. 1991. *Planning Basic Education in China: A Case Study of Two Counties in the Province of Liaoning.* Paris, UNESCO/IIEP.

—— 1997. Qualitative Research and Educational Policy-making: Approaching the Reality in Developing Countries. In: M. Crossly and G. Vulliamy (eds.), *Qualitative Research in Developing Countries*, pp. 65–86. New York, Garland.

MIN, W. F. 1997. *The Major Strategic Issues in Chinese Higher Education Development in the 21st Century.* (Keynote paper presented at the 5th International Conference on Chinese Education, Hong Kong, 13–19 August 1998.)

YAMAGUCHI, S. Y. 1998. *Economic Development and Education Development: Case Study of the Province of Jiangsu.* Colombia University, Teachers' College. (Unpublished Ph.D. dissertation.)

Development assistance to primary education in India: transformation of enthusiastic donors and reluctant recipients
Jandhyala B. G. Tilak[1]

Introduction

The 1990s is a decade that marks a new phase of developments in education in general – and primary education in particular – in India. Preceded by a serious economic crisis, the Government of India adopted in 1990 structural adjustment policies that inflicted serious cuts in budgetary resources for education in general and elementary education in particular. Consequently, a social safety net programme was launched to protect vulnerable but important sectors such as primary education and basic health care from the adverse effects of stabilization and structural adjustment policies.[2]

Thus began international assistance to primary education in India. This has been the most significant development in education in independent India as, during its fifty years of independence, external assistance was not sought for a long time by the Government of India, even for other levels of education. Although quite a few international aid organizations were eager to enter the primary education scene in India from the mid-1980s onwards, the Government of India felt no need for external assistance to primary education. The foreign exchange crisis in 1989 followed by the adoption of structural adjustment policies, which were regarded as 'a necessary evil', changed this situation and also thereby the approach of the government. For the first time, the primary education sector was rather reluctantly opened to the enthusiastic external aid organizations on a large

1. This chapter partly draws on articles by the author in *NORRAG News*, Nos. 19 and 22. The views expressed are those of the author and should not necessarily be attributed to the organization with which he is associated.
2. For a review of Asian experience with structural adjustment policies and their effects on education, see Tilak (1997).

TABLE 1. Geographical coverage
of the District Primary Education Programme (DPEP)
(number of districts)

State	Phase I	Phase II	Phase III
Assam	4	5	–
Haryana	4	3	–
Karnataka	4	7	–
Kerala	3	3	–
Tamil Nadu	3	3	–
Maharashtra	5	4	–
Madhya Pradesh	19	15	–
Himachal Pradesh	–	4	–
Gujarat	–	3	–
Orissa	–	8	–
Andhra Pradesh	–	5	–
West Bengal	–	5	–
Uttar Pradesh	–	15	–
Bihar	–	–	27
Total	42	80	27

Source: Government of India, 1997.

scale.[3] Starting with World Bank assistance for primary education in ten districts in Uttar Pradesh and UNICEF assistance in Bihar, a plethora of international – both multilateral and bilateral – aid organizations are currently in operation in India working for the improvement of the primary education system.[4]

In order to ensure better co-ordination from the point of view of the Government of India and governments of various states (provinces) on the one hand, and the host of international aid organizations on the other, the Government of India has launched a District Primary Education Programme (DPEP), as a broad overall umbrella of international aid programmes in primary education in the country.[5] A number of other programmes assisted by external agencies – which were in existence before the formation of DPEP – are also brought under this common umbrella. Three projects have, however, remained separate.[6] Starting in 1994 with 42 districts in 7 states in phase I of the DPEP, the programme has

3. There were some minor projects in operation earlier. They include non-formal education projects in a few selected villages financed by UNICEF and primary-education projects in selected schools in Andhra Pradesh funded by DFID.
4. Some important organizations are: the World Bank, the European Union, UNICEF, UNDP, DFID and Sida.

expanded to cover 149 districts, as shown in Table 1. It is being planned soon to cover 194 districts in 15 states, out of the total of approximately 500 districts in the country.

In this chapter a few random and somewhat tentative but important dimensions of DPEP are briefly discussed. The analysis includes a description of some of the major strengths and weaknesses of the programme relating to either funding agencies or the recipient governments. It is hoped that preliminary valuable lessons can be drawn for other governments, and funding agencies as well, that might lead to a refinement of their policies. After all, policies of governments and funding agencies such as the World Bank 'have never been static. Time and experience have subjected many to refinement' (Jones, 1992, p. 219). As the programme and its procedures are still evolving, the analysis should be understood as tentative.

DPEP: critical issues and emerging trends

In countries where a multitude of external agencies work on primary education in an uncoordinated way, confusion, if not chaos, often arises because of conflicting policies, procedures, approaches and plans of action. By contrast, the formation of the overall umbrella of DPEP by the Government of India could be seen as an important step in a positive direction. It has facilitated better co-ordination among the three partners (the Government of India, the governments of the states and the funding agencies), has prevented duplication, and ensured some kind of coherence and consistency in the overall programme. From the point of view of planning and management, this is indeed an important step, although it also worked as a catalytic force contributing to some weaknesses of the whole programme, as will be discussed below.

The most important consequence of DPEP is relaxation of resource constraints in planning education. Educational planning under austerity (or under conditions of severe resource constraints) has for a long time been the characteristic feature of planning education in India, as in many

5. For a description of the logic and logistics of the DPEP programme, see Government of India (1993, 1995); World Bank (1994); and Varghese (1994, 1996).
6. The exceptions are the Shiksha Karmi project and the Lok Jumbish project in Rajasthan, boh funded by Sida, and the Mahila Samakhya project, financed by the Netherlands Government.

other developing countries. Perhaps for the first time, the districts in India were informed that each district participating in DPEP would be given about Rs 350–400 million[7] for a seven-year project period under DPEP. While Rs 350–400 million is a substantial additional amount for a district, Rs 50–60 million per annum is not really that high compared to the present level of public spending of about Rs 600 million per district in India (1994–95). In all, as shown in Table 2, about Rs 40,000 million are being contributed by external sources, which would flow, not necessarily evenly, over a ten-year period until the year 2003, i.e. at an annual average of Rs 4,000 million.

This may be compared to the current level of total expenditure on elementary education in the country, which is about Rs 150 billion (1995–96). Thus, despite the geographical expansion of the programme as noted earlier, it still cannot be regarded as a massive large-scale programme of improvement of primary education all over India, as the funds constitute less than 3 per cent of the total expenditure of the government on elementary education. More than the effects of resource availability, the influence of DPEP – both positive and negative – on the education scene as a whole is indeed very significant. These effects could be either direct or catalytic in nature.

District planning in primary education has been restored to a respectable place under DPEP. While there has been much talk about the need for district planning in education in India ever since independence, including constitution of a few important national-level committees on district- or block-level planning,[8] few significant efforts have been made until recently, except for a few district plans in education prepared by researchers and planners.[9] DPEP has been envisaged to be based on district planning and accordingly district planning in primary education became very important. This is the single most important positive contribution of DPEP.

One of the primary strategies of DPEP is decentralization of policy-making, planning, administration and implementation of the educational policies and plans. This is very important in a vast country like India, where some of the states and even districts are larger than many countries

7. At the time of writing $1 equals about Rs 35.
8. See e.g. Tilak (1984, 1992) for a review of earlier efforts.
9. See e.g. Tilak and Varghese (1985) and Tilak (1992).

TABLE 2. External assistance for DPEP (figures in millions)

Phase/period/states	Funding agency	Total amount	Average per annum
Phase I (1994–95/2001–02)	World Bank	$260 (Rs 8 060)	$32.5
Assam			
Haryana			
Karnataka			
Kerala			
Maharashtra			
Tamil Nadu			
Madhya Pradesh (1994–99)	European Community	150 mill. ecus (Rs 5 850)	25 mill. ecus
Phase II (1996–97/2001–02)			
Gujarat	Netherlands	$25.8 (Rs 900)	$4.3
Himachal Pradesh	World Bank	$425 (Rs 14 800)	$70.8
Orissa	–		
Uttar Pradesh	–		
Phase II (1996–2003)			
Andhra Pradesh	DFID	£42.5 (Rs 2 200)	£5.3
West Bengal	DFID	£37.71 (Rs 2 070)	£4.7
Phase III (1997–98/2001–02)			
Bihar	World Bank	$152.4 (Rs 5 300)	$30.5
Bihar	UNICEF (in process)	$10 (Rs 360)	$2.0

Source: Government of India, 1997.

in the world in terms of population. However, when a uniform format was prepared under DPEP essentially by the Government of India, some of the fundamental aspects relating to decentralization went into oblivion. While the plans are formulated at decentralized levels, the formats for the formulation of the plans were given by the central government. The formats included detailed procedures and guidelines to be followed at every step. They also included specific limits on the availability of external resources and their broad pattern of allocation between different major items of expenditure – which is the same for all districts. At best, the responsibility for implementation of the programme is decentralized, with limited degrees of freedom. The implementation is consistently monitored by the central government and bodies specially constituted by the central government. In addition, there are appraisal and reappraisal missions by the funding agencies.[10] This could not be avoided, not only because of the involvement of the central government and several state governments, but also because the funding agencies find it convenient to follow a commonly agreed format. A common format is likely to have enabled more state governments and new funding agencies to enter the scene and progress quickly. The governments and the funding agencies find it convenient, although they may at the same time be aware of the loss of scope for innovation and experimentation in their activities.

Planners, administrators, educationists and community leaders at decentralized levels – the states, the districts and even lower levels – are, however, also involved in the preparation of the plans and in their execution. This adds a rich flavour of decentralization, particularly because these local bodies did not previously participate in such activities in any significant way. The 73rd and 74th Amendments of the Constitution of India strengthened the mechanisms of decentralization with the creation of village/local level socio-political bodies such as the Panchayat (local government bodies at village level) and village education committees.

The creation of autonomous 'societies' at national, state, district and village levels, which are to play an active role in management and implementation, is an important feature of the programme within a framework of decentralization. But simultaneously with the creation of these parallel structures, the government machinery seems to have been slowly sidelined. The parallel structures erode the importance of the government, which may lead to an increasingly reduced government role in education in general, including primary education specifically.

The programme is in operation in about 150 of the 536 districts of the country. The government and the external agencies as well can run this massive programme without facing serious problems and constraints, partly due to the existence of highly trained, skilled and talented manpower, unlike in many other countries. As a result, there is no large-scale

10. Most of the supervision and monitoring is undertaken jointly by missions with the participation of government, local administration and representatives of the foreign funding agencies. Such a joint mechanism is claimed to 'open a new vista in developmental cooperation' (Ayyar, 1996, p. 352).

need for consultants from abroad on behalf of either the government or the external agencies. Furthermore, capacity-building of manpower at local levels has been an important component of the programme and has gradually fulfilled the increasing demand for trained middle-level personnel. This has been an important outcome, as it is an important prerequisite for the preparation of meaningful district plans within a decentralized framework. As planning has generally been undertaken from above, expertise has also been concentrated at national and state levels. Under DPEP it has become imperative to train and develop local-level manpower for planning, project preparation and execution of the plans and projects. This is another important contribution of DPEP.

Similarly, the massive programme has been run relatively smoothly, as much research on various aspects of primary education – or, in the terminology of the international funding organizations, so-called 'sector work' – has been readily available. The gaps in research could be filled very quickly, owing to the existence of a large network of universities and research institutions in the country with sufficiently well-trained researchers. The external agencies might not have felt the need for extensive technical assistance to start the project, but rather for collation of research. Furthermore, the programme has a component of strengthening research and the research capacities of institutions and individuals, as elaborate research assists both the funding agencies and the recipient governments (King, 1991; Tilak, 1994).

Other important trends seem to be emerging that may have serious long-term implications. In a sense, the approach of DPEP is sectarian rather than holistic to the cause of education development. First, because of the different kinds and quantities of inputs which are provided to the DPEP districts, inequalities might be created between DPEP districts and non-DPEP districts, even within a given state. The programme is not geographically holistic. Second, primary education is not approached in a holistic manner. For example, 'Education for All', 'Universalization of Elementary Education' and DPEP are perceived by state administrations as different projects/programmes and are in operation in several states in a rather uncoordinated fashion. So even the programme of elementary education is not viewed in a holistic manner. Furthermore, the upper primary level, which is a part of the compulsory elementary ('basic') education in India, seems to have been given insufficient attention. Third, while DPEP cells/bureaux have been endowed with a higher level of physical, human and financial resources, and are also associated with modernization and efficiency, systemic improvement is not noticeable in the same way as for primary education as a whole and of those directorates of school education that include primary education. This is also the case for the Department of Higher Education and the Department of Education as a whole. Fourth, other levels of education, particularly secondary and higher, are being increasingly ignored. Budgetary resources for secondary and higher education are either stagnant or have declined in recent years. Even the planning and management aspects of secondary and higher education seem not to be receiving the usual level of (inadequate) attention from the government. Such a sectarian approach causes serious imbalances in education development in the society. The flow of external funds for primary education as 'an adjunct to the structural adjustment operations' (Ayyar, 1996, p. 352) perhaps complicated the issues, as structural adjustment policies include the reduced role of the state in all spheres including education, specifically post-elementary education. Thus, although funding for DPEP is programme-based, it might work like the policy-based lending operations of external organizations.

An immediate fall-out of DPEP could reduce domestic efforts to finance primary education. The central government could encourage states to join DPEP and obtain external financing, in order that it may reduce its transfers (or additional transfers) from the central revenues to the states for primary education. Similarly, states have been willing to seek external financing because it relieves pressures on themselves to (a) mobilize additional resources on their own and (b) reallocate budgetary resources in favour of primary education more efficiently. In addition, external assistance has been attractive to states as it has been transferred from the central government as grants instead of loans. A fall in domestic efforts to finance primary education is possible despite the condition of 'additionality' in external assistance, as the condition of additionality might refer to the absolute level of expenditure incurred in the base year and not to the rate of growth in expenditure experienced. On the whole, the states seem to view the programme essentially as a centrally sponsored programme with generous resources flowing into the states through central government. What seems to be overlooked by both the central and state governments is the long-term debt burden on the people.

Neither district planning nor capacity-building require external assistance. It is unfortunate that they have materialized only under externally assisted programmes of primary education. While the contribution of DPEP has to be acknowledged, it must be emphasized that the fact that revitalization of district planning and capacity-building has taken place under an externally assisted programme also reveals the inability and failure of the government in these areas during the last fifty years. Moreover, most, if not all, of the components of DPEP – whether they relate to quantitative expansion, improvements in quality or equity, or decentralization – do not require foreign exchange. Many of the components have been funded from domestic resources. Thus a clear and sound rationale for external assistance for primary education does not exist. This is perhaps the greatest weakness of the programme. The eagerness of the international aid organizations to finance primary education in India on the one hand, and the severely deteriorated general budgetary conditions of the government at the beginning of the 1990s on the other, were responsible for launching the programme of external assistance for primary education.

Correspondingly, a very important and damaging consequence of DPEP (and the economic reform policies introduced since the beginning of the 1990s) has been of a different kind. A view which people used to question has now become widely accepted and barely questioned, namely that the government does not have money even for primary education and for the development of any qualitative or quantitative or other dimension of primary education. An unfortunate and not necessarily correct impression is being created that improvements in primary education in the country will be possible only with external assistance. As a result, district after district and state after state are eager to enter DPEP, as external assistance is believed to be the only source available for financing primary education. Resource-poor (as well as resource-rich) states compete with each other to enter the DPEP arena. This (in familiar terms) dependency culture has spread widely and rapidly, both horizontally – across all parts of the country in all states, irrespective of the political ideology of the ruling parties in the states – and vertically – at all layers of government and administration, and among the general population in the whole country. This belief that primary education in the country cannot develop without external assistance can be described as an unfortunate and sudden turn in the history of primary education in independent India.

Concluding observations

This short chapter has presented a brief and critical account of a programme of development assistance for primary education in India. The programme began rather modestly in the early 1990s, but now seems to be emerging as a large-scale programme. Even if the quantity of financial assistance is not massive, the impact of the programme is likely to be sizeable. However, the impact is mixed. The trends seem to indicate that, while there are strong positive aspects of the programme, there are equally strong if not more powerful adverse effects, some of which affect the polity of the country as briefly reviewed above.

During the final three to four years of the programme's operation, a balance could be slowly and steadily reached between the two actors who initially started as enthusiastic donors and reluctant recipients. One can only hope that the reverse will not happen, i.e. that the recipients become too enthusiastic and critically dependent, and the donors reluctant. It is the responsibility of both the external agencies and the government to ensure that this is avoided. The government may rely on external funds to the extent that this is absolutely necessary. The external agencies should finance in such a way that the dependency of the national government on external resources does not increase and the system becomes self-reliant. This is after all the explicitly stated objective of the governments and the funding agencies. But this may become a serious challenge to both, requiring a clear approach and special efforts on both sides.

References

AYYAR, R. V. V. 1996. Educational Policy Planning and Globalisation. *International Journal of Educational Development*, Vol. 16, No. 4, pp. 347–53.

GOVERNMENT OF INDIA. 1993. *District Primary Education Programme*. New Delhi, Ministry of Human Resource Development.

——. 1995. *DPEP Guidelines*. New Delhi, Ministry of Human Resource Development.

——. 1997. *DPEP Moves on . . .* New Delhi, Ministry of Human Resource Development.

JONES, P. W. 1992. *World Bank Financing of Education: Lending, Learning and Development*. London, Routledge.

KING, K. 1991. *Aid and Education in the Developing World: The Role of the Donor Agencies in Educational Analysis*. London, Longman.

TILAK, J. B. G. 1984. Block Level Planning in Education. *Indian Journal of Public Administration*, Vol. 30, No. 3, pp. 673–84.
——. 1992. *Educational Planning at Grassroots*. New Delhi, Ashish Publishing House.
——. 1994. External Financing of Education: A Review Article. *Journal of Educational Planning and Administration*, Vol. 8, No. 1, pp. 81–6.
——. 1997. Effects of Adjustment on Education: A Review of the Asian Experience. *Prospects*, Vol. 27, No. 1, pp. 85–107.
TILAK, J. B. G.; VARGHESE, N. V. 1985. Educational Planning at District Level: A Preliminary Exercise on Gurgaon District. *Margin*, Vol. 17, No. 3, pp. 57–76.
VARGHESE, N. V. 1994. District Primary Education Programme: The Logic and the Logistics. *Journal of Educational Planning and Administration*, Vol. 8, No. 4, pp. 449–55.
——. 1996. Decentralization of Educational Planning in India: The Case of the District Primary Education Programme. *International Journal of Educational Development*, Vol. 16, No. 4, pp. 355–65.
WORLD BANK. 1994. *District Primary Education Programme: Staff Appraisal Report (India)*. Washington, D.C., World Bank.

Contributors

Beatrice Avalos is currently Co-ordinator of the Programme for Improvement of Initial Teacher Training, Higher Education Division, Ministry of Education in Chile. Formerly, she developed teacher professional activities in the Secondary MECE Programme (1994–96), was Professor of Education, University of Papua New Guinea (1988–94) and Senior Lecturer in Education, University of Wales, Cardiff (1974–88). Her publications include: *Women's Education and Economic Development in Melanesia* (with K. G. Gannicott) (Canberra, National Centre for Development Studies, The Australian University, 1994) and *Issues in Science Teacher Education* (Paris, UNESCO/IIEP, 1995). Contact: Ministerio de Educación, Programa Fortalecimiento de la Formación Inicial Docente, Avda. Libertador Bernardo O'Higgins 1371, Santiago, Chile.
Tel: (+56 2) 688 3406/3410. Fax: (+56 2) 696 3542.
E-mail: bavalos@chilesat.net

Kingsley Banya is Professor and Chairperson of Educational Leadership and Policy Studies, Florida International University, United States. His research focus has been on comparative and international education, curriculum theory and teacher education. He has published articles on education in West Africa and recently completed a book entitled *Implementing Educational Innovation in the Third World: A West Africa Experience*. Contact: Department of Educational Leadership and Policy Studies, College of Education, ZEB 310A, University Park, Miami, FL 33199, USA.
Tel: (+1 305) 348 1921. Fax: (+1 305) 348 3205.
E-mail: kbanya@fiu.edu

Lene Buchert is Senior Programme Specialist in the Division for the Reconstruction and Development of Education Systems, UNESCO, and Leader of the Working Group on Education Sector Analysis under the umbrella of ADEA. She is also an executive member of NORRAG. In recent years, her writings have focused particularly on issues related to educational aid policies and practices. Her most recent (edited) publication is *Education Reform in the South in the 1990s* (UNESCO Publishing, 1998). Contact: UNESCO, ED/ERD/ESD, 7 Place de Fontenoy, 75352 Paris 07 SP, France.
Tel: (+33 1) 4568 0826. Fax: (33 1) 4568 5631.
E-mail: l.buchert@unesco.org

Michel Carton is currently Professor and was former Deputy Director at the Graduate Institute of Development Studies in Geneva and has been Co-ordinator of NORRAG since 1992. His research and teaching deal mainly with education and training policies, management of vocational training programmes and the articulation between formal and non-formal education. His areas of geographical specialization include West and Central Africa, Indonesia, the Lao People's Democratic Republic, Lebanon and Viet Nam. Contact: Institut Universitaire d'Études du Développement (IUED), Post Box 136, Rue Rothschild 24, 1211 Geneva 21, Switzerland.
Tel: (+41 22) 731 5940. Fax: (+41 22) 741 0480.
E-mail: Michel.Carton@iued.unige.ch

Kai-ming Cheng is Chair Professor of Education and Pro-Vice-Chancellor at the University of Hong Kong. He is also currently Visiting Professor at Harvard Graduate School of Education. He has undertaken various studies and consultancies on education policies in China for the World Bank, the Asian Development Bank, UNESCO, UNICEF, UNDP and the Hong Kong Research Grants Council. His academic interest has also extended to qualitative research methodology and cultural studies in education. Contact: University of Hong Kong, Faculty of Education, Pokfulam, Hong Kong.
Tel: (+852) 2859 2246. Fax: (+852) 2559 9315.
E-mail: hradckm@hkucc.khu.hk

Wyn Courtney is an independent consultant in the areas of education policy and planning. She has worked in the south-west Pacific, Brazil and China, as well as in English-speaking countries in East, southern and central Africa, as headmistress, researcher and education planner. Until recently she was Senior Programme Specialist in the Unit for Extra-budgetary Activities in the Education Sector of UNESCO. Contact: 58 rue Denis Gogue, 92140 Clamart, France.
Tel.: (+33 1) 46 44 10 51.
E-mail: gkutsch@wanadoo.fr

Cristián Cox has since 1990 been National Co-ordinator of the Programme for Improvement of Equity and Quality of Education (MECE) and has headed the Secondary Curriculum Reform Task Force, both within the Ministry of Education in Chile. Formerly, he worked as a researcher at the Centro de Investigación y Desarrollo de la Educación (CIDE) in Santiago. Among his publications are a historic account of teacher training in Chile, and articles and monographs on the Chilean educational reform. Contact: Ministerio de Educación, Programa MECE, Avda. Libertador Bernardo O'Higgins 1371, Santiago, Chile.
Tel: (+56 2) 698 9219. Fax: (+56 2) 699 7984.
E-mail: ccox@meca.mineduc.cl

Juliet Elu is Assistant Professor of Economics and Director of Management and Organization Programs at Spelman College, Atlanta, Georgia, United States. Her research emphasis is on international trade and finance for developing countries, in particular structural adjustment programmes and trade integration. Contact: Department of Economics, Spelman College, 350 Spelman Lane, SW, Atlanta, GA 30314-4399, USA.
Tel: (+1 404) 215 7804. Fax: (+1 404) 215 7863.
E-mail: jelu@spelman.edu

Jacques Forster is Professor of Development Economics, Graduate Institute of Development Studies (IUED), Geneva and was previously its Director (1980–92). He is the editor of *Annuaire Suisse-Tiers Monde*

published by IUED. Contact: IUED, Post Box 136, 1211 Geneva 21, Switzerland.
Tel: (+41 22) 906 5926. Fax: (+41 22) 906 5947.
E-mail: jacques.forster@iued.unige.ch

Wolfgang Gmelin is Deputy Director of the Centre for Education Science and Documentation of the German Foundation for International Development (DSE) – an institution specializing in further training of specialists and executive personnel from developing countries. He is a member of the executive committee of NORRAG. His experience is related to issues of educational development and cooperation, mainly in higher education. Contact: DSE, Hans-Böckler-Strasse 5, D-53225 Bonn, Germany.
Tel: (+49 228) 4001 210. Fax: (+49 228) 4001 111.
E-mail: w_gmelin@zed.dse.de

Aklilu Habte is at present an independent consultant and President of NORRAG. He has long academic, managerial and international civil service experience. He has served UNICEF as Chief of the Education Division and Special Adviser to the Executive Director (1990–93) and was Director of the Education and Training Department in the World Bank and Special Adviser in Human Resources Development to the Vice-President of the Africa Region (1977–87). He was Minister of Culture, Sports and Youth Affairs in the Government of Ethiopia (1974–77) and President of the Haile Selassie I University, Addis Ababa (1969–74), having served, before that, in other academic and executive functions at the same university. He is the author of papers, monographs and reports on education and development. Contact: 9410 Corsica Drive, Bethesda, MD 20814, USA.
Tel: (+1 301) 564 9192. Fax: (+1 301) 564 1174.
E-mail: swolde@aol.com

Myra Harrison has been Chief Education Adviser at DFID/ODA since 1993, and was Senior Education Adviser at the ODA for five years before that, advising on programmes in West and South Africa and in Latin America. She previously worked in education in the

Sudan, Zambia, Malawi and South Africa as a teacher, in teacher training, and in syllabus planning, course development and materials writing. Contact: DFID, Education Division, 94 Victoria Street, London SW1E 5JL, United Kingdom.
Tel: (+44 171) 917 0543. Fax: (+44 171) 917 0287.
E-mail: m-harrison@dfid.gtnet.gov.uk

Stephen P. Heyneman was the former Lead Education Specialist for the Europe and Central Asia Region of the World Bank. He contributed analytic justifications for lending and policy work on education, training and labour markets for countries in eastern and central Europe, the Russian Federation and central Asia, and the Baltic and Caucasus regions. He has worked in eleven OECD countries and in thirty-six different developing countries. He has published widely in the fields of economics, sociology, history and political science, and on wide-ranging issues of education. Contact: International Operations, IM&D, 1729 King Street, No. 200, Alexandria, VA 22314–2720, USA.
Tel: (+1 703) 684 8400. Fax: (+1 703) 684 9489.
E-mail: SH@ind-net.com

Henry Kaluba was formerly on the staff of the University of Zambia and is now Chief Programme Officer in the Education Department, Human Resource Development Division, of the Commonwealth Secretariat. His present area of special interest is teacher management and support. He is Co-ordinator of the ADEA Working Group on the Teaching Profession (English-speaking), for which the Commonwealth Secretariat is the lead agency. Contact: Commonwealth Secretariat, Marlborough House, Pall Mall, London SW1Y 5HX, United Kingdom.
Tel: (+44 171) 747 6276. Fax: (+44 171) 747 6287.
E-mail: h.kaluba@commonwealth.int

Ulla Kann spent the last twenty-five years as an educational planner and researcher in Botswana and Namibia. She is now an independent educational consultant and researcher, currently focusing on

educationally marginalized children and youth unemployment. Contact: P.O. Box 23815, Windhoek, Namibia.
Tel/fax: (+264) 61 22 89 10.
E-mail: ukann@emis.mec.gov.na

Kenneth King is Director of the Centre of African Studies and Professor of International and Comparative Education at the University of Edinburgh. His research interests over the years have focused on aid policy towards all subsectors of education; on technical and vocational education and training; and on the special character of micro-enterprises and the informal economies in Africa. He is currently working on a DFID-funded research project on Learning to Compete: Small Enterprises in the Age of Globalization, which has a particular focus on South Africa, Ghana and Kenya. Contact: Centre of African Studies, University of Edinburgh, Edinburgh EH8 9LW, United Kingdom.
Tel: (+44 131) 650 3879. Fax: (+44 131) 650 6535.
E-mail: Kenneth.King@ed.ac.uk

Simon McGrath is Research Fellow on joint appointment to the Centre of African Studies and Department of Education and Society, University of Edinburgh. He is currently engaged in research for DFID on education, training and small enterprise in Ghana, Kenya and South Africa. He is also editor of the discussion paper series of the Working Group for International Cooperation in Technical and Vocational Skills Development. Contact: Centre of African Studies, University of Edinburgh, Edinburgh EH8 9LW, United Kingdom.
Tel: (+44 131) 650 4321. Fax: (+44 131) 650 6535.
E-mail: S.McGrath@ed.ac.uk

Karen Mundy is Assistant Professor of International and Comparative Education at Stanford University School of Education. She has worked extensively in Africa, as a teacher in Zimbabwe during 1985–88; for a Canadian non-government organization involved in South Africa during 1990–92; and as a consultant for a variety of development organizations. Her research interests include literacy and adult education in East and southern Africa and the political

economy of international co-operation in education. Contact: Stanford University School of Education, International and Comparative Education, Stanford, CA 94305-3096, United States.
Tel: (+1 605) 725 4411. Fax: (+1 605) 725 7412.
E-mail: kmundy@leland.stanford.edu

Nobuhide Sawamura is Associate Professor at the Center for the Study of International Cooperation in Education, Hiroshima University and was before that Deputy Director of the Grant Aid Department of JICA. His research interests concern aid policy in sub-Saharan Africa. Contact: Center for the Study of International Cooperation in Education, Hiroshima University, 1-5-1 Kagamiyama, Higashi-Hiroshima 739-8529, Japan.
Tel/fax: (+81 824) 24 6246.
E-mail: nsawamur@ipc.hiroshima-u.ac.jp

Jandhyala B. G. Tilak is Senior Fellow and Head of the Educational Finance Unit at the National Institute of Educational Planning and Administration, New Delhi. Among his recent publications are *Education for Development in Asia* (Sage, 1994) and *Educational Planning at Grassroots* (Ashish, 1991). Professor Tilak is also the Editor of the *Journal of Educational Planning and Administration* and a member of the Editorial Advisory Board of *Higher Education Policy*. Contact: National Institute of Educational Planning and Administration, 17B Sri Aurobindo Marg, New Delhi 110 016, India.
Tel: (+91 11) 686 3562. Fax: (+91 11) 685 3041.
E-mail: niepa@delnet.ren.nic.in

Peter Williams is now an independent consultant on international education and Deputy Executive Chairman of the Council for Education in the Commonwealth. He retired as Director of the Human Resources Development Division, Commonwealth Secretariat, in 1994. Contact: 6, Upper Rose Hill, Dorking, Surrey RH4 2EB, United Kingdom.
Tel/fax: (+44 1306) 881 315.

Lennart Wohlgemuth has been Director of the Nordic Africa Institute since 1993. Prior to that he worked for many years for Sida, most

recently as Assistant Director-General and Head of the Sector Department and between 1981 and 1987 as Head of Sida's education division. He has been a Board Member of IIEP since 1989. He has published widely on issues related to education aid and policies. Contact: Nordic Africa Institute, Box 1703, 751 47 Uppsala, Sweden.
Tel: (+46 18) 562 200. Fax: (+46 18) 695 629.
E-mail: Lennart.Wohlgemuth@nai.uu.se

Yumiko Yokozeki is Development Specialist in the field of education in JICA and worked before that for non-governmental organizations and UNICEF in Kenya and Zimbabwe. She has a particular interest in education in sub-Saharan Africa and has conducted research on issues of secondary education in Zimbabwe and Ghana. Contact: Institute for International Co-operation, JICA, 10-5 Ichigayahonmura cho, Shinjuku, Tokyo 162, Japan.
Tel: (+81 3) 3269 3851. Fax: (+81 3) 3269 6992.
E-mail: yokozeki@jica.go.jp